W9-BYT-162

Language Policy and Planning for Sign Languages

Ceil Lucas, General Editor

VOLUME 1 *Sociolinguistics in Deaf Communities*

VOLUME 2 *Multicultural Aspects of Sociolinguistics in Deaf Communities*

VOLUME 3 *Deaf Children in Public Schools*

VOLUME 4 *Pinky Extension and Eye Gaze: Language Use in Deaf Communities*

VOLUME 5 *Storytelling and Conversation: Discourse in Deaf Communities*

VOLUME 6 *Bilingualism and Identity in Deaf Communities*

VOLUME 7 *Sociolinguistic Variation in American Sign Language*

VOLUME 8 *Turn-Taking, Fingerspelling, and Contact in Signed Languages*

VOLUME 9 *Language and the Law in Deaf Communities*

VOLUME 10 *To the Lexicon and Beyond: Sociolinguistics in European Deaf Communities*

VOLUME 11 *The Rising of Lotus Flowers: Self-Education by Deaf Children in Thai Boarding Schools*

VOLUME 12 *Multilingualism and Sign Languages: From the Great Plains to Australia*

VOLUME 13 *Sign Languages in Contact*

VOLUME 14 *Hearing, Mother Father Deaf: Hearing People in Deaf Families*

VOLUME 15 *Extraordinary from the Ordinary: Personal Experience Narratives in American Sign Language*

VOLUME 16 *Language Policy and Planning for Sign Languages*

Language Policy and Planning for Sign Languages

Timothy G. Reagan

GALLAUDET UNIVERSITY PRESS

Washington, DC

Sociolinguistics in Deaf Communities
A Series Edited by Ceil Lucas

Gallaudet University Press
Washington, DC 20002
http://gupress.gallaudet.edu

Printed in the United States of America

Library of Congress Cataloging-in-Publication Data

ISSN 1080-5494

∞ The paper used in this publication meets the minimum requirements of American National Standard for Information Sciences—Permanence of Paper for Printed Library Materials, ANSI Z39.48-1984.

This book is dedicated to Kimberly,
who has taught me
that listening
does not mean hearing,
that hearing does not mean listening,
and that neither means understanding.

Contents

List of Figures, ix

List of Abbreviations, xi

Editorial Advisory Board, xiii

Editor's Note, xv

Preface, xvii

1. Sign Language and the DEAF^WORLD as a Special Case: An Overview, 1

2. Language Planning and Language Policy: An Introduction, 31

3. American Sign Language, Language Planning, and Language Policy, 97

4. The Creation and Use of Manual Sign Codes as Language Planning, 129

5. International Perspectives on Sign Language, Language Planning, and Language Policy, 155

6. Conclusion: The DEAF^WORLD, Language, and Power, 180

Appendices, 186

Bibliography, 196

Index, 241

List of Figures

Figure 1.1. Diagram of the ASL-Contact Sign-MSC continua, 8

Figure 1.2. ASL sign HEAFIE, 19

Figure 1.3. The I-LOVE-YOU sign, 21

Figure 2.1. Traditional demarcation of the major Romance languages, 40

Figure 2.2. The Languages of Wider Communication and their speaker numbers (estimate), 46

Figure 2.3. Types of language planning activity, 51

Figure 2.4. Language endangerment, 64

Figure 2.5. Orientations in language planning and language policy, 78

Figure 2.6. Ideologies of language planning, 79

Figure 2.7. The language planning process, 83

Figure 3.1. ACTFL standards, 122

Figure 4.1. American Manual Alphabet, 132

Figure 4.2. International Manual Alphabet, 133

Figure 4.3. British Two-Handed Manual Alphabet, 134

Figure 4.4. ASL sign BUTTERFLY, 137

Figure 4.5. SEE-I combination sign for BUTTER + FLY, 138

Figure 4.6. SEE-2 affixes, 139

Figure 4.7. Four different ASL glosses for the English word *manage*, 141

Figure 4.8. Cued Speech markers, 145

Figure 5.1. Status of sign languages in the European Union, 158

Figure 5.2. ASL signs for FAMILY, GROUP, ASSOCIATION, and TEAM, 166

List of Abbreviations

ACTFL	American Council on the Teaching of Foreign Languages
AFOOD	Arab Federation of Organizations Working With the Deaf
ASD	American School for the Deaf
ASL	American Sign Language
ASLTA	American Sign Language Teachers Association
Auslan	Australian Sign Language
B.C.E.	Before the Common Era (i.e., B.C.)
BSL	British Sign Language
CAL	Center for Applied Linguistics
CASE	Conceptually Accurate Signed English
C.E.	Common Era (i.e., A.D.)
CODA	Child of Deaf Adults
dB	Decibel
De'VIA	Deaf View/Image Art
EU	European Union
IDEA	Individuals with Disabilities Act
IEP	Individualized Educational Program
IMA	International Manual Alphabet
LOVE	Linguistics of Visual English
LWC	Language of Wider Communication
MCE	Manual Code for English
MSC	Manual Sign Code

NAD	National Association of the Deaf
NTD	National Theatre of the Deaf
NTID	National Technical Institute for the Deaf
PANSALB	Pan-South African Language Board
RIT	Rochester Institute of Technology
SASL	South African Sign Language
SEE-I	Seeing Essential English
SEE-2	Signing Exact English
SimCom	Simultaneous Communication
TC	Total Communication
WFD	World Federation of the Deaf

Editorial Advisory Board

Editor's Note

And so, with this volume, I pass the editorship of the Sociolinguistics in Deaf Communities series to the capable hands of Dr. Kristin J. Mulrooney, faculty member in the Department of Linguistics at Gallaudet University. We co-edited this volume. As I look back at the contents of the sixteen volumes produced since 1994, I can say that the series has done what I wanted it to do when I conceived of it those sixteen years ago: provide reports of current research on all aspects of sociolinguistics in Deaf communities—multilingualism, bilingualism and language contact, variation, discourse analysis, language policy and planning, language attitudes—with a truly international perspective. I am very grateful to all of the contributors to the volumes, including the guest editors, and to members of the editorial board, who have provided invaluable advice over the years. I am also very grateful to everyone at Gallaudet University Press, the folks who do the very hard work of getting the volumes produced and publicized: John Vickrey Van Cleve, David Armstrong, Ivey Wallace, Dan Wallace, Deirdre Mullervy, Donna Thomas, Frances Clark, and Valencia Simmons. The series would simply not have been possible without their consistent support and good humor.

My departure is being marked by this excellent and useful volume by Tim Reagan and now I get to sit back and see what comes next, with volume 17 . . .

Ceil Lucas
Washington, D.C.
July 2010

Preface

This book is an attempt to address an important and timely topic: language planning efforts, and the related language policies that arise from these efforts, for the sign languages used by deaf people. This is a huge topic on its own, but it is made more difficult in this book by my desire to provide an understandable introduction to these issues for two very different and distinct audiences. The first audience that I am trying to address are those who are already familiar and concerned with the literature on language planning and language policy studies, but who are not particularly familiar with either the DEAF⁀WORLD or sign language, and who wish to learn about the case of sign language and the deaf with respect to issues of language planning and language policy more broadly conceived. The second audience that I am trying to reach are those who are either members of the DEAF⁀WORLD, or who are familiar with the DEAF⁀WORLD and sign language, but who are unfamiliar with matters of language planning and language policy studies.

We are in a period during which an immense amount of language planning activity is taking place around the world related to sign language and the deaf, and while much of this language planning is very positive in nature, not all of it is. In addition, the resistance to many efforts to gain recognition for sign languages—both official recognition and recognition for sign language as a medium of instruction in educational settings—is profoundly worrying, and demonstrates how far we have to go in many places and with many people in challenging traditional, and misguided, ideas about the nature of sign language, deafness, and the deaf community. As Graham Turner recently wrote, "Deaf communities undoubtedly benefitted from the multicultural turn and the politics of difference during the late twentieth century, but this last decade seems to have thrown them squarely back into a medicalised realm from which, it has been argued, there is no escape" (2006, p. 409). I am not ready to concede that there is no escape from the current medicalization of deafness that seems increasingly popular, in part as a response to cochlear implants, genetic advances, and other developments, but I also believe that it would be a mistake not to be aware of and sensitive to such changes.

The organization of *Language Policy and Planning for Sign Languages* is, I hope, both straightforward and logical. Because the book is written for two quite different audiences, the first two chapters seek to provide the necessary background for each audience: Chapter 1 provides an overview of the DEAF⁀WORLD (the deaf cultural community), as well as a brief introduction to sign language in general, while Chapter 2 provides a broad overview of language planning and language policy studies as both an academic discipline and an applied type of social engineering. Chapter 3 then examines the specific case of American Sign Language (ASL), both in terms of the history of language planning and language policy related to ASL (both in the nineteenth century and in the post-Congress of Milan period), and in more recent years. Chapter 4 provides a detailed, and critical, examination of the creation of manual sign codes for use in deaf education, both in the United States and elsewhere. Next, Chapter 5 takes a much broader international view, examining language policy and language planning in settings around the world. Finally, Chapter 6 seeks to provide a conclusion to the book, including recommendations for future language planning efforts for sign languages.

In writing this book, I have benefited from the helpful comments and support of a number of individuals. I am grateful to Karen Beyard, Jane Edwards, Bonnie Fonseca-Greber, Nancy Hoffman, Paloma LaPuerta, Ceil Lucas, Daniel Mulcahy, Kristin Mulrooney, Frank Nuessel, Dale Ogilvy-Foreman, Terry Osborn, Claire Penn, Tony Rigazio-Digilio, and Humphrey Tonkin. I especially want to thank my friend and colleague Stephen Nover, the director of the Language Planning Institute (LPI) and the Center for ASL/English Bilingual Education and Research (CAEBER) at Gallaudet University for his unstinting generosity of time, resources, and spirit. I also want to thank Ivey Pittle Wallace at Gallaudet University Press for her help, support, and encouragement. Finally, as always I am incredibly grateful to Jo Ann, Joshua, Bryan, and Kimberly for their patience and tolerance during the writing of this book. Any mistakes, of course, are entirely my own.

Chapter 1

Sign Language and the DEAF^WORLD as a Special Case: An Overview

The traditional way of writing about Deaf people is to focus on the fact of their condition—that they do not hear—and to interpret all other aspects of their lives as consequences of this fact . . . In contrast to the long history of writings that treat them as medical cases, or as people with "disabilities" who "compensate" for their deafness by using sign language, we want to portray the lives they live, their art and performances, their everyday talk, their shared myths, and the lessons they teach one another. We have always felt that the attention given to the physical condition of not hearing has obscured far more interesting facets of Deaf people's lives. (Padden & Humphries, 1988, p. 1)

Lately . . . the deaf community has begun to speak for itself. To the surprise and bewilderment of outsiders, its message is utterly contrary to the wisdom of centuries: Deaf people, far from groaning under a heavy yoke, are not handicapped at all. Deafness is not a disability. Instead, many deaf people now proclaim, they are a subculture like any other. They are simply a linguistic minority (speaking American Sign Language) and are no more in need of a cure than are Haitians or Hispanics. (Dolnick, 1993, p. 37)

For those interested in language planning and language policy, deaf people, as a cultural and linguistic community, are an especially fascinating case study.[1] Both the DEAF^WORLD and sign language exist only in the plural; that is, although deaf people in different countries and settings certainly share certain experiences, attitudes, values, and concerns, they are also quite distinct in nature. In addition, and making the situation even more complex, whereas language planning and language policy studies for sign languages are similar to such activities for spoken languages, they are not identical. Thus, language planning and language policy studies for sign languages essentially creates something of a parallel universe to that with which language planners and policy makers are normally most familiar. And yet, at the same time, this universe in which deaf culture and natural sign languages exist is not completely independent of the universe in which we live and operate. It overlaps the world of the hearing and spoken languages, in important ways. Furthermore, because deaf people inevitably live in the hearing world as well as in the DEAF⁀WORLD, the decisions that we make with respect to language planning and language policy for both spoken and sign languages have immense impacts on them.

This book, as mentioned in the preface, addresses two very different audiences. The first are those readers who are familiar and concerned with the literature on language planning and language policy studies but not particularly familiar with either the DEAF⁀WORLD or sign language and wish to learn about the case of sign language and deaf people with respect to issues of language planning and language policy more broadly conceived. The second audience for this book are those readers who are either members of or those close to the DEAF⁀WORLD and sign language but unfamiliar with matters of language planning and language policy studies. Thus, the first two chapters of this book will attempt to provide introductions for each of these groups: Chapter 1 provides a general overview of the nature of sign language and the DEAF⁀WORLD, whereas Chapter 2 provides a broad overview of the language planning and language policy literature as it has developed for spoken languages.

Although this chapter is not focused explicitly on language planning and language policy, such issues are addressed implicitly here in two ways. First, in order to understand issues related to language planning and language policy for sign languages, both in the U.S. and around the world, it is essential to have a foundational understanding of the nature of sign language and the DEAF⁀WORLD, and in this chapter I will provide that foundation. Second, although many of the aspects of language planning and language policy for sign languages do reflect and overlap those for spoken languages, there are some important differences between spoken and sign languages in terms of language planning and language policy, and this chapter will address some of these.

CONCEPTIONS OF DEAFNESS

The literature on deafness now commonly identifies two quite different ways to view deafness (see Baker, 1999; Benvenuto, 2005; Branson & Miller, 2002; Corina & Singleton, 2009; Janesick & Moores, 1992; Kyle, 1990; Lane, 1992; Lane, Hoffmeister, & Bahan 1996; Lindgren, DeLuca, & Napoli, 2008; Mather, 1992; Padden & Humphries, 1988, 2005; Reagan, 1988, 1990a, 1995a, 2002c, 2005b [1985]; Senghas & Monahgan, 2002; Skelton & Valentine, 2003). The dominant perspective is grounded in the view that deafness is essentially a medical condition, characterized by an auditory deficit—that is, deaf people are people who cannot hear. Such a perspective, which has been labeled the "pathological" or "medical" view of deafness, leads naturally enough to efforts to try to remediate the deficit. In short, the pathological view is premised on the idea that deaf people are not only different from hearing people, but, at least in a physiological sense, are also *inferior* to hearing people. If one accepts the pathological view of deafness, and the myriad assumptions that undergird it, then the only reasonable approach to dealing with deafness is indeed to attempt to remediate the problem—which is, of course, precisely what is done when one focuses on the teaching of speech and lipreading or speechreading in education, utilizes technology such as hearing aids and cochlear implantation to maximize whatever residual hearing a deaf individual may possess, and otherwise seeks to develop medical solutions to hearing impairment. In other words, the pathological view of deafness inevitably leads to efforts to attempt to assist the deaf individual to become as "like a hearing person" as possible. Such a perspective is common in general in the hearing world, and, perhaps most importantly, among hearing parents, who "typically view being deaf through the lens of audiology, hearing loss, and difference, not as a cultural phenomenon" (Leigh, 2008, p. 23).

The alternative way of understanding deafness has been termed the "sociocultural perspective" on deafness. This view of deafness operates from an anthropological rather than a medical perspective, and suggests that for some (though not all) deaf people, it makes far more sense to understand deafness not as a handicapping condition, let alone as a deficit, but as an essentially cultural condition (Ladd, 2003, 2005; Lane et al., 1996; Padden & Humphries, 1988, 2005; Reagan, 1988, 1996, 2005 [1985]). Thus, from the perspective of advocates of the sociocultural perspective, the appropriate comparison group for deaf people is not individuals with disabilities but individuals who are members of other dominated and oppressed cultural and linguistic groups. In short, the sociocultural view leads to efforts that focus on issues of civil rights and to assist deaf people to function fully in the dominant (hearing) culture (Bauman, 2004; Ladd, 2005; Shapiro, 1993, pp. 74–104; Simms & Thumann, 2007).

SITUATING THE TARGET POPULATION: THE MANY FACES OF DEAFNESS

The case of deaf people presents an especially interesting example of the limitations of traditional discourse about "mother tongue" and "native language." The vast majority of deaf individuals are born to hearing, and nonsigning, parents.[3] Once a child is identified as having significant hearing loss, intervention begins (under the best of circumstances)—perhaps through the introduction of a sign language, perhaps through intensive oral and aural rehabilitation, and perhaps through surgical interventions such as those provided by cochlear implants.[4] In some instances, a combination of these different approaches is used. What is important to note here is that in most cases the deaf child's exposure to language (whether spoken or sign) is delayed. Such delays, in turn, have developmental consequences that are difficult to address later on in the child's education. The exceptions here—and by far the luckiest of deaf children—are those who are born to parents who are themselves signers (and, in most cases, presumably also deaf themselves).

In everyday discourse, however, the terms *deaf* and *hearing impaired* refer to a wide array of different kinds of hearing loss and responses to hearing loss—including, for example:

- A person who uses ASL (or some other natural sign language) as his or her primary language and identifies with the deaf cultural community.
- A person who communicates primarily through speech (i.e., in a spoken language) and identifies with the hearing community.
- A person who does not know either ASL (or some other natural sign language) or English (or some other spoken language), but rather communicates through gestures, mimes, and their own "home" signing systems.

- A person who became deaf later in life, generally as a result of aging (i.e., the elderly deaf).

The population with which I am concerned in this book is a subset of the hearing impaired population: children who are prelingually deaf—that is, deaf prior to the acquisition of spoken language—and profoundly or severely deaf, not with those with a broadly defined hearing impairment.[5] I am also concerned both with children who are raised in homes in which the dominant language is not a sign language, regardless of the hearing status of the parents, and those who are raised in homes in which the first language is indeed ASL. This may seem to narrow my focus, but it actually does not do so all that dramatically—the vast majority of children in residential schools for the deaf, for example, fit into this definition. Although, as we will see in Chapter 3, the numbers of such children is declining, it is these children who are most likely to constitute core members of the DEAF⌒WORLD.

THE NATURE AND CHARACTERISTICS OF SIGN LANGUAGE: A BRIEF OVERVIEW

Since the 1960 publication of William Stokoe's landmark study, *Sign Language Structure* (Stokoe, 1993 [1960]), there has been a veritable explosion of historical, linguistic, psycholinguistic, and sociolinguistic research dealing with ASL (see, e.g., Fischer & Siple, 1990; Liddell, 1980, 1995, 2003; Lucas, 1989, 1990, 1995, 1996; Lucas & Valli, 1992; Metzger, 2000; Siple & Fischer, 1991; Valli et al., 2005), as well as with other natural sign languages (see, e.g., Emmorey & Reilly, 1995; Lucas, 1990; Plaza-Pust & Morales-López, 2008; Reagan, Penn, & Ogilvy, 2006). The result is that we now know far more about the nature and workings of natural sign languages than we did a half-century ago. In his recent book on grammar, gesture, and meaning in ASL, Liddell notes:

> By the early 1970s many other linguists and psychologists began studying the properties of ASL. At that time, their published papers tended to begin with brief justifications explaining that ASL was a language. Such explanations were needed since most people still held the view that ASL was not a language. By perhaps the mid-seventies, and most certainly by the early eighties, the weight of published descriptions of ASL and its grammar was sufficient to turn the tide of opinion about the language status of ASL. Studies of various aspects of the grammar of ASL left no

doubt that signers using ASL were using a real human language. . . . The recognition that sign languages were real human languages set off a flurry of activity in a number of academic arenas beginning in the seventies . . . More and more sign languages continue to be identified and investigated as researchers around the globe pursue answers to a wide variety of interesting scientific questions. (2003, pp. 4–5)

Although I do not have the space here to provide a comprehensive overview of what linguists now know about ASL and other natural sign languages (see, however, in particular Johnston & Schembri, 2007; Lillo-Martin, 1991; Meir & Sandler, 2008; Nakamura, 2006), a very brief discussion of some of the principal, and generally common, linguistic features of natural sign languages will be useful. Because the greatest amount of linguistic research to date has been concerned with ASL, this discussion will necessarily focus on ASL, although examples from other sign languages will be provided as appropriate.

Different Kinds of Signing

There are, broadly speaking, four different kinds of "signing": the natural sign languages used by deaf people themselves in intragroup communication, which are unrelated to surrounding spoken languages; contact sign languages typically used by deaf and hearing people in intergroup communication; manual sign codes, which are efforts to represent spoken languages in a visual/manual format; and signed communication used by (and between) hearing people in certain situations. One useful way of thinking about these different kinds of signing is in terms of the diversity of signing and sign language. The diversity of sign languages actually refers to a number of different, and significant, kinds of diversity.

First, there are large numbers of sign languages that are natural sign languages used by deaf people in different settings around the world. Although these different natural sign languages share certain generic features (such as their gestural and visual nature, their use of space for linguistic purposes, etc.), and while some sign languages are genetically related to others, these languages are nevertheless distinctive languages in their own right. Many of these natural sign languages have been studied by linguists; among these are not only ASL, but also Australian Sign Language, British Sign Language, Danish Sign Language, Dutch Sign Language, French Sign Language, German Sign Language, Hausa Sign Language, Hong Kong Sign Language, Indo-Pakistani Sign Language, Israeli Sign Language, Italian

Sign Language, Kenyan Sign Language, Modern Thai Sign Language, Russian Sign Language, South African Sign Language, Swedish Sign Language, Taiwanese Sign Language, and Venezuelan Sign Language, and this is far from an exhaustive list. Indeed, although impressive in its own right, this list is but the proverbial tip of the iceberg, since most natural sign languages (like most spoken languages) remain unstudied. Skutnabb-Kangas suggests that "there probably are something between 6,500 and 10,000 spoken (oral) languages in the world, and a number of sign languages which can be equally large" (2000, p. 30). This is likely a gross overgeneralization, because many spoken languages are far too small to have a concomitant deaf community using its own sign language, but the underlying point is well taken: there is a huge number of natural sign languages in the world, of many of which we are not even aware.

The number of natural sign languages is but one sense in which we can talk about sign language diversity (see Reagan, 2007; Schermer, 2004). The second way in which diversity enters the picture is with respect to the diversity present *within* particular natural sign languages. In the case of ASL, for instance, we know that there is not only extensive lexical diversity related to region of the country, but also diversity related to age, gender, and ethnicity (see Lucas, 1989, 1995, 1996; Lucas, Bayley, & Valli, 2001, 2003; McCaskill et al., in press). A far more extreme case is provided by South African Sign Language (SASL). SASL, at least in part as a consequence of the social and educational policies of the apartheid regime (see Penn & Reagan, 2001), has been characterized by extensive lexical variation coupled with an underlying syntactic unity. Indeed, the situation is so complex that sign language linguists concerned with SASL have engaged in arguments about whether it is a single sign language or a related collection of different sign languages (see Aarons & Akach, 1998, 2002; Branson & Miller, 2002, pp. 244–45; Heap & Morgans, 2006; Morgan, 2008; Reagan, 2004).

The third sort of diversity that plays a role in understanding sign language, and one to which I have already alluded, is not so much a diversity in terms of sign language as it is a diversity with respect to what the term *signing* actually means. The distinction between *sign language* and *signing* is a significant one. Up to this point, I have been concerned only with natural sign languages, the sign languages that have emerged and are used in communities of deaf people for intragroup communication. Deaf people, however, do not live apart from hearing people; rather, they are integrated into the hearing world in a number of ways and on a number of different levels. The vast majority of deaf people have hearing parents, and the vast majority of deaf people will have hearing children. In addition, deaf people need to have access to at least some hearing people in order to function socially and economically. Although the children of deaf people may well learn their parents' sign language as a native language, most parents of deaf children and other hearing people who are in contact with deaf people will generally not learn a natural sign language. Instead, they will learn to sign using a contact sign language—that is, a sign language that has elements of both the natural sign language and the surrounding spoken language (see Lucas & Valli, 1989, 1991, 1992). Such contact languages, originally labeled *pidgin sign*, are in fact the primary kind of sign language used in many hearing–deaf communicative interchanges. These contact languages, like natural sign languages, are the result of normal linguistic development, and their emergence parallels that of spoken contact languages.

Next, *manual sign codes* were developed in educational settings as a way of providing deaf children with access to spoken language (the development of such manual sign codes will be discussed in detail in Chapter 4). These are simply efforts to represent a spoken language in a gestural/visual modality—comparable, really, to writing a spoken language (see Figure 1.1).

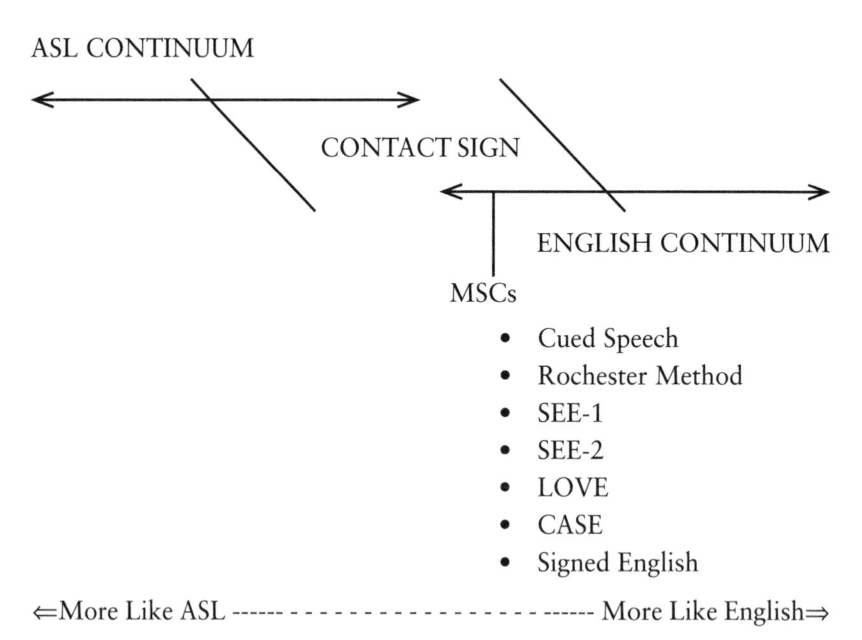

FIGURE 1.1. *Diagram of the ASL-Contact Sign-MSC continua*[6]

Finally, there is signed communication that has been used by hearing people, not to communicate with deaf people, but rather to communicate with other hearing people in certain settings. Examples include the kinds of signing used by the Plains Indians in North America (see Davis, 2006, 2007, in press), the signing used in monasteries (both historically, from at least the tenth century, and in some contemplative orders such as the Benedictine, Cistercian, Franciscan, and Trappist orders, even today; see Barakat, 1975a, 1975b; Barley, 1974; Kendon, 1990; Nitschke, 1997; Umiker-Sebeok & Sebeok, 1987), and so on. Although different in both nature and purpose from other kinds of signing, and more accurately described as *gestural lexicons* than as *sign languages*, there is no doubt that all these are also kinds of signed communication.

THE CULTURE OF THE DEAF⁀WORLD

The extraordinary impact of ASL on American deaf culture is just one example of the complex interaction between language and identity. Indeed, in discussions about this relationship deaf people stand out as an exceptionally complicated and intriguing case (Bragg, 2001; Goodstein, 2006; Harris, 1995; Monaghan, Schmaling, Nakamura, & Turner, 2003; Neisser, 1983; Padden, 1980; Parasnis, 1988; Reagan, 2002c). As Charlotte Baker observes, "Deaf people do not necessarily identify with the hearing world and increasingly regard the hearing world as a different language community. Rather than allowing themselves to be defined by the majority hearing group, Deaf people are progressively expressing and valuing their own self-constructed identity" (Baker, 1999, p. 129). Since the 1970s, social science scholars have recognized that many individuals identify themselves as members of a common deaf cultural community (see Baker & Battison, 1980; Ladd, 2003; Lindgren et al., 2008; Padden & Humphries, 1988, 2005; Paul & Jackson, 1993; Reagan, 1988, 1990a, 1995a, 2002c, 2005b [1985]; Schein, 1989; Siple, 1994; Stokkoe, 1980; Vernon & Andrews, 1990; Wilcox, 1989). Such a cultural conceptualization of deafness presents a significant challenge to the more popular view among hearing people of deafness as a disability. The difference is not merely a semantic one; it is fundamental to one's conception of what deafness is, what it means to be deaf, and how both individuals and society as a whole ought to address deafness. As Lane, Hoffmeister, and Bahan note in their powerful book *A Journey into the DEAF-WORLD*, "When hearing people think about Deaf people, they project their concerns and subtractive perspective onto Deaf people. The result is an inevitable collision with the values of the DEAF⁀WORLD, whose goal is to promote the unique heritage of Deaf language and culture. The disparity in decision-making power between the hearing world and the DEAF⁀WORLD renders this collision frightening for Deaf people" (1996, p. 371).

The complexities of the situation become even greater when one takes into account the fact that not all *deaf* people are *Deaf*. Audiological deafness and cultural deafness are distinct and different conditions. The deaf population can be subdivided into a wide range of different groups, distinguished in part of degree of hearing loss, but also by language preference, educational experience, and relative integration into either the DEAF⁀WORLD or the hearing world (see Goodstein, 2006; Monaghan et al., 2003). My focus in this book is on understanding the multiple, competing conceptions of deafness that divide the DEAF⁀WORLD and hearing world, with emphasis on the dominant constructions of deafness that exist in each of these worlds. It is important to note at the outset, then, that the concern here is primarily with *Deaf* people rather than with *deaf* people. As Harlan Lane observes in his masterful book *The Mask of Benevolence*, "Most Americans who have impaired hearing are not members of the American deaf community. They were acculturated to hearing society, their first language was a spoken one, and they became hard of hearing or deaf in the course of their lives, often late in life. This book is not about them; it is about people who grow up deaf, acculturated to the manual language and society of the deaf community" (1992, p. xi). Although there are many interesting issues that might be addressed with respect to the identities of deaf people, as well as with regard to the complex identities of the hearing children of deaf people (generally referred to as Codas, for *children of deaf adults*), these issues are beyond the bounds of this book (Bishop & Hicks, 2008). It is, nevertheless, important to recognize that the dichotomy separating the hearing and deaf worlds is in fact a false one; rather than two completing distinct identities, the reality of deafness is one of a continuum of multiple identities ranging from "hearing" to "deaf."

At issue here is the broader issue of disability. As numerous scholars have explored in detail in recent years, "disability" is a social construct grounded in cultural, political, ideological, and economic assumptions and biases (Barton, 1997; Charlton, 1998; Davis, 1995, 1997; Linton, 1998; Safford & Safford, 1996). In the case of deaf people, the relative emphasis and importance accorded to audiological versus social factors is the central feature of differentiation between what can be labeled the *etic* and *emic* views of deafness (Gregory & Hartley, 1991; Ohna, 2003; Reagan, 2002c; Schein, 1989). At stake, ultimately, is the question of who defines "deafness": the dominant hearing world or the DEAF⌒WORLD. It is, fundamentally, the relationship of power and discourse that is at stake.

Deaf constructions of deaf identity, which are grounded in the experiences and history of the DEAF⌒WORLD (see Fischer & Lane, 1993; Van Cleve, 1993, 2004), stress the sociocultural and linguistic aspects of deafness (Andersson, 1990, 1994; Burch, 2000; Corker, 2000; Ladd, 2003; Lindgren et al., 2008; Padden & Humphries, 1988, 2005; Paul & Jackson, 1993; Reagan, 1988, 1990a, 1995a, 2002c, 2005b [1985]; Schein, 1989; Skelton & Valentine, 2003; Vernon & Andrews, 1990; Wilcox, 1989). Such emic constructions of deafness focus primarily on deaf people as a cultural and linguistic minority community (and, indeed, on that community as an oppressed one). The deaf cultural community is, from this perspective, characterized by the same sorts of elements that might characterize any cultural community, among which are:

- a common, shared language
- a literary and artistic tradition
- a shared awareness of cultural identity
- culturally specific humor
- endogamous marital patterns
- distinctive behavioral norms and patterns
- cultural artifacts
- a shared historical knowledge and awareness
- a network of voluntary, in-group social organizations.

We turn now to a brief discussion of each of these elements of the DEAF⌒WORLD.

ASL as the Language of the DEAF⌒WORLD

The single most significant element of deaf cultural identity in the United States is, without a doubt, communicative competence in ASL (Lane et al., 1996; Schein & Stewart, 1995; Valli, Lucas, & Mulrooney, 2005). ASL serves multiple roles within the deaf community, functioning not only as the community's vernacular language, but also as an indicator of cultural group membership. An indication of the important role of ASL in the establishment and maintenance of cultural identity can be seen in the use of "name signs" (see Hedberg, 1994; Meadow, 1977; Stokoe, Casterline, & Croneberg, 1976, pp. 291–93; Supalla, 1990, 1992; Yau, 1982, 1990, pp. 271–72; Yau & He, 1990). Name signs constitute a special category of signs in ASL (and in other natural sign languages). They

> seem to develop wherever a group of Deaf people have extended contact with each other and use sign language as their vernacular language. They are created for individuals within each generation or social grouping of Deaf people. Most typically, name signs originate in deaf school settings where Deaf children form an autonomous social world beyond the gaze of teachers . . . the name signs that Deaf adults bestow on each other later in life are determined by Deaf social norms and visual language structures rather than those of the "outside" hearing society. (McKee & McKee, 2000, pp. 4–5)

Further, "the acquisition of a name sign may mark a person's entry to a signing community, and its use reinforces the bond of shared group history and alternative language use (in relation to mainstream society)" (McKee & McKee, 2000, p. 3).

The critical roles ASL plays in reinforcing and strengthening the bonds of the deaf community are really restricted to ASL; other types of signing commonly used in the United States (including both the contact sign language normally employed by hearing signers and the artificially constructed manual sign codes) fulfill very different functions and are viewed very differently by members of the deaf community (Lucas, 1989; Lucas & Valli, 1992; Reagan, 1988, 1990a, 1995a, 1995b, 2002c, 2005b [1985]). For instance, contact sign language is viewed as an appropriate means of communication with hearing individuals, while manual sign codes are often rejected by the deaf community as awkward efforts to impose the structures of a spoken language on sign.

ASL also plays an important role in the construction of what could be termed the *DEAF⌒WORLD worldview*—that is, the way in which deaf people make sense of the world around them. It does this in two distinct ways: first, through its role as linguistic mediator, and second, as an identifying facet of cultural identity. For instance, ASL mediates experience in a unique way, as of course do all languages. The structures and vocabulary of ASL provide the framework within which experience is organized, perceived, and understood, and this framework is inevitably distinct from the frameworks employed by other languages. For example, in ASL if one describes a person as VERY HARD-OF-HEARING, it means that the person has substantial residual hearing, whereas LITTLE HARD-OF-HEARING suggests far less residual hearing. In other words, the concepts themselves are based on different norms than is the case in English (where the meanings of these two expressions are reversed).

The use of ASL as one's primary vernacular language is arguably the single most important element in the construction of deaf cultural identity. Deaf cultural identity presupposes communicative competence in ASL, and is impossible without it. As Jerome Schein explains, "Being deaf does not in itself make one a member of the deaf community. To understand this, one has to remember that the distinguishing feature of membership in the deaf community is how one communicates" (1984, p. 130). It is not merely *signing* that is necessary, though—it is, specifically, the use of ASL. Many hearing people sign, but relatively few are competent in ASL. ASL has historically functioned as a language of group solidarity.

The Literary and Artistic Tradition of the DEAF⁀WORLD

Regarding the literary and artistic tradition of the DEAF⁀WORLD, Lane and colleagues write:

> The arts . . . also play a critical role in bonding the members of any culture, and the members of the DEAF⁀WORLD are no exception. In fact, in at least two respects, the arts have a privileged relation to Deaf culture. Deaf people are, as we have seen repeatedly, best thought of as a visual people, so it should be no surprise that there has always been a substantial number of Deaf artists, many with worldwide renown. Then, too, ASL is an unwritten language, so literature such as storytelling and humor carry much cultural information that, in cultures with written languages, would be passed down through the generations in books. (1996, pp. 138–39)

There is a fundamental distinction between individuals who happen to be deaf and who produce works of art (whether literary, visual, multimedia, or of whatever sort), and those individuals who produce what is termed *Deaf Art* (see Sonnenstrahl, 2003; see also Bauman, 2008a; Davidson, 2008; Novak, 2008; Perlmutter, 2008). My focus here is, needless to say, solely on the latter group of artists. Several efforts have been made to articulate this difference and to provide opportunities for deaf artists to perform and display their work. For instance, in the 1970s, in the midst of the rise of Deaf Art, *Spectrum: Focus on Deaf Artists* was started in Austin, Texas, and was able, under the deaf painter Betty Miller, to assemble some two dozen deaf artists within a few years, leading to the establishment of the Spectrum Visual Arts Institute in 1977 (see Lane et al., 1996, p. 139). Later, the creation of the Deaf Artists of America in Rochester, New York, in 1985 made possible the presentation of more than twenty exhibitions prior to its closing in 1992 (Lane et al., 1996, p. 140). Perhaps the clearest articulation of the difference between Deaf Art and art created by deaf people is that provided by the De'VIA (Deaf View/Image Art) Manifesto, which was written by eight deaf artists at a four-day workshop prior to the "Deaf Way" arts festival held at Gallaudet University in May 1989 (Miller, Sonnenstrahl, Wilhite, & Johnston, 2006; Sonnenstrahl, 1996, 2003). The Manifesto argued that

> De'VIA represents Deaf artists and perceptions based on their Deaf experiences. It uses formal art elements with the intention of expressing innate cultural or physical Deaf experience. These experiences may include Deaf metaphors, Deaf perspectives, and Deaf insight in relationship with the environment (both the natural world and Deaf cultural environment), spiritual and everyday life. . . . De'VIA can be identified by formal elements such as Deaf artists' possible tendency to use contrasting colors and values, intense colors, contrasting textures. It may also most often include a centralized focus, with exaggeration or emphasis on facial features, especially eyes, mouths, ears, and hands. (Quoted in Sonnenstrahl, 1996, p. 132)

The deaf literary canon has only recently begun to be recognized and studied, but it is already clear that novels, plays, poetry, and theatrical presentations in ASL can be and often are very powerful and compelling (see Bahan, 1992; Peters, 2000). Deaf literature now includes a number of novels, such as *Islay* (see Bullard, 1986), which meet the standards of traditional literary works and present and focus on issues of the DEAF⌒WORLD, and which in some ways may surpass traditional written works in their use of visual metaphors (see Christie & Wilkins, 1997; Frishberg, 1988; Peters, 2000). There is also a rich tradition of stories and storytelling in ASL (see Krentz, 2000; Winston, 1999). To some extent, such storytelling parallels that found in other oral traditions, but there are also distinctive aspects of such stories in ASL. Apart from their focus on the DEAF⌒WORLD and deaf people, and the history of the DEAF⌒WORLD (see Rutherford, 1993), such stories also include particular genres not found, for obvious reasons, in spoken language traditions. One example is the *A-to-Z story* (also called the *ABC story*):

> In an A-to-Z story each sign represents one of the twenty-six handshapes in the manual alphabet, from A to Z. The stories cover a wide range of topics, including an operation, a haunted house, a romantic couple, a car race, and a basketball game. The transition from A to Z must be very smooth, as in a

regular story. A-to-Z stories are not easy to translate into English since their meaning depends on the visual effect created by the alphabet handshapes. (Valli et al., 2005, pp. 184–85)

The *numerical story* is similar in format but employs numbers, using 1 to 15. Another genre, the *classifier story*, employs classifiers, one of the more significant linguistic characteristics of ASL (see Emmorey, 2003; Sandler & Lillo-Martin, 2006, pp. 76–93):

> The classifier story is a very rich, creative art form. The story is told exclusively with classifier predicates. One of the many classifier predicate stories is about a golf ball. In this story the storyteller's head becomes a golf ball. It creates a point of view as it is put on a tee and watches a club approach several times before it is hit. After the ball is hit, it flies high over trees, and then descends and lands on the ground, bounces, rolls slowly, and finally stops. It is hit again, rolls toward the cup, and circles the rim of the cup before going down into the hole. (Valli, et al., 2005, p. 185)

The theatrical tradition in ASL is quite strong, in large part because of the active agenda of the National Theatre of the Deaf and other historical theatrical groups (see Bragg, 1996; Corrado, 1990). Examples of plays that clearly focus on the DEAF⁀WORLD include such productions as *My Third Eye* (Barman et al., 1973; the debut production of the National Theatre of the Deaf), *Sign Me Alice* (a deaf version of Shaw's *Pygmalion*; Eastman, 1974), and *Children of a Lesser God* (Medoff, 1980). Note here the difference between a theatrical production that is *interpreted* into ASL and one which is actually *performed* in ASL (see Novak, 2008).

Interpreted performances are certainly of value in many ways (not the least of which is that they expose hearing people to ASL), but the nature of the performance itself is quite different from that of a truly ASL performance. Consider, for instance, Caliban's line in *The Tempest* that reads, "You taught me language and my profit on't is, I know how to curse." In ASL, this would be interpreted as YOU FINISH TEACH-TEACH ME LANGUAGE, ME BENEFIT WHAT? ME KNOW-HOW SWEAR. Willy Conley comments:

> [This] doesn't exactly capture the rich beauty of Shakespeare's language, but at least it is practical enough to deliver the concept. The deaf audience member now has to figure out who said the line—was it Caliban, Prospero, or Miranda? Next, the line needs to be put into context. And then, very quickly, the audience member needs to look over to the group of characters to see what happened as a result of saying that line. Most good actors in Western theatre act on the line, so this bit of action gets finished by the time a deaf person's eyes return to the stage. (2001, p. 59)

On the other hand, Peter Novak points out that

> the translation of Shakespeare's *Twelfth Night* into American Sign Language (ASL) reflects a confluence of cultures, where the nature and process of theatrical translation have been revisited and, to some extent, re-envisioned . . . The translation stands at the center of two distinctly different cultures: the hearing world with Shakespeare as one of its greatest poets, and the American Deaf community with its visual/manual language and literature. The product of these two languages and literatures creates a new "text"—a literature of the body—a corporeal artifact that will expand conventional notions of language, text, and performance. (Novak, 2008, p. 220)

ASL poetry is another powerful artistic product of the DEAF⁀WORLD (see Bauman, 2008a; Davidson, 2008; Low, 1992; Perlmutter, 2008; Valli, 1990). Although difficult, if not impossible, to translate adequately into a spoken language, the following translation of the ASL poem "Windy, Bright Morning" by Clayton Valli gives some sense of what ASL poetry is capable of expressing:

Through the open window
with its shade swinging, sunshine, playful,
taps my sleepy eyes.

[The hand, used to represent the shape, moves in a slightly irregular but not unpleasant rhythm.]

Breezes dance in my room,
around me, not shy, but gentle,
letting me know that it's time
to get up! Slowly I wake
my eyes stung by sunlight
flashing past the swinging shade
that seems to know I'm deaf.

[The presence of the light is unmistakable; the movement revolves around the center of the light.]

I stand up, tired, ignoring the light,
chilled in the dancing air
that meets me by the window
I closely shut it. And with the shade still,
my room darkens.

[The irregular movement abruptly ceases, and the room becomes silent. As Valli moves back to the familiar bed, movement is slow and comforting.]

Happy
back under the covers,
I'm drowsy, purring, warm . . .

[The audience, lulled by Valli's slow delivery, is unprepared for the next verse:]

But suddenly, how strange!
The shade flaps wildly,
bright, dark, bright, dark, bright
Fierce wind flung open the window . . .
so bitter cold, so cold, the wind, the shade,
the storm!

[The movement is wild and unpredictable. Valli as experiencer widens his eyes and moves his body with a sense of urgency.]

Slowly I rise, and try to make them calm down.

[As he moves toward the window, the movement, formerly dissonant, changes again, beginning to come together in one organized and focused form:]

The wind, the shade, dancing gracefully, happy.
One bright ray gently pulls me
to raise up the shade
like unwrapping a gift.
Warm sunlight tickles me,
morning breeze laughs with me . . .
Joyful, I welcome the day.

(Quoted in Padden & Humphries, 1988, pp. 104–6; translated by Karen Wills and Clayton Valli)

Such poetry employs the structural components of ASL, as well as its visual and gestural nature, to essentially paint a picture or series of pictures in a way simply not possible in a spoken language. In addition, the use of ASL metaphors further adds to the beauty and power of such poetry (see Taub, 2001; Wilbur, 1990; Wilcox, 2000).

Finally, there is visual Deaf Art, which includes photographs, paintings, ceramics, stained glass, and a host of other kinds of artistic production. A common theme in much of such Deaf Art is the punitive nature of much of deaf education historically. The theme of the oppression of deaf people by the hearing world includes a variety of styles, techniques, and images, and transcends national boundaries. It is also a recurring theme, often focused on the denial of sign language as a language and the related denial of deaf people as a cultural community (see Barton, 1997; Baynton, 1996). The explicit use of the hand, either as a central focal point of the artwork or in terms of the use of a particular sign, also characterizes much Deaf Art. For instance, Susan Dupor has used signs extensively both in paintings related to deer and other wildlife, as well as in a series related to hands themselves. Another theme that emerges in much Deaf Art is that of the DEAF⁀WORLD itself. Finally, there are in Deaf Art examples of more traditional artistic themes, albeit from a deaf perspective, and these should not be overlooked. For example, Ethan Sinnott's *The Last Supper* portrays Jesus' last meal with his disciples from the perspective of a deaf outsider. Sinnott explains this complex painting:

> The moment during *The Last Supper* I have chosen to portray is Jesus' revelation that he would come to be betrayed by one of his twelve disciples. Instead of the usual full-frontal and linear arrangement of the same scene found in Renaissance paintings, I set the scene up as if being observed by a Deaf outsider in a Hearing world. Jesus' back is turned to the viewer, who cannot see his face and what he's saying. The disciples' violent, vehement protestations—as human nature tends to shy away from fallibility and culpability—become more mysterious, confusing even, with everyone talking over each other. Judas is not made so clear-cut; it could easily be a table full of Judases. This dramatic event, as it unfolds, is an absurd, bizarre spectacle to the Deaf person who obviously cannot hear what is obviously being spoken. (1999)

A similar painting is Mary Thornley's *Milan Italy, 1880* (named in reference to the Congress of Milan, which basically sought to eliminate sign language in deaf education), which is reminiscent of Goya's *Third of May, 1803*, except that it is ASL itself that is being shot by a firing squad (see Lane et al., 1996, p. 141).

Attitudinal Deafness and the DEAF^WORLD

Members of the deaf cultural community identify themselves as socially and culturally deaf, maintaining a clear-cut distinction between audiological deafness and sociocultural deafness—a phenomenon that is sometimes referred to as "attitudinal deafness" (Janesick & Moores, 1992, pp. 49–65; Reagan 1988, 1990a, 1995a, 2002c, 2005b [1985]). Thus, within an emic construction of deafness, the fact of audiological deafness is actually neither a necessary nor a sufficient condition for cultural deafness. Codas, who grow up with ASL as their first language, are (at least in some significant ways) potential members of deaf culture, just as older hearing people who lose their hearing are, under normal circumstances, not deaf—they are, rather, hearing people who can no longer hear. It is interesting to note that in ASL there is actually a very pejorative and insulting sign, HEAFIE (see Figure 1.2), used to denigrate a deaf person who "thinks like a hearing person" (rather like the highly pejorative term "Oreo" in the African American community). Further, a common facet of cultural identity for many ethnic groups is the presence and maintenance of endogamous marital patterns, and the same is true in the case of deaf people. Indeed, estimates of the rate of in-group marriage in the deaf community generally indicate a remarkably high rate in contemporary American society. Such a high rate of in-group marriage is certainly facilitated by the role of the residential schools for the deaf, but it is also tied to the common, shared language of deaf people as well as to the power of the concept of attitudinal deafness.

FIGURE 1.2. *ASL sign* HEAFIE. *Reproduced from Phyllis Perrin Wilcox,* Metaphor in American Sign Language *(Washington, DC: Gallaudet University Press, 2000), p. 93.*

Deaf Humor

The concept of attitudinal deafness is a key element in understanding much of deaf humor (Bienvenu, 1994, pp. 16–23; Bouchauveau, 1994, pp. 24–30; Lane et al., 1996, pp. 116–19). Jokes and funny stories abound in the DEAF^WORLD, and many involve the presumed difference between deaf people and the DEAF^WORLD and hearing people and the hearing world—almost inevitably, as one would expect, with the punch line focusing on hearing people's ignorance of signing, deafness, and deaf people. Deaf humor tends to have the deaf person win out *because of his or her deafness*. This does not mean that deaf humor is necessarily anti-hearing; rather, it is simply a case of a culturally and socially oppressed group poking fun both at the dominant group and, sometimes, at themselves. It is often the very condition of deafness itself that is at the core of deaf humor.

One story, for instance, involves a hearing man who is hitchhiking and is given a ride by a deaf man. As they drive along, the deaf driver exceeds the speed limit and is stopped by a police officer. The police officer comes to the car and the deaf man signs to him, indicating that he is deaf. Unable to communicate with the driver, the police officer just says, "Oh, never mind—just slow down!" Some time later, the hearing man offers to drive so that the deaf man can rest. The deaf driver accepts the offer, and the hearing man begins driving. Before too long, they are again stopped by a police officer. The hearing man, recalling what occurred before, copies what he saw the deaf man sign to the police officer. This police officer, though, immediately signs back, "Oh, you're deaf? So are my parents. So why are you going so fast, anyway?" The joke is, of course, on the hearing man, who had tried, for selfish reasons, to "pass" as a deaf person.

Another example of deaf humor is a story about a deaf couple on their honeymoon. One night, the husband leaves his wife in the hotel room to get them a drink. When he returns, he realizes he has forgotten which room is theirs. So he begins honking the horn of his car until all the room lights in the motel turn on except one—and thus he finds his room. He triumphs *because of* his wife's deafness.

Behavioral Norms in the DEAF^WORLD

There are also differences between the hearing world and the DEAF^WORLD with respect to behavioral norms, most notably differences in eye contact patterns, rules governing the permissibility of physical contact of various sorts (including certain kinds of touching to gain attention), the use of facial expressions, gesturing, and so on (Kersting, 1997, pp. 252–63). Similarly, the cultural artifacts of the deaf community are primarily technological devices designed in recent years to facilitate the ability of deaf people to function in the hearing world. The key difference between the audiologically deaf and culturally deaf with respect to the use of such technologies is that there is a reluctance on the part of many culturally deaf people to utilize some technological devices (such as hearing aids) that focus primarily on *hearing*. Other kinds of technological innovations, although they are cultural artifacts to some extent, are widely and commonly used both within deaf culture and by those who are audiologically deaf but not culturally deaf—technologies such as TDD/TTYs (which are now becoming obsolete) and, more recently, videophones, computers that enable video teleconferencing, e-mail and instant messaging, text messaging, and vlogging and the like; televisions with built-in closed-caption decoders; and doorbells and alarms tied to lights are examples of these. Cultural artifacts emphasizing membership in deaf culture, such as jewelry, T-shirts, bumper stickers, and so on, which often involve visual images of signs (and especially of the I-LOVE-YOU sign), are additional artifacts that are somewhat more likely to be found among culturally deaf people, though such artifacts are also used more generally by both deaf and hearing people with an interest in deafness—sometimes even inappropriately, as Tom Willard articulates in a wonderful short essay entitled, "I've Had Enough of the I-LOVE-YOU Sign, Thanks" (1993, p. 2; see Figure 1.3).

FIGURE 1.3. *The* I-LOVE-YOU *sign. Reproduced from Clayton Valli, ed.,* The Gallaudet Dictionary of American Sign Language *(Washington, DC: Gallaudet University Press, 2005), p. 229.*

Historical Awareness and the DEAF^WORLD

Members of the deaf community have a strong sense of the history of their community, and this awareness was previously passed from generation to generation largely through "oral" means. However, the 1981 publication of Jack Gannon's *Deaf Heritage: A Narrative History of Deaf America* began a continuing process of the written transmission of this historical awareness of the deaf community to the hearing world, and, more recently, there have been a number of outstanding scholarly works on the history of deaf people that are also reinforcing pride in the community's history and heritage (see, e.g., Baynton, 1993, 1996, 2002; Bragg, 2001; Fischer & Lane, 1993; Nover, 2000; Van Cleve, 1993, 2007; Van Cleve & Crouch 1989; Winefield, 1987). At the same time, it is worth noting that some elements of the community's "historical memory" may not be completely accurate or true, as is the case with any cultural community. In the case of the DEAF^WORLD, for instance, the very common notion that the hands of Abraham Lincoln in the Lincoln Memorial are fingerspelling *A* and *L*, the initials for "Abraham Lincoln," because the sculptor (Daniel Chester French) had sculpted the 1889 statue of Thomas Hopkins Gallaudet and Alice Cogswell, his first pupil, is at best highly contentious. The National Park Service (NPS), for instance, sees this claim as simply a myth. According to the NPS website, "the artist studied casts of the former President's hands to get the proper appearance. They were both in a closed shape for the casting, the artist decided to open one up a bit to give a more life-like aspect."

Voluntary Network of Deaf Social and Cultural Organizations

Finally, an extensive voluntary network of social organizations serving deaf people works to maintain the cohesiveness of the deaf community and provide, to a very significant extent, for the companionship needs of group members. This network includes local deaf clubs, the state and national organizations of deaf people (such as the National Association of the Deaf [NAD]), sports associations, political organizations, and so on (Lane, 2005; Lane et al., 1996, pp. 131–38). Although local deaf clubs are now less popular than they once were, perhaps due to other ways for deaf people to keep in touch and interact (e.g., using videophones, text messaging, etc.), they still play an important role both with respect to passing on deaf culture and providing a kind of "second home" for many deaf people. Deaf community organizations are found in virtually any part of the world in which deaf people live in reasonable numbers.

THE DEAF^WORLD AND THE HEARING WORLD: A STUDY IN TENSIONS

It is clear, then, that in an anthropological sense, that the DEAF^WORLD is a legitimate and viable culture (see Senghas & Monaghan, 2002). Thus, attempts to medically "cure" or "remediate" audiological deafness are seen as not merely misguided but as culturally and linguistically oppressive as well. This point was made quite vividly by I. King Jordan, the retired president of Gallaudet University, in an interview some years ago. Jordan was asked by the interviewer whether he wouldn't like to have his hearing restored, to which Jordan replied, "That's almost like asking a black person if he would rather be white . . . I don't think of myself as missing something or as incomplete . . . It's a common fallacy if you don't know deaf people or deaf issues. You think it's a limitation" (quoted in Lane 1993a, p. 288). From the perspective of deaf culture, this response was appropriate, meaningful and indeed relatively uncontroversial; from outside the culture, it no doubt strikes many hearing people as somewhat odd, bizarre, or puzzling. An indication of the fundamentally different way in which many hearing people see deafness is represented by the following statement from a chairman of a National Institutes of Health planning group, quoted in the *New York Times*: "I am dedicated to curing deafness. That puts me on a collision course with those who are culturally Deaf. That is interpreted as genocide of the Deaf" (quoted in Lane et al., 1996, p. 379). It is the tension between these two kinds of constructions of deafness that is at play here, and it is this tension that is, on a fundamental level, probably ultimately irreconcilable.

Perhaps the clearest contemporary manifestation of this tension between the two competing perspectives of deafness has been the debate about the use of cochlear implants in young children. Cochlear implants do not restore hearing; rather, they can create the perception of sound which, coupled with effective rehabilitation, can assist some hearing impaired individuals to function more effectively (see Christiansen & Leigh, 2006; Woodcock, 2001 [1993]). In the case of young children, advocates of cochlear implants argue that "early implantation of deaf children should be considered as a way to expose them to the spoken word, enable them to learn spoken languages, and develop better speech skills" (Woodcock, 2001 [1993], p. 325; see also Jones, 2002).

Cochlear implantation involves a three to four hour surgical procedure, during which

> the hospitalized child is placed under general anesthesia . . . The surgeon cuts the skin behind the ear, raises the flap, and drills a hole in the bone. Then a wire carrying electrodes is pushed some twenty-five millimeters into the coiled inner ear. The tiny endings of the auditory nerve are destroyed and electrical fields from the wire stimulate the auditory nerve directly. A small receiver coil connected to the wire is sutured to the skull and the skin is sewn over it. A small microphone worn on an ear piece picks up sound and sends signals to a processor worn on a belt or in a pocket. The processor sends electrical signals back to the implanted receiver via a transmitter mounted behind the ear, and those signals stimulate the auditory nerve. (Lane et al., 1996, p. 388)

In short, the cochlear implant functions as a kind of equivalent for a hearing aid, though it is by no means the same. There is no doubt that cochlear implants can be helpful for some late-deafened individuals, for whom the procedure was originally designed. The debate is not about the choice of adults to seek cochlear implants; it is about whether the procedure is appropriate for very young children (Aiello & Aiello, 2001 [1999], pp. 406–7; Howe, 1992, pp. 67–68; Lane, 1993a, 1993b; Lane et al., 1996, pp. 386–407; Woodcock, 2001 [1993]). From an outsider's perspective, the arguments in favor of cochlear implants for young deaf children are fairly compelling. The procedure does have the potential to help the hearing impaired individual function more effectively in the hearing world, offering if not a cure for deafness, then at least the possibility of the individual acquiring the skills necessary to "pass" as hearing and, hence, as "normal," though this is neither the articulated goal of the procedure nor a particularly likely outcome (see Woodcock, 2001[1993]), and while its long-term effects remain unclear (see Padden & Humphries, 2005, pp.178–79). There is some evidence for the educational effectiveness of cochlear implants (see Paul, 2001, pp. 220–22), and the option of a cochlear implant is clearly one that both many physicians and hearing parents of deaf children see as desirable. This said, the surgery itself is only the beginning of what is required for success with a cochlear implant:

> Each year thousands of deaf children are surgically implanted with electronic devices that direct electronic impulses to the cochlea to simulate hearing . . . After surgery, the child begins a long course of rehabilitation that tailors the

electronic device to the capabilities of the child, and then the child is trained to recognize sounds transmitted by the device. The child interacts first with the surgeon, then the specialists who train the child for the device. The child's teachers may also be enlisted in the task, to coordinate training with education. (Padden & Humphries, 2005, p. 166)

From a deaf perspective, however, cochlear implants raise a number of both practical and ethical questions, as Padden and Humphries note:

In the early years of the cochlear implant technology, some Deaf people spoke out, raising questions about the immediate and long-term effects of the devices, especially for young deaf children. A position paper written in 1985 on behalf of a Deaf organization asked questions about the medical risks of the procedure: the possibility of infection, and other hazards related to surgery such as facial paralysis, or if in the event of failure or technical obsolence of the device, the child would need to be reimplanted. This attempt at voice had limited effect and was roundly dismissed by supporters of cochlear implant surgery as exaggerating the risks of the medical procedure and obstructing the desires of parents of deaf children and deaf individuals who wanted the devices. Harlan Lane, an eloquent hearing speaker and scientist, wrote several articles questioning the goals and claims of cochlear implant specialists, but he was severely criticized by parents of deaf children with implants as being romantic about deafness and alarmist about the dangers of the surgery. (2005, pp. 166–67)

Even more, deaf people tend to be concerned about the lack of information about the DEAF⁀WORLD that most hearing parents of deaf children have:

The majority of parents of children with cochlear implants report not meeting deaf adults, whether oral or signing, at the time of diagnosis of deafness or when deciding on cochlear implantation for the deaf children . . . For deaf children of hearing parents, exposure to deaf peers or to Deaf culture comes, if at all, when the children get older and are provided with opportunities for interacting either in educational programs that include deaf children or during social functions that involve large groups of deaf people . . . Very often, this exposure hinges on the advice, guidance, and information provided by professionals specializing in working with deaf and hard of hearing individuals, typically within early intervention, audiology, or educational settings . . . How these professionals convey implicit messages about successfully integrating into hearing worlds or interacting with other deaf peers can play a significant role in framing the meaning of deaf identity, whether as a minuscule difference (not hearing), a stigmatized concept to be minimized, or as a significant core identity. (Leigh, 2008, p. 23)

It is the very conception of what constitutes "normal," however, that is at the heart of much of the deaf community's resistance to such procedures. Michel Foucault explored the epistemological power of socially established norms in terms of mental illness, punishment, and sexuality; here the deaf community likewise illuminates "the power of normalization and the formation of knowledge in modern society" (Foucault, 1969) with regard to the equation of "hearing" with "normal." As Jim Cummins (2009) notes in a recent article in the *International Journal of Bilingual Education and Bilingualism*, the devaluation of community languages in the wider society often results in ambivalence among parents and teachers about the extent to which such languages should, in fact, be supported in the school—a point with direct ramifications for both ASL and the DEAF⌒WORLD. Returning once again to Harlan Lane's observation, from a deaf perspective it is clear that

> if the birth of a Deaf child is a priceless gift, then there is only cause for rejoicing, as at the birth of a black child, or an Indian one. Medical intervention is inappropriate, even if a perfect "cure" were available. Invasive surgery on healthy children is morally wrong. We know that, as members of a stigmatized minority, these children's lives will be full of challenge but, by the same token, they have a special contribution to make to their own community and the larger society. (1993b, pp. 490–91)

Although the tension between the dominant hearing and deaf constructions of deaf identity may well be irreconcilable on a conceptual level, it is nevertheless important to recognize that the reality of deaf experience is more complex and less clear than this might suggest. The vast majority of deaf people become members of the DEAF⌒WORLD relatively late in comparison with membership in most cultures. This is the case because most deaf people have hearing parents and are introduced to deaf culture not by adults but rather by peers, most often in the context of residential schools for deaf children. Further, membership in deaf culture is not really an either/or proposition: individual deaf people identify as culturally deaf in different ways, and to different extents. Perhaps the clearest example of this complexity is manifested in the case of individuals who are hard of hearing, for whom membership in deaf culture is related to often conflicting attitudes about deafness itself. The extent to which the process of normalization of deafness to hearing norms (or "hearization") is accepted or rejected is key here, as Nover makes clear: "hearization leads many deaf children into wishing or thinking they will become hearing some day.

Others prefer to be called 'hearing impaired' or 'hard of hearing' rather than deaf. Unfortunately, deaf and hard of hearing children may learn to view hearing people as superior to those who are deaf" (1993).

The cultural and linguistic identity of individuals who are hard of hearing is, in short, both potentially and practically ambiguous, as indeed is the identity of many other individuals who straddle multiple cultural and linguistic worlds. It is this ambiguity that makes simple descriptions of cultural identity misleading, not only in the case of deaf people, but with respect to virtually all minority cultural and linguistic groups (Motoyoshi, 1990, pp. 77–94; Ogbu, 1978, 1987, 1988, 1992, 2008).

Thus far, I have been concerned with presenting what I take to be the standard description and analysis of the DEAF-WORLD, and its relationship with the hearing world. As the field of Deaf Studies has emerged in many universities in the United States as a legitimate academic discipline, however, there have inevitably been developments in the field, including calls for a reconceptualization of the standard dichotomous view that has been the norm (see Bauman, 2008b)—for example, in two recent articles by Jane K. Fernandes and Shirley Shultz Myers published in the *Journal of Deaf Studies and Deaf Education* (see Fernandes & Myers, 2010; Myers & Fernandes, 2010). Fernandes and Myers make a number of compelling points that should be taken into account in understanding the nature of the DEAF⁀WORLD. In essence, they recommend that the field of Deaf Studies "take a more expansive, nuanced, and interdisciplinary approach that encompasses the many ways deaf people live today" (Fernandes & Myers, 2010, p. 17). Few could object to such a call, but Fernandes and Myers go on to note that the "founding scholarship [in Deaf Studies] validates and instills pride in native ASL users and demarcates the boundaries of Deaf culture. What remains in the shadows is the fact that the pride of ASL users has evolved into a powerful hierarchy through which native White ASL users and those born into Deaf culture receive privileged status at the expense of other deaf people" (Fernandes & Myers, 2010, p. 17). Fernandes and Myers are also critical of the use of the past in making arguments about the present. Although they recognize that deaf people have historically been oppressed, they argue that "the ahistorical view needs to be brought current in order to generate fuller, multiple understandings of the reality of deaf people and their complex lives" (Myers & Fernandes, 2010, p. 32); further, deaf people in the United States are not currently an oppressed population:

> The status quo for deaf people today reflects a reality where they are known as safe drivers who get insurance from companies other than their own National Fraternal Society of the Deaf—now dissolved because of this progress. Deaf people also own property and have children. And they have moved into all types of professions including the law, dentistry, and medicine. Deaf people's rights to live with full citizenship are widely acknowledged and guaranteed by law. ASL courses are taught in many school systems and universities . . . Moreover, many ASL courses are taught by Deaf individuals so that these courses are a valuable way to bring Deaf people into desirable and rewarding employment. (Myers & Fernandes, 2010, p. 34)

The alternative view is that the integration of deaf people into American society remains at best problematic, whether educationally, economically, professionally, culturally, or in whatever domain—a point acknowledged even by Fernandes and Myers: "These criticisms are not meant to imply that audism does not exist. It most certainly does" (Myers & Fernandes, 2010, p. 34). This point is important to bear in mind in our discussion here.

The second half of the twentieth century has been, in many ways, the most liberating for deaf people—for their language, their culture, and their rights—in the history of the world. This is no small matter, and it is important to recall. This is not the same thing, however, as saying that deaf people have finally achieved equality with hearing people. The distance between the hearing world and the DEAF⌒WORLD remains not really so much as a gap as a chasm much of the time. Robert Panara, one of the best-known deaf writers and poets in the United States, makes the tension between the two worlds clear in his poem "Lip Service," in which he castigates the hearing world for its hypocrisy:

> You want to rap
> you said
> and let it all hang out
> this thing about
> the communication gap
> that keeps us separate
> your kind
> from mine.
> You want to rap
> you said
> you want to integrate
> but you decline

to change your line
of crap
from speech
to sign. (1992, p. 29)

In short, as Robert Frost so eloquently put it in his 1922 poem "Stopping By the Woods on a Snowy Evening" (1969), we still have "promises to keep, and miles to go" to address the issues of inequality and oppression that separate the DEAF⁀WORLD from the hearing world.

NOTES

1. A common distinction made in writing about deafness is between *deaf* and *Deaf*: the former refers to deafness solely as an audiological condition, the latter to deafness as a cultural condition. The basic idea underlying this distinction is that when writing about cultural groups in general, uppercase letters are employed (African American, Hispanic, Native American, and so on). Thus, a person can be deaf without being Deaf (as in the case of an older person who gradually loses his or her hearing). Although I believe that this is a valuable distinction conceptually and heuristically, I also think that it oversimplifies and dichotomizes the complexity of membership in the DEAF⁀WORLD. I have therefore chosen simply to use the lowercase *deaf* throughout this book, with the understanding that deafness is not only socially and individually constructed, but that its construction is complex and multilayered (see Branson & Miller, 2002; Ladd, 2003; Lane et al., 1996; Padden & Humphries, 1988, 2005; Reagan, 1988, 1990a, 1995a, 2002c, 2005b [1985]).

2. The phrases "deaf culture" and DEAF⁀WORLD are both commonly used, and I have chosen to use them interchangeably in this book.

3. The disconnects between hearing parents and deaf children, and then, in the next generation, between deaf parents and hearing children contribute to the complexity of life as a culturally and linguistically deaf person. For further discussions of this topic, see Bishop and Hicks (2005), Cohen (1994), Preston (1994), and Walker (1986).

4. For a discussion of early identification of hearing impairment and its implications, see Cone-Wesson (2003); for intensive speech perception and spoken word recognition strategies, see Bernstein and Auer (2003); for cochlear implants, see Spencer and Marschark (2003). For discussions of the implications of deafness and the early identification of deafness on literacy, see Paul (2001, 2003).

5. The degree of hearing loss is clinically measured in decibels (dBs); severe hearing loss is between 71 and 90 dBs, whereas profound hearing loss is 90 dBs

or above. Between 1/800 and 1/1000 infants in the U.S. are born with profound or severe hearing loss.

6. Although the relationship of different types of signing (ranging from ASL through contact sign to various manual sign codes) is typically presented as a falling along a single continuum (see, e.g., Baker & Cokely, 1980, p. 73), I believe that this is an erroneous representation of the linguistic reality (see Reagan, 2005b [1985]). The use of a single continuum makes sense when we are dealing with two historically (i.e., in a linguistic sense *genetically*) related languages. Thus, a continuum showing the relationship between Spanish and Portuguese, or between German and Dutch, makes perfectly good sense. However, when one is dealing with two languages (in this case, ASL and English) that are *not* genetically related, what is required, in my view, is the use of two separate continua. This allows us to see that there are two quite distinct and separate languages involved, and that while there may be what seem to be common linguistic behaviors found among some speakers (in terms of contact sign, in this case), what is actually taking place is that native users of ASL are modifying ASL in ways that make it appear more like English, while native users of English are modifying their signing in ways that make it appear closer to ASL. This does not, to be sure, eliminate the possibility that an individual might "jump" from one continuum to the other (that is, become truly bilingual), but in the case of ASL and English, this is in fact relatively rare.

Chapter 2

Language Planning and Language Policy: An Introduction

> *Language planning refers to deliberate efforts to influence the behavior of others with respect to the acquisition, structure, or functional allocation of their language codes.* (Cooper, 1989, p. 45)

> *Language issues have some of the characteristics of sex—everyone does it, and consequently everyone is an expert. However, it is not teachers nor even parents who teach most adolescents about sex; rather it is a cadre of other adolescents, mostly characterised by knowing little about the matter. From there on, it is largely a matter of on-the-job training. It is not until one reaches maturity that one even discovers that there are real experts who might teach one something about the subject. So it is with language issues. Every segment of society has language and individuals competently use language for a variety of purposes. However, when users engage in talking about language, which they frequently do, that talk is largely marked by profound ignorance.* (Kaplan & Baldauf, 1997, p. 3)

Language planning is both an academic discipline and a practical activity resulting in the development and implementation of specific language policies. It is thus at the same time an effort to guide individual and communal behavior with respect to language use (typically undertaken by governmental bodies and agencies), and the engagement in the study of such efforts (typically undertaken by academics). This duality has led to confusion in the field and to debates about the legitimacy of language planning efforts from various academic and political perspectives. The problem has been made even more complex by the fact that many scholars interested in language planning and language policy studies have themselves participated in discussions, and even in decision-making, with respect to national language planning and language policy efforts. In short, many of us have played roles as both language planners and as those who study the very language planning efforts in which we have been engaged. In addition, as Roberts (2005) has noted with respect to literacy and definitions of literacy, the wide variety of definitions of the concepts involved used by policy makers, politicians, academics, and teachers, not to mention the general public, make it almost impossible to present clear and cogent summaries of the nature of the field (see also Maruatona, 2005; Rosenquest, 2002). This makes discussing language planning and language policy complex and difficult, but also means that as a common form of social engineering language planning and policy studies are of crucial concern to us in understanding the world around us. The purpose of this chapter, then, is to present a broad overview of language planning and language policy studies. Our focus in this chapter will be on language planning and language policy studies as these relate, for the most part, to spoken languages. In later chapters, our focus will shift to language planning and language policy studies as these relate to sign languages.

In 1971, Rubin and Jernudd edited a book entitled *Can Language Be Planned*? That was, and remains, an important question, although the answer, which once seemed clearly affirmative, is now considerably more mixed. As such efforts have been developed, implemented, and evaluated, it has become increasingly clear that language planning and the establishment of language policies are incredibly complex matters, and that what works in one setting may very well fail miserably in another similar setting. Furthermore, the road from the early language planning efforts of the 1970s to the present concern for and interest in language planning and language policy studies has not been a smooth one (see Canagarajah, 2005; Kaplan & Baldauf, 1997; Lambert, 1990; Ricento, 2006; Ricento & Burnaby, 1998; Shohamy, 2006; Spolsky, 2004; S. Wright, 2004). Robert Cooper notes, "That language planning should serve so many covert goals is not surprising. Language is the fundamental institution of society, not only because it is the first human institution experienced by the individual, but also because all other institutions are build upon its regulatory patterns . . . To plan language is to plan society" (1989, p. 182)—and the planning of society is, if anything, an increasingly common phenomenon in both the developed and developing worlds. In fact, perhaps rather than ask whether language can be planned, we should assume it can be and turn to the more significant questions of *how* and *by whom* language will be planned. There is, in addition, an ethical argument at play here: "In order to give individuals fair equality of opportunity to realize their own conception of a good life, the state must try to provide equally effective support for the structures of each component ethnolinguistic community making up the country. This would seem to provide powerful and reasoned support for a language policy in support of multiple languages in a multilingual country" (Schmidt, 2006, p. 106). Thus, at the heart of issues of language planning and language policy are inevitably issues of language diversity and how such diversity is to be (or not to be) accommodated.

A good place to begin our discussion is to note that while language planning and language policy studies are generally considered to be relatively recent phenomena, this is true only in a very limited sense:

> In one sense, our knowledge of language planning is probably as old as recorded human history as it is a part of how people use language. In Europe, when the Romans conquered the circum-Mediterranean world, Latin and Greek acted as lingua francas and the authorities of the Empire did a certain amount of language planning as Latin spread throughout the vast conquests of the Empire . . . For example, when Julius Caesar invaded Britain in 55 BC, the legions came to Britain speaking Latin, and there was some attempt to teach the language to the local inhabitants, not so much in formal schooling settings as through the practical realities of everyday life. The Romans drew maps in which they used the rules of Latin nomenclature to designate places and to describe features; they built fortifications and cities using Latin names for architectural features and for completed buildings; they enslaved local residents into Roman households in which those local residents had to learn Latin in order to understand their masters. (Kaplan & Baldauf, 1997, p. ix)

Nor were the Romans the only people historically who engaged in such informal language planning; such efforts long predate the Roman Empire (in Mesopotamia, for instance) and continued through the spread of Islam, the European colonial enterprise, and during a host of other eras and in many other locations.

The terminology of language planning and language policy itself often makes linguists and others uncomfortable. Language is, after all, a core part of an individual's identity, and phrases like "language planning" and "language policy" can suggest an almost Orwellian kind of social control. In spite of this, what is really intended is both quite common and even necessary. Consider the following questions:

- What is the correct spelling for a word?
- What is the correct pronunciation for a word?
- What does a word actually mean?
- What variety or varieties of a language should be used in formal or official settings?
- What kind of orthographic (writing) system should one use to write a particular language?

For speakers of a language like English, French, Spanish, German, or Russian, all of which have been standardized for a relatively long period of time, the responses to these questions may seem to be very straightforward. In such languages, with only rare exceptions, there are clear-cut answers to questions of these sorts. For the correct spelling, pronunciation, and meaning of a word, we rely on a dictionary, which tells us the socially accepted norms for usage. The dominant variety of a language, generally labeled the "standard language," is typically that taught in schools and used in government and the media. As for the writing system to be used, again, we rely on a socially agreed-upon system. Thus, English is written in the Latin alphabet rather than in the Cyrillic, like Russian. English could, of course, be written in Cyrillic script—or in Arabic or Hebrew script, or even with Chinese characters. Although every writing system has its own advantages and disadvantages, any language could, in principle, be represented in any kind of orthography, and many languages have been written using different orthographies from time to time. This was the case, for example, with a number of languages in what was formerly Soviet Central Asia, where the languages have been written in Arabic script, Cyrillic script, and Latin script, often reflecting the political ideology of the time (see Garibova & Asgarova, 2009; Maurais, 1992; Schlyter, 1998; Sebba, 2006; Shorish, 1984). In Turkey, Turkish language reform under Atatürk in the early twentieth century replaced Arabic script with Latin script (see Baskan, 1986; Doğançay-Aktuna, 1995; Heyd, 1954; Iz, 1991; Lewis, 1984; Perry, 1985).

For languages that have been standardized, the socially accepted norms have been, at least in part, determined and are widely shared and generally accepted by speakers of the languages. In societies with standardized languages, we tend to assume that such socially accepted norms are not only necessary and appropriate, but even that they represent the "real language" in some sense. This is, of course, not really the case at all; language is not static and fixed, but rather is, by its very nature, complex, diverse, and changing. Further, while the languages with which most of us are familiar (such as French, Spanish, German, Russian, Japanese, Chinese, and so on) are standardized, the vast majority of languages spoken today, and historically, by human beings are not. Efforts to standardize language, including efforts to create new terminology where needed, are examples of *language planning activity*. So, too, are efforts by institutions and governments to determine what language or languages can be used in particular spheres (for instance, in schools, courts, legislatures and other governmental settings, business, etc.); in other words, attempts to institute particular *language policies*. Such language planning activities are increasingly widespread today, and are taking place in some manner in virtually every nation in the world (Canagarajah, 2005; Kaplan & Baldauf, 1997; Ricento, 2006; Ricento & Burnaby, 1998; Shohamy, 2006; Spolsky, 2004; Weinstein, 1990; S. Wright, 2004). In essence, a language policy is a deliberate effort to mandate specific language behaviors in particular contexts. Such policies can, and do, involve decisions about language development and allocation, language use, language rights, language education, and a host of other important issues. Cooper, quoted at the start of this chapter, is correct in arguing that "language planning refers to deliberate efforts to influence the behavior of others with respect to the acquisition, structure, or functional allocation of their language codes" (1989, p. 45).

In the remainder of this chapter, I investigate an underlying problematic in the discipline of language planning and language policy: the nature of "language" itself, and the extent to which such a construct can actually vex the study of language planning and language policy. I then offer a broad overview of the nature and purposes of language planning and language policy activities in general, including examinations of the role of ideology in language policy and of the use (and misuse) of language planning and language policy to achieve social, political, and educational ends.

THE PROBLEMATIC NATURE OF "LANGUAGE"

One of the more compelling intellectual debates of the twentieth century was that which took place among philosophers of science and others interested in understanding both the nature and limits of human knowledge. Originating in the 1920s with the work of a group of philosophers known as the "Vienna Circle" (*Wienerkreis*), logical positivism (or logical empiricism, as it was also called) provided a foundation for the development of a positivistic approach to epistemology that dominated philosophical discourse, at least in the Anglophone world, well into the 1960s (see Audi, 1998). Although perhaps best recognized for his contributions to the philosophy of science, the Austrian-born British philosopher Karl Popper was actually primarily concerned with issues of epistemology. In his seminal book *The Logic of Scientific Discovery*, Popper argued, "The central problem of epistemology has always been and still is the problem of the growth of knowledge. *And the growth of knowledge can be studied best by studying the growth of scientific knowledge*" (2002 [1935], p. xix, emphasis in original). Thus, for the positivist, the way in which science contributes to and makes possible the growth of knowledge is essential. Positivism, in its simplest form, presupposes the existence of an external reality that we can seek to recognize and understand. Reality is thus singular, divisible, and, to some extent, knowable. It is knowable through the use of common methods of observation and public confirmation. Science, properly understood and carried out, has as its mission the articulation of this singular reality.

Linguists and language specialists, as well as the lay public, have generally viewed language from a perspective that is, at its heart, fundamentally positivist in orientation. We tend to assume that language as an abstract entity, in a sort of Chomskian sense, exists as just such a knowable, and singular, object.[1] Neil Smith writes, "There is an intuitive appeal to the notion that there is an external language that different people speak. Indeed, it is so self-evidently true that it would be pointless to deny it. However, when taken to its logical conclusion, the idea turns out to be problematic, as the notion of 'language' involved is different from the notion that linguists theorize about" (2002, pp. 102–3). Even more problematically, we assume that *particular* languages also exist as knowable entities that can be described and analyzed. Such assumptions and presuppositions are embedded in our discourse and have important implications for any sort of applied language studies, including of course the study of language planning and language policy. We commonly make claims about English, Spanish, Russian, Navajo, and so on, just as we make claims about the nature of human language in more general terms. Indeed, when we engage in teaching foreign languages, for example, our goal is to move the student's linguistic behavior in the second language closer to the preconceived norms of the singular reality of that target language. What we do, in short, is to engage in the objectification of the construct of "language," which in turn, I believe, has led us to misunderstand the nature of language and to accept technicist and positivistic views of languages in many disciplines, which focus on a problem-solving approach to language rather than to a more broad and thoughtful one.

An excellent starting point for understanding how this objectification of language has taken place, and why it matters, is to consider the meaning of the term *language* itself. The historian Carl Becker makes clear the importance and potential power of definitions:

> Now, when I meet a word with which I am entirely unfamiliar, I find it a good plan to look it up in the dictionary and find out what someone thinks it means. But when I have frequently to use words with which everyone is perfectly familiar—words like "cause" and "liberty" and "progress" and "government"—when I have to use words of this sort which everyone knows perfectly well, the wise thing to do is to take a week off and think about them. (1955, p. 328)

Language is a wonderful case of such a "week-off" word. It is one of those terms that we use all of the time, and whose meaning we seem to know and understand. And yet, the deeper one pursues the matter, the fuzzier and more problematic the concept of language becomes:

> Language plays an important role in the lives of all of us and is our most distinctive human possession. We might expect, therefore, to be well-informed about it. The truth is we are not. Many statements we believe to be true about language are likely as not false. Many of the questions we concern ourselves with are either unanswerable and therefore not really worth asking or betray a serious misunderstanding of the nature of language. Most of us have learned many things about language from others, but generally the wrong things. (Wardhaugh, 1999, p. viii)

In its most commonplace and everyday uses, the term *language* is in fact both ahistorical and atheoretical. It is ahistorical in that it presupposes that language is in some sense fixed and static—that is, that it is a singular reality, in positivistic terms. Consider the case of Spanish. The speech community of Spanish has evolved from varieties of Latin (especially varieties of Vulgar Latin) to modern Spanish varieties spoken around the world over the past two thousand years in a number of ways (see Penny, 2002; Pharies, 2007); "Latin is the ancestor of Spanish (and, by definition, of all other Romance languages) in the sense that there is an unbroken chain of speakers, each learning his or her language from parents and contemporaries, stretching from the people of the Western Roman Empire two thousand years ago to the present population of the Spanish-speaking world" (Penny, 2002, p. 4). Latin was first introduced to northeastern Spain by Roman troops in 218 B.C.E., but between then and the present, there was no clear-cut break between speakers of Latin and speakers of Spanish; there has been a continuity in the speaker community, and at no point were speakers of one generation unable to understand speakers of the next generation. The same, of course, is true of any case of linguistic evolution. From a strictly historical perspective, any language is thus something of a moving target. Codification, of course, can and does slow this process down, but it does not prevent it. Language—*any* language—is constantly changing and in flux, and thus any effort to demarcate the boundaries of a particular language are inevitably at best able to provide a snapshot of the language at a particular time and place. A fairly good analogy is provided by the coastline of Britain; we all know that there *is* such a thing, and can talk about it and even show pictures of it—and yet, it really does not exist except as an abstraction. The waves at the edge of the coast, and the coastline itself, are constantly in a state of flux. In a sense, it is simply not possible to "measure" the coastline since it is always changing. The same is true of language.

Conceptions of language are not only ahistorical, though, they are also atheoretical in nature. Language varies, as we all know, not only over time, but also from place to place, class to class, and individual to individual. H. Ekkehard Wolff, in a discussion of the relationship of language and society in the African context, notes that "no two speakers of the same language speak alike, nor does the same speaker use his/her language the same way all the time: variation is part of language and language behaviour" (2000, p. 299). Responding to the question "How many Romance languages are there?" Rebecca Posner writes:

> An answer to this question that has been slightingly labeled *sancta simplicitas* is that there is only one: the languages are all alike enough to be deemed dialects of the same language. Another equally disingenuous answer might be "thousands"—of distinctive varieties—or "millions"—of individual ideolects. The usual textbook answer is "ten, or possibly eleven," according priority to putative chronologically early differentiation from the common stock, allegedly linked to ethnic differences among the speakers. (1996, p. 189)

Posner's point is extremely well taken: even in a case as well documented as that of the Romance languages, the specific demarcation of distinct languages is fundamentally an arbitrary one (for the traditional demarcation of the major Romance languages, see Figure 2.1). We see this same problem in delimiting languages as distinct in settings around the world. Although the criterion of mutual intelligibility is useful in some instances, it is far from adequate in many others. Norwegian, Swedish, and Danish have a very high degree of mutual intelligibility, and yet are recognized as different languages by both their own speakers and others. The language boundaries in Africa and many other parts of the developing world are often even fuzzier, which helps to explain why we are incapable of articulating a meaningful response to the question, "How many languages are there in the world?" In South Africa, for instance, the differences between isiZulu and isiXhosa are minimal, at least in their spoken forms (see Campbell-Makini, 2000, p. 115)—and yet, in part as a consequence of different orthographic norms, and in part as a result of issues related to ethnic identity, not to mention the historical legacy of apartheid that stressed cultural and linguistic differences among the black majority, the two are seen as distinct languages (and both are among the eleven official languages of South Africa; see Kamwangamalu & Reagan, 2004; Reagan, 2001b, 2002b). At the same time, many of the regional varieties of modern German are mutually unintelligible, and yet we speak of "German" as a single language (see Barbour & Stevenson, 1990; Stevenson, 1997, 1998).

Perhaps one of the best recent examples of this phenomenon is the change that has taken place with respect to the language varieties that were known collectively, at least during the latter half of the twentieth century, as Serbo-Croatian (see Hawkesworth, 1998; Norris, 1993; Partridge, 1972). The deliberate construction of a single Serbo-Croatian language had been an important element of social engineering during the Communist regime and was part of the broader effort to create a sense of Yugoslav national identity. Although Serbian and Croatian language varieties are indeed quite close, they are distinguished not only by their orthography (Serbian is written in the Cyrillic alphabet, while Croatian uses the Latin alphabet), but also by lexical differences. Even during the period in which the languages were officially unified, there were tensions (primarily on the part of Croatian intellectuals) related to the apparent dominance of Serbian forms. John Lampe explores this history, asking, "Could a common Serbo-Croatian orthography and dictionary fairly be called Croato-Serbian as well? Croatian reservations turned into public protests when the first two volumes of the dictionary were published [in 1967]. Serbian variants of these two, overlapping, grammatically identical languages were consistently chosen over the Croatian variants" (2000, p. 305).

Name of Language	Approximate Number of Speakers	Status
Aragonese	10,000 (active), 30,000 (passive)	Spoken in the Aragon region of Spain.
Balearic	750,000	Spoken in Andorra, in France (in northern Catalonia), in Italy (in the city of Alghero), and in Spain (in Aragon, the Balearic Islands, Carche, Catalonia, Murcia, and Valencia).
Catalán	9,200,000	The official language in Andorra, and the co-official language in Catalonia, the Balearic Islands, and Valencia in Spain. It is also spoken in southern France and on Sardinia. It has been recognized as one of Spain's four "official languages."
Corsican	340,000	Spoken in Corsica and northern Sardinia.
French	110,000,000	French is a major world language and a language of wider communication (LWC). It is an official language in 28 countries.
Galician	3,000,000	Spoken in northwestern Spain in Galicia, and in northern Portugal. Galician is recognized as one of Spain's four "official languages."
Italian	70,000,000	Italian is the official language of Italy and San Marino, one of the four official languages of Switzerland, and the primary daily language of the Vatican City.
Occitan	1,500,000	Occitan is also known as *Langue d'oc.* A co-official language with Catalán in Catalonia, Occitan is also spoken in southern France, Monaco, and Italy.
Portuguese	210,000,000	Portuguese is the official language in Brazil, Macau, Portugal, Angola, and Mozambique, among others. Portuguese is among the LWCs.
Romanian (Moldovan)	28,000,000	Romanian (called Moldovan in Moldova) is the official language of Romania, Moldova, and Vojvodina in Serbia, and is a recognized minority language in Ukraine.
Romansh	35,000	Romansh is the fourth (and, in terms of number of speakers, smallest) official language of Switzerland.

(*continued on next page*)

FIGURE 2.1. *Traditional demarcation of the major Romance languages*

Name of Language	Approximate Number of Speakers	Status
Sardinian	1,850,000	Spoken in most parts of the island of Sardinia, Sardinian has official status in Sardinia.
Spanish	329,000,000	Spanish is the official language in 21 countries around the world. Spanish is an LWC.
Walloon	600,000	Walloon is spoken in the Walloon region in Belgium, as well as in small parts of France.

FIGURE 2.1. *Traditional demarcation of the major Romance languages* (continued)

In the years following the break-up of the former Yugoslavia, efforts to emphasize the distinctive nature of each variety of the language intensified (see Glenny, 1996; Lampe, 2000), and there are now separate dictionaries, grammars, and so on, for Croatian, Serbian, and Bosnian (see, for example, Kroll & Zahirovič, 1998; Šušnjar, 2000; Uzicanin, 1996; Vitas, 1998), not to mention the emergence of the related Macedonian language in the Republic of Macedonia (see Kramer, 1999a, 1999b). Typical of the rhetoric found in such works is the following description of the "Bosnian language":

> The Bosnian language is spoken by 4.5 million people: Muslims, Serbs, and Croats living together for centuries in Bosnia and Herzegovina. . . . The Bosnian language is a symbiosis of the Serb and Croat languages, which are Slavic tongues, with strong Turkish and German influences. Bosnian is written in two alphabets: Cyrillic and Roman. (Uzicanin, 1996, p. 7)

As a consequence of these developments, we are now presented with a number of separate (albeit for the most part mutually intelligible) languages spoken by ethnically distinct groups, among which are Croatian, Serbian, and Bosnian. Regardless of the extent to which these languages are in fact mutually intelligible, their speakers have, by and large, decided that they are separate languages, and each speaker population has sufficient political legitimacy at the present time to enforce such a determination. In short, in distinguishing between "languages" and "dialects," we are ultimately left with the distinction attributed to Max Weinreich (1945): "A language is a dialect with its own army and navy."[2]

Up to this point, our discussion has focused on the difficulties of fixing the boundaries between and among historically related languages in areas and times of political unrest, and yet the difficulties are not unique to such settings. Consider, for instance, the case of sign language in general, and of ASL in particular. "Signing" and the use of ASL are by no means the same thing: there many different natural sign languages in the world, some of which are historically related (such as French Sign Language and ASL), and some of which are not historically related (such as British Sign Language and ASL). The language boundaries of natural sign languages are also necessarily arbitrary to some extent; a good example of this is the recent debate among sign language linguists in South Africa about whether there is a single South African Sign Language (SASL), characterized by extensive lexical variation but closely related syntax, or rather a number of distinct, probably (but by no means certainly) related, SASLs (see Aarons & Akach, 1998, 2002; Aarons & Reynolds, 2003; Ogilvy-Foreman, Penn, & Reagan, 1994; Penn & Reagan, 1994; Reagan, 2004, 2007; Reagan & Penn, 1997; Storbeck, Magongwa, & Parkin, 2009). The debate, ultimately, is really a silly one in that there is no possible linguistic (or perhaps even conceptual) answer (Reagan, 2004). Whether SASL is a single language or a group of sign languages depends not on the answer to any particular linguistic question but rather on extralinguistic factors, the most important of which is how deaf people in South Africa themselves see the situation. For a time, under the apartheid regime and as a result of social and educational pressures, many deaf people in South Africa believed that their sign languages were quite distinct (see Penn, 1992, 1993, 1994a, 1994b, 1994c; Penn & Reagan, 1990, 1994, 2001; Reagan, Penn, & Ogilvy, 2006); in the post-apartheid era, there has been a strong impetus among deaf people for seeing SASL as a single, shared sign language. In the context of ASL, we have long recognized that there is in fact a continuum of sign language usage, ranging from ASL through various contact sign languages to the artificial manual codes designed to represent English (see Baker & Cokely, 1980; Reagan, 1995a, 1995b, 2002c; Valli et al., 2005, p. 14). While the manual sign codes are clearly not, by any definition, ASL, distinguishing the exact boundary between ASL and a particular contact sign language (especially one used by a proficient user of ASL) depends on understanding the signer's linguistic behavior and thus is considerably more problematic.

This is not at all a small matter, though it is not the whole story. Language boundaries are ultimately determined not by linguistic criteria, but rather by extralinguistic criteria, as Weinreich suggests in the quotation cited above. Furthermore, since no two speakers of a language possess and use the language in identical ways—indeed, since no *single* speaker does so—we are left with the reality of language as existing only in the plural. A language, in short, is ultimately a collection of idiolects that have been determined to belong together for what are ultimately non- and extralinguistic reasons. The growing number of scholars and researchers who have suggested that we need to speak of English*es*, rather than of English, are correct (see, for example, Bamgbose, Banjo, & Thomas, 1997; Kachru, 1982; McArthur, 1998)—but they do not go quite far enough. Not only are there multiple Englishes, but there are quite literally millions of different Englishes. Nor does this observation apply solely to English; it is true of French, Russian, Navajo, indeed, of every language. The only kind of language that could really exist in the singular would be one spoken by only one person—and by that single person if he or she were capable of absolutely consistent linguistic behavior.

The implications of this problematic conceptualization of "language" for any discipline dealing with language-related issues are significant. In the case of language planning and language policy studies, the issue becomes especially important when we deal with smaller languages, languages whose borders and boundaries are unclear, and languages that have not been codified. In short, the positivistic conception of language is most dangerous and most problematic specifically in the cases most likely to involve language planning and language policy efforts.

THE HISTORICAL DEVELOPMENT OF LANGUAGE PLANNING AND LANGUAGE POLICY STUDIES

The first major scholarly publication to deal with language planning is Einar Haugen's (1966) *Language Conflict and Language Planning: The Case of Modern Norwegian*, which deals with the development of a new standard language in Norway after independence from Denmark had been achieved in 1814. Haugen's work is a historical study; it was not until shortly after its publication that a number of scholarly works appeared that began to explore more contemporary language planning efforts (see Cobarrubias & Fishman, 1983; Fishman, 1971, 1972, 1974, 1978; Rubin & Jernudd, 1971; Rubin, Jernudd, Das Gupta, Fishman, & Ferguson, 1977). Although some of these early works also deal with historical cases, especially with the Israeli and Irish examples of language revitalization (to which I will return later in this chapter),[3] most are concerned primarily with more contemporaneous language planning efforts. In addition to articles and books dealing with particular cases of language planning and language policy, several journals with a primary focus on such issues also emerged, most notably *Language Problems and Language Planning*, which began publishing in 1977 and continues to the present.[4]

In the immediate postcolonial era, the development and implementation of language policies played a key role in national development in a wide range of formerly colonial societies. Decolonization, especially in Africa and Asia, created significant challenges with respect to language planning and language policy writ large. Newly constituted nations had to find answers for such questions as these:

- What language or languages will serve as the official language of government?
- What role, if any, will be played by the language of the former colonial power?
- What role, if any, will be played by indigenous languages in the country?
- What efforts, if any, will be needed to employ indigenous languages in new domains of language use?
- In what language or languages will primary, secondary, and tertiary education take place? How will linguistically appropriate materials for use in educational settings be prepared?
- What language or languages will be used in different media (e.g., print media, radio, television)?
- What role, if any, will the state play in supporting or encouraging the use of a particular language or languages?
- What role, if any, will the state play in discouraging the use of a particular language or languages?
- What language rights will be recognized for citizens of the new nation?

The answers to these questions had implications for how resources (inevitably limited, of course) would be allocated to language-related projects. Issues of language, language policy, and language planning were especially significant in the domains of government and education (see Mazrui & Mazrui, 1998). In some countries, the language of the former colonial power (most commonly, English, French, or Portuguese) continued to function as an official language, and often as the language of education, even though this meant disempowering large numbers of people in the society, largely as a consequence of social class and education. (Such policies were especially common in Francophone Africa [see Ball, 1997; Djité, 1990, 1991; Weinstein, 1980].) In other countries, the government selected a particular indigenous language and devoted resources to its development (as was the case in Tanzania with KiSwahili [see Harries, 1983; Hinnebusch, 1979; Khalid, 1977; Mkilifi, 1978; Polomé & Hill, 1980]). Many nations sought a middle ground, in which one or more indigenous languages were used in a limited number of domains, but where the former colonial language still functioned as an élite language (as in Nigeria, for example, where English was used alongside the three major indigenous languages, Hausa, Ibo, and Yoruba [see Akinnaso, 1989; Fakuade, 1989]). Regardless of the choice made, the implementation of the chosen policy almost inevitably created problems; in the Nigeria case, one writer voiced his frustrations when he published an article entitled "The National Language Question in Nigeria: Is There an Answer?" (Oladejo, 1991). The Nigerian case is, to be sure, an especially troublesome one: not only are there more than 500 languages spoken in Nigeria, but the three largest indigenous languages are identified not only with different ethnic groups, but also with different religions—Hausa with Islam, Ibo primarily with Christians (both Roman Catholics and Protestants), and Yoruba fairly evenly with Christians and Muslims. The legacy of the civil war between 1967 and 1970, which involved the attempted secession of Biafra (largely Ibo) from the rest of the country, reflected ethnic tensions that continue to the present. Finally, in addition to a standard Nigerian English, there is also a Pidgin English that is widely spoken in the country. The policy dilemmas in such a situation are, of course, immense, whether we are discussing language in government, in the military, in commerce, or in education. Although rarely as complex and multifaceted as the Nigerian case, policy makers in many other countries would be tempted to ask the same question about whether there is an answer to the language challenges in their own national contexts.

Decisions about language planning and language policy in the postcolonial world were not, of course, neutral in nature. They were embedded in highly ideological and political contexts, and served ideological and political purposes—a criticism that was often directed toward both specific language policies and language planning as an academic discipline in the 1980s and 1990s. Perhaps most serious during this period was the growing power of the "Languages of Wider Communication" (LWCs) in general, and English in particular. (The Center for Applied Linguistics [CAL] has identified as LWCs Arabic, Bengali, English, French, Hindi,

Malay, Mandarin, Portuguese, Spanish and Russian, though Bengali, Hindi, Malay, and Mandarin are often excluded from the list because of their use only in fairly limited regional settings, whereas the other languages have more international foci; see Figure 2.2.) The increasing dominance of English in virtually all spheres of life has been, and continues to be, subjected to serious scholarly critique (see Canagarajah, 1999; Holborow, 1999; Karmani, 1995; Kazmi, 1997; Pennycook, 1994, 1998, 2004, 2008; Phillipson, 1992, 2003; Prendergast, 2008). As a result of its relationship with language policies that were clearly ideological in nature, language planning as an academic discipline lost a great deal of credibility during this period (see Ferguson, 2006, pp. 3–4). Tollefson articulates the problem this way:

> Language policy is a form of disciplinary power. Its success depends in part upon the ability of the state to structure into the institutions of society the differentiation of individuals into "insiders" and "outsiders" . . . To a large degree, this occurs through the close association between language and nationalism. By making language a mechanism for the expression of nationalism, the state can manipulate feelings of security and belonging . . . the state uses language policy to discipline and control its workers by establishing language-based limitations on education, employment, and political participation. This is one sense in which language policy is inherently ideological. (1991, pp. 207–8)

Language	Number of Native Speakers	Non-Native Speakers	Total Speakers
Arabic	280,000,000	250,000,000	530,000,000
Bengali	181,000,000	49,000,000	230,000,000
English	400,000,000	1,400,000,000	1,800,000,000
French	110,000,000	390,000,000	500,000,000
Hindi	490,000,000	225,000,000	715,000,000
Malay / Indonesian	62,300,000	197,700,000	260,000,000
Mandarin	885,000,000	480,000,000	1,365,000,000
Portuguese	210,000,000	30,000,000	240,000,000
Spanish	329,000,000	171,000,000	500,000,000
Russian	164,000,000	114,000,000	278,000,000

FIGURE 2.2. *The Languages of Wider Communication and their speaker numbers (estimate)*

In the years since the early 1990s, however, language planning and language policy studies and the scholars involved in these disciplines have begun to address many of the concerns raised in the past. They have become increasingly concerned with issues of minority language groups, language oppression, linguistic hegemony, language rights, and language endangerment. In characterizing the disciplines, Ferguson writes:

> Language planning is a resurgent academic discipline revived by the policy challenges of the late twentieth- and early twenty-first-century global developments: globalisation, migration, resurgent ethno-nationalisms, language endangerment, the global spread of English, new states and failing states. . . . It is, however, a different discipline in several respects from the early years of the immediate post-colonial era of the 1960s and 1970s. First of all . . . there is now greater skepticism regarding the efficacy of [language planning]. A second striking difference is the much more positive stance toward linguistic diversity, manifested in increased interventions on behalf of regional minority languages, the languages of migrants and the endangered languages of indigenous peoples. Evident also, and clearly linked to the above, is a greater interest in questions of power, access, inequality, discrimination and disparity, and how all these are impacted by language policies. (2006, p. 13)

Jan Blommaert credits changes in post-apartheid South Africa to this far more empowering approach to language planning and policy, which replaced a tradition of oppressive and disempowering language planning:

> The 1990s . . . have been marked by a renewed interest in language planning. The historical changes in South Africa triggered a new enthusiasm among language scholars, and almost automatically drove them into the direction of language planning issues because of the nature of the political-ideological debate surrounding the end of apartheid. Issues of national and subnational identity, of culture and language, featured prominently in almost any debate on the future of South Africa, and the new Republic set an important precedent by allowing eleven languages to be used as official languages instead of the usual one, two or four of most other African states. Here was a country which championed multilingualism as a symbol of political and cultural pluralism. (1996, p. 203)

Language planning and language policy studies are activities of growing significance not only in terms of spoken languages around the world, but also with respect to sign languages. The broad framework within which sign language planning and sign language policies are developed and implemented is essentially the same as that for spoken languages, although the exact details and challenges faced by sign language planners and policy makers differ from those faced by other language planners and policy makers in important ways, as we shall see (see Batterbury, Ladd, & Gulliver, 2007; Corker, 2000; Covington, 1976; Deuchar, 1980; Eichmann, 2009; Erting, 1978; Gutiérrez, 1994; Nash, 1987; Nover, 1995, 2000; Nover & Ruiz, 1994; Ramsey, 1989; Reagan, 1990a, 2001a, 2005c; Turner, 2009; Van Herreweghe & Vermeerbergen, 2009; Wesemaël, 1985; Woodward, 1973).

THE NATURE AND PURPOSES OF LANGUAGE PLANNING

Questions of national and official language selection; orthographic selection and spelling standardization; language use in government, judicial, and educational settings; and language status and power are rarely made easily, and they seldom avoid a considerable degree of controversy and conflict. As Altbach observed in the mid-1980s, "Language is a key to the intellectual situation in many Third World nations. Language also plays a role in the distribution of knowledge, since the medium through which material is communicated determines accessibility. Many Third World nations are multilingual states in which questions of language policy are often politically volatile" (1984, p. 234). Such controversy is common where language policies are concerned with the provision of education (see Cooper, Shohamy, & Walters, 2001; Corson, 1999; Ferguson, 2006; Lambert & Shohamy, 2000; Lubbe & Truter, 2007; Tollefson, 2002; Tollefson & Tsui, 2004), and this is understandable because "the close relationship between use of a language and political power, socioeconomic development, national and local identity and cultural values has led to the increasing realization of the importance of language policies and planning in the life of a nation. Nowhere is this planning more crucial than in education, universally recognized as a powerful instrument of change" (Kennedy, 1983, p. iii). In the preface to their book *Medium of Instruction Policies: Which Agenda? Whose Agenda*? James Tollefson and Amy Tsui write:

> Since the early 1990s, a revival of interest in language-policy research has contributed to growing awareness that medium-of-instruction policies in education have considerable impact not only on the school performance of students and the daily work of teachers, but also on various forms of social and economic (in) equality. Because much of the daily work that takes place in education involves verbal interaction among students and teachers,

medium-of-instruction decisions play a central role in shaping the learning activities that take place in all classrooms and on all playgrounds. Moreover, because educational institutions play such a crucial role in determining social hierarchies, political power, and economic opportunities, medium-of-instruction policies thus play an important role in organizing social and political systems. (2004, p. vii)

The role of language planning as a component of more general social and educational planning and policy analysis is an important facet of understanding development in general, and education in particular, in many societies. Language planning as an element of national development strategy can best be understood as the deliberate attempt to change or in some way alter existing language usage, and thus to resolve various types of language problems and controversies. It is an activity that is potentially deeply involved in both identity construction and conflict management. As Eastman cogently asserted more than twenty-five years ago, "Language planning is the activity of manipulating language as a social resource in order to reach objectives set out by planning agencies which, in general, are an area's governmental, educational, economic, and linguistic authorities" (1983, p. 29).

TYPES OF LANGUAGE PLANNING ACTIVITIES

Language planning activities can focus on any of four different kinds of activities: status planning, corpus planning, acquisition planning, and attitude planning (Cooper, 1989; Ferguson, 2006; Kaplan & Baldauf, 1997; Reagan, 2001b; S. Wright, 2004). However, this suggests that each of these kinds of language planning activities is separate and distinct, and in practice that is actually far from the case.

> Status planning refers to the appropriate uses for a named variety of language. Corpus planning refers to the choices to be made of specific linguistic elements whenever the language is used; it was corpus planning when the Serbians wanted the Croatian elements omitted. But obviously, as Kaplan and Baldaulf (1997) noted, the two activities are virtually inseparable: "any change in the character of a language is likely to result in a change in the use environment, and any change in the use environment is likely to induce a change in the character of a language." (Spolsky, 2004, p. 11)

In fact, the early literature in language planning actually described only status planning and corpus planning; acquisition planning as a separate aspect of the language planning process was only added later, by James Cooper in 1989. He wrote:

> This additional category seems to me useful for at least two reasons. First, considerable planning is directed toward *language spread*, i.e. an increase in the users or the uses of a language or variety, but not all planning for language spread can be subsumed under the rubric of status planning. When planning is directed towards increasing a language's uses, it falls within the rubric of status planning. But when it is directed toward increasing the number of users—speakers, writers, listeners, or readers—then a separate analytic category for the focus of language planning seems to me to be justified . . . Second, the changes in function and form sought by status and corpus planning affect, and are affected by, the number of a language's users. New users may be attracted by the new uses to which a language is put . . . Since function, form, and acquisitions are related to one another, planners of any one should consider the others. (Cooper, 1989, p. 33)

I suggest that there is in fact a fourth kind of language planning, one that it often plays an extremely prominent role in both language planning and language policy development and implementation. Surprisingly, it has not been identified in the literature as a distinct kind of language planning, though it should be, because it goes significantly beyond the objectives of status planning as it is traditionally understood. I am referring here to efforts to change or alter the attitudes of individuals or groups either toward a particular language (their own or that of someone else), or toward monolingualism, bilingualism, or multilingualism (see Reagan, 2001b). Such efforts at what I call *attitude planning* are quite common, and they should be recognized as such (see Figure 2.3).

Status planning refers to efforts by a government or institution to determine what language or languages are to be used in particular spheres. The identification of a country's official language, for example, constitutes status planning, as would a decision about what language should be used in schools, decisions about signage, and so on (see Cooper, 1989, pp. 99–121; Kaplan & Baldauf, 1997, pp. 30–38; S. Wright, 2004, p. 43). The breakup of the former Soviet Union has led to massive efforts at status planning as well as efforts at corpus planning and acquisition planning. Language policy changes in the Baltic nations (Ozolins, 2003), Belarus (Brown, 2007), and other parts of the former Soviet Union that are now newly established (or, more accurately, re-established) nations clearly embody status planning objectives (see Ciscel, 2007; Garibova & Asgarova, 2009; Schlyter, 1998; Sebba, 2006). Although the changes

Types of Language Planning	Description
Status Planning	Status planning refers to efforts by a government or institution to determine what language or languages are to be used in particular spheres of use. The identification of a country's official language, for instance, constitutes status planning, as would a decision about what language should be used in schools, decisions about signage, and so on.
Corpus Planning	Corpus planning is often a result of, and tied to, status planning; it refers to efforts to standardize, elaborate, and perhaps to "purify" a language selected for use in a particular sphere of language use. While status planning has to do primarily with extralinguistic concerns (cultural, demographic, and economic considerations in particular), corpus planning is basically linguistic in nature, focusing on the specifically linguistic features of the target language.
Acquisition Planning	Acquisition planning, a somewhat more recent term in the language planning literature, takes place when the language planning activity is explicitly focused on language spread, and, more specifically, on the spread of the number of users of the language. In fact, as Spolsky notes, what is really intended by the term "acquisition planning" is language education policy (2004, p. 46).
Attitude Planning	Attitude planning refers to efforts to change or alter the attitudes of individuals or groups either toward a particular language (their own or that of someone else), or toward monolingualism, bilingualism, or multilingualism.

FIGURE 2.3. *Types of language planning activity*

in language policy in different parts of the former Soviet Union vary dramatically, Ozolins's description of the changes in the Baltic states provides a powerful example of how significant such changes can be:

> Soviet language policy, including the marked features of asymmetrical bilingualism (Russians remaining largely monolingual, while non-Russians needed to become bilingual to function at any level in the Soviet system) has been well researched. . . . Baltic language laws, strengthened after independence, required that all those working in situations of public contact must be able to demonstrate their competence in the national language; other requirements covered the increase of teaching of the national language in all school systems, signage,

and measures promoting the national languages in broadcasting, publication and public life. (2003, p. 218)

Status planning decisions are, by their very nature, far simpler and far less controversial in traditional "nation states," such as France, than in the more common postcolonial multiethnic states. In the case of the former sort of state, there is a widely shared assumption about what it means and entails to be a citizen or member of the national community, while in the latter, it is just such questions that language policies help answer, and are thus debatable. To be sure, even in those countries that see themselves and are seen by others as "nation states," the situation is in fact considerably more complicated than this might suggest:

> The ideal of nationalism, that cohesive national groups should strive to have their own state, was and remains immensely problematic as a way of organising groups politically. No European country naturally matches the ideal of congruence between territory and people, except perhaps Iceland, where a small and unified cultural and linguistic group inhabits the clearly defined territory of an island. In all other situations the congruence of nation and state has only been approximated through strategies to assimilate divergent elements. (S. Wright, 2004, p. 19)

Status planning efforts can and do occur at a variety of levels: they take place internationally (for example, in determining official and working languages at the United Nations, in the European Union, and so on), nationally (at the level of the state, with the selection of an official language or languages), regionally (with the selection of particular regional languages with, typically, more limited roles and rights than the national official language), and even locally (especially with respect to educational settings).

Corpus planning is often a result of, and tied to, status planning; it refers to efforts to standardize, elaborate, and perhaps to "purify" a language selected for use in a particular sphere of language use (see Cluver, 1993b, p. 59; Kaplan & Baldauf, 1997, pp. 37–51). While status planning has to do primarily with extralinguistic concerns (cultural, demographic, and economic considerations in particular), corpus planning is basically linguistic in nature, focusing on the specifically linguistic features of the target language. Kaplan and Baldauf include the following as some of the major kinds of corpus planning activities:

- orthographic innovation, including design, harmonisation, change of script and spelling reform;
- pronunciation;

- changes in language structure;
- vocabulary expansion;
- simplification of registers;
- style; and
- the preparation of language material. (Kaplan & Baldauf, 1997, p. 38)

Examples of corpus planning efforts abound, and include centralized efforts at lexical expansion to fill lexical gaps; the production of dictionaries, grammars, and school textbooks; and a government-supported (or at least government-encouraged) media, all in the target language, in the selected form of the target language.

Acquisition planning, a somewhat more recent term in the language planning literature, takes place when the language planning activity is explicitly focused on language spread, and, more specifically, on the spread of the number of users of the language. In fact, as Spolsky notes, what is really intended by the term "acquisition planning" is language education policy (2004, p. 46). In other words, acquisition planning seeks to provide answers to such questions as:

- What should the medium of instruction in the school be?
- If there is to be a change in medium of instruction from one language to another at some point in the educational process, what should that point be?
- At what point are children taught to read and write, and in what language or languages?
- What additional languages should students study, how should they study them, and what are the objectives of such language study?

These questions can be answered in any number of perfectly legitimate ways in any particular context (see Kaplan & Baldauf, 1997, pp. 113–17), although there is also a substantial body of very credible research that can guide such decision-making. For example, we know that children learn best if their schooling begins in their mother tongue (see August & Hakuta, 1998; Baker & Hornberger, 2001; Corson, 2001; Cummins, 2000; Krashen, 1996; Tse, 2001). This may or may not be feasible in a particular setting, but it is a well-documented, research-based finding that needs to be taken into account.

Last, although it is not clearly recognized in the language planning literature except perhaps as a special kind of status planning, *attitude planning* seems to me an additional kind of language planning activity that plays a significant role in many national and international settings. One of the best examples of contemporary attitude planning efforts are those currently taking place in South Africa, a country with a long history of language planning (see Alexander, 2004; Beukes, 1996; Heugh, 2002; Kamwangamalu, 2004; Kamwangamalu & Reagan, 2004; Msimang, 1992; Pan-South African Language Board, 2005; Reagan, 1984, 1987, 1991, 2001b, 2002b; Webb, 2002, 2004). A significant focus of contemporary language planning activities in South Africa is on language attitude planning (Finchilescu & Nyawose, 1998; Louw-Potgieter & Louw, 1991; Verhoef, 1998b). Language attitude planning in the South African context actually has both an articulated and an unarticulated purpose. The articulated purpose is to raise consciousness about the multilingual nature of South African society, to increase toleration and acceptance of language differences, and to encourage the growth of individualism bilingualism and multilingualism in the country's languages (see Beukes, 1991, 1996; Heugh, Siegrühn, & Plüddemann, 1995; King & van den Berg, 1992; Mawasha, 1996; Smit, 1994; Verhoef, 1998a). The unarticulated but nevertheless powerful purpose of language attitude planning in contemporary South Africa is to attempt to address the concerns about the future of specific languages in the country—most notably Afrikaans (see Brink, 1984; Cluver, 1993a; Combrink, 1991; Kriel, 1998; Maartens, 1994; van Rensburg, 1993, 1997; Webb, 1992), but also many of the African languages (Baai, 1992; Msimang, 1992; Mutasa, 1996; Robinson, 1996). Indeed, changing common, negative attitudes about the African languages in South Africa is one of the greater challenges faced by language planners in the post-apartheid regime, as indeed has been the case in many other post-independence countries. Hardly surprisingly, it has been in the educational sphere where such efforts face the greatest resistance, due both to the historical significance of mother tongue schooling and the very real practical advantages of English, even with respect to the study of other major European languages (see Reagan, 1984, 1987, 1991, 2001b, 2002b; Ridge, 2004; Strike, 1996; Webb, 2002, 2004; L. Wright, 2002, 2004).

In the context of the United States, there was a bumper sticker in support of foreign language education in the United States some time ago that read, "Monolingualism is curable"—a clear example of an attempt to mold language attitudes. A similar suggestion was made by the late Senator Paul Simon in his book *The Tongue-Tied American: Confronting the Foreign Language Crisis*: "We should erect a sign at each port of entry into the United States: 'Welcome to the United States. We cannot speak your language'" (1980, p. 1).

THE FUNCTIONS OF LANGUAGE PLANNING

Language planning activities of all types—status planning, corpus planning, acquisition planning, and attitude planning—serve a number of different, although sometimes overlapping, functions. Kaplan and Baldauf identify a total of eleven purposes of language planning:

- language purification;
- language reform;
- language spread;
- language revival;
- language standardisation;
- lexical modernisation;
- stylistic simplification;
- language maintenance;
- terminological unification;
- interlingual communication; and
- auxiliary code standardisation. (1997, p. 82)

These are not completely independent and distinct purposes of language planning and language policy, however, so I would distill this list into what I, as well as others (see Canagarajah, 2005; Kaplan & Baldauf, 1997; Shohamy, 2006; Spolsky, 2004; Spolsky & Shohamy, 2000; S. Wright, 2004), see to be the four major functions: language purification, language revival and revitalization, language reform, and language standardization and modernization.

Each of the major functions of language planning and language policy (both in terms of spoken [or signed] and, where appropriate, written language) is reflected and manifested in virtually every sphere of human life. Language policies are reflected in the political sphere (the language of political and legislative debate and discourse, etc.), the judicial sphere (the language of law, as well as the language used by the police and courts), the military sphere (the language used in a country's armed forces), the religious sphere (the language used for worship, as well as the language in which key religious texts are written), the cultural sphere (the language of literature, poetry, and other aspects of what are often called "high culture"), the commercial and economic sphere (the language of business and industry), the educational sphere (the language of instruction, additional languages studied by pupils, etc.), and the interpersonal and familial sphere (the language used in the home, with relatives, and so on). Finally, it is important to bear in mind that all of these kinds of language planning activities can be either covert or overt in nature:

> In some contexts, language policy is stated *explicitly* through official documents, such as national laws, declaration of certain languages as "official" or "national," language standards, curricula, tests, and other types of documents. In other contexts, language policy is not stated explicitly, but can be derived *implicitly* from examining a variety of de facto practices. In these situations language policy is more difficult to detect as it is subtle and more hidden from the public eye. Implicit language policies can occur also at national level as many nations do not have explicit policies that are formulated in official documents. In the case of the USA, for example, there are no explicit and stated language policies that specify that status and uses of the English language [at the national level]. (Shohamy, 2006, p. 50)

Although there is no "official" language policy in the United States at the national level, there is nevertheless a very clear de facto national policy in operation: that English is, under most circumstances and in most settings, the society's operating language.

Language purification is a prescriptive effort on the part of policy makers to delimit "proper" or "correct" linguistic usage, often based on beliefs about what constitutes what is believed to be the historically pure variety of the language. Linguistic purification can involve both spoken (or signed) language and written language. With respect to the former, concern is typically on phonology or accent, lexical choice, and grammatical usage. In terms of the latter, the focus is generally on spelling and grammatical usage. In both instances, what is really at issue is the promotion of a standard variety of the target language (see Shohamy, 2006). Such efforts, which generally focus principally (though by no means exclusively) on corpus planning, are often concerned with eliminating foreign or alien usages in both the spoken and written language, and are commonly tied to other manifestations of what might be termed "purist" or ethnocentric ideologies, although they can also be outgrowths of anticolonialist sentiments and movements. An example of a call for language purification in language planning is provided in Abdallah Khalid's *The Liberation of Swahili from European Appropriation*, published in Nairobi in 1977, in which Khalid presents a case for the adoption of a pure variety of KiSwahili uncontaminated by European influences: "Once our thinking has been freed from foreign domination, the reintroduction of the true Swahili language in the place of its colonialist falsification will follow as a matter of logic and self-respect" (1977, p. xiii). Language purists often have strong emotional attachments to the traditional form of their language, as Sibayan makes clear in his discussion of Pilipino in the Philippines:

> The purists are emotionally attached to Tagalog while the antipurists do not hold such sentimental attachments. Generally, the purists are native speakers of Tagalog while most of the nonpurists are nonnative speakers. The purists would like to use original Tagalog words for many borrowed ones which are in general use and acceptance such as *guro* for the more generally used *maestra* (or *maestro*, if a man) "teacher," *aklat* for *libro* "book," and the now abandoned teaseword *salipawpaw* for what everyone calls *eroplano* "airplane." (1974, p. 233)

To some extent, one might hypothesize that purist movements are strongest in those instances in which national pride and self-confidence have suffered in some way, though it is also important to note that even languages that have high economic and political status have on occasion been the objects of purist movements (see Jernudd & Shapiro, 1989). For example, there have been numerous efforts in recent years to stop the use of anglicisms in modern French (which is critically referred to as "*franglais*" in French), though terms like *le week-end* continue to be far more popular in daily speech than the historically preferred *la fin de semaine* (see Ball, 1997, pp. 207–20), and similar phenomena have been noted in Spanish (Mar-Molinero, 1997, pp. 168–70) and German (in which the equivalents to "*franglais*" are "*Spanglish*" and "*Engleutsch*") (Stevenson, 1997, pp. 212–16). Indeed, even in English there have been such purist efforts, as with the Saxonist movement in the late nineteenth century, which attempted (generally unsuccessfully) to reform English by replacing foreign terms borrowed from French and Latin roots with terms of Germanic origin (Baron, 1981).

Linguistic purism, in fact, is ultimately—and hardly surprisingly—about issues of power and status:

> It is . . . important to note the continuous battles taking place regarding language correctness between emerging new language varieties that are constantly being creating vs. those who oppose them and seek to maintain languages as they are used at certain times by certain people and following certain prescribed rules. The latter resent changes in languages while

seeking to maintain and preserve language, viewing such changes as "inappropriate," "bad," "wrong," and "corruptions."

These varieties are positioned in comparisons with "official" languages, which are referred to as the "better" languages, often labeled "good," "correct," "standard," and "pure." The process that often occurs is that groups in power take measures to ensure that "their" language varieties are maintained and preserved while these "new" varieties are erased, eradicated and stigmatized. The prestigious languages are recorded in dictionaries, textbooks and other formal texts and are viewed as good models that are here to stay while "the other" varieties are rejected and forbidden from use, especially in the educational system. (Shohamy, 2006, p. 9)

The extent to which language purism is tied to issues of power and hierarchy, as well as to social class and ideology, is perhaps nowhere clearer than in the case of the Quechua language in Perú, where "a group of mestizo intellectuals claims that *Qhpaj'simi* is the Quechua used centuries ago by the Inca nobility and therefore is the purest form of the language. Based on this premise a social hierarchy has been established, the use of this "imperial language" being the marker separating its users from the common people, speakers of the *runa simi*" (Niño-Murcia, 1997, p. 134). Thus,

> linguistic purism in Cuzco [Perú] is the expression on another plane of reality—that of language itself—of the indigenous being used as a referent, with language functioning as an emblem of the Inca past. The purist discourse in Cuzco, although it appears on the surface to legitimize indigenous culture (solidarity function), in reality contributes to the marginalization (separating function) of the indigenous language and ultimately of its rural speakers, whose language one sees marked by the stigma of poverty and equate with a lack of culture. Ironically, it is a group of mestizos and not a Quechua-dominant group promoting this myth of purity. (Niño-Murcia, 1997, pp. 156–57)

Language revitalization refers to various kinds of activities intended to promote the status and usage of a language that has been, in some sense, previously in decline (or even, in extreme instances, a language that has actually ceased to have native users). As King defines it, language revitalization is "the attempt to add new forms or functions to a threatened language with the ultimate aim of increasing its uses or users" (1999, p. 111). Language revitalization is primarily an example of both status planning and acquisition planning, though elements of corpus planning (especially in terms of lexical expansion) and attitude planning are also likely to be involved.

Discussions of language revitalization and language revival often deal with the two cases of the revitalization of Irish (Gaelige) in Ireland following the establishment of the Republic of Ireland in 1921, with the declaration of Irish as the "national and first official language" of the country, and the revival of Hebrew as a modern language beginning in the nineteenth century and culminating in its use in as both an official and vernacular language following the formal establishment of the State of Israel in 1947. Although the two cases do share some similarities, they are also quite different in a number of important ways. In the case of Irish, the language had remained the dominant spoken language in most of Ireland under British occupation well into the seventeenth century. The replacement of Irish with English took place gradually after that point, as a result of a number of factors including the shift by the aristocracy from Irish to English, military campaigns by the Tudor monarchs, the growth of towns and urban centers that tended to support English, and so on. While estimates are that around 45 percent of the population of Ireland was still Irish-speaking in the last quarter of the eighteenth century, by the Census of 1851 that percentage had dropped to under 30 percent. The famine, which took place between 1845 and 1849, impacted the poor (and most likely Irish-speaking) especially severely, and some two and a half million people died in a five-year period, leading to an even greater decline in the percentage of Irish speakers. By the time of the establishment of the Republic of Ireland in 1921, the percentage of Irish speakers had declined further to less than 18 percent of the total population (see Ó Riagáin, 1997; also of interest are Edwards, 1984; Hindley, 1990; Maguire, 1991; O'Huallacháin, 1991, 1994). With the establishment of the Republic of Ireland and the declaration of Irish as an official language (together with English), the language revival movement that had emerged in the nineteenth century in conjunction with Irish nationalism more generally gained official status and governmental support. Irish became a required school subject, radio programming in Irish received governmental support, and the government identified an area called the *Gaeltacht*, in the west of the country, in which Irish was still widely spoken and needed to be supported, maintained, and further developed. Despite such efforts, however, the percentage of Irish citizens whose first language is Irish is now approximately 2 to 3 percent of the Republic's population. Although Irish is used largely for ceremonial purposes much of the time, more than 40 percent of the population claim to have competence in Irish as a second language, and support for Irish remains fairly strong in Ireland. There is in fact a fundamental dilemma in Ireland with respect to Irish. As Suzanne Romaine quotes one Irish person, "although we are all *for* Irish as we are for cheaper bus fares, heaven, and the good life, nobody of the masses is willing to make the effort" (1994, p. 42). The problem is that in a country in which virtually everyone is a native speaker of English, convincing people of the advantages of learning a quite difficult language that has little practical use outside of the country is, to put it mildly, a difficult sell.

The case of Hebrew is very different. Hebrew (עִבְרִית) was spoken in ancient Israel from around the tenth century B.C.E., and continued to be a spoken language until as late as 200 C.E. (although this is actually somewhat debatable; see Hoffman, 2004, pp. 165–66). In point of fact, the ancient world was in many places a multilingual setting, and this was true for Israel. During the Persian period, Jews most commonly spoke both Hebrew and Aramaic, while under the Greeks they spoke Hebrew, Aramaic, and Greek. In fact, even parts of the Hebrew Bible are in Aramaic rather than Hebrew. With the destruction of the Second Temple in 70 C.E. and the Bar Kokhba revolt in the second century C.E., much of the Jewish population was exiled from Israel, and Jews adopted (and often modified) the languages surrounding them elsewhere in the Roman Empire. Hebrew continued to be used as a written language, however, and especially as a liturgical, scholarly, and religious language, and this tradition continued into the nineteenth century (and for some groups, to the present). After the exile, however, for most Jews Hebrew was the לשון הקודש ("Holy Tongue"), and so was not seen as an appropriate vernacular language. Instead, Jews in exile tended to speak languages that included elements of Hebrew but were based on the languages that surrounded them (or had surrounded them historically), such as Ladino (Judeo-Spanish) for Sephardic Jews, Yiddish (Judeo-German) for Ashkenazi Jews, and so on.

In the late nineteenth and early twentieth centuries, this situation changed dramatically as the revival of Hebrew as a daily, spoken language became an important element of Zionist ideology. Most closely associated with Eliezer Ben-Yehuda (1858–1922), the revival of Hebrew was a complex and controversial undertaking. Spurred on by the First Aliyah (1881 to 1903) and the Second Aliyah (1904 to 1914) to Ottoman Palestine, the Zionists created both kibbutzim and schools as well as cities and the settlers began using Hebrew in their daily affairs (see Fellman, 1973; Harshav, 1993; Hoffman, 2004, pp. 187–213; Nahir, 1988, 2002;

Sáenz-Badillos, 1993, pp. 267–87). Newspapers, books, poetry, and so on, in modern Hebrew rapidly emerged as well, both in Europe and in Palestine. Although later immigrants brought a host of languages, it was Hebrew, from the time of the British Mandate of Palestine (1917–48), that was the official language of the Jews (during the Mandate, there were three official languages: English, Arabic, and Modern Hebrew). One of the interesting aspects of the revival of Hebrew is its relationship to Yiddish. Yiddish was the mother tongue of many of the early advocates of the revival of Hebrew, and modern Hebrew does show elements of influence from Yiddish. However, in Israel Hebrew was identified most strongly with the secular advocates of Zionism, while Yiddish was identified with an older, religious worldview. The result was that active efforts were undertaken in Israel to eradicate the use of Yiddish in favor of Hebrew, and these efforts were quite successful.

The revival of Hebrew is perhaps the best example of a successful language revival effort. Hebrew, along with Arabic, is an official language of the State of Israel, and it is an effective and thoroughly modern language in any sense of the term. There is an extensive literature in Hebrew (including work by Shmuel Yosef Agnon, who won the Nobel Prize for Literature in 1966, as well as Ephraim Kishon, Yaakov Shabtai, Amos Oz, Irit Linur, and Etgar Keret, among others), a number of newspapers representing virtually any and all political and ideological perspectives (including *Ha'aretz* and *Maariv*, for example), magazines, and so on. Hebrew, in short, is now a language fully suited for individuals and organizations in a modern, sophisticated urban society. At the same time, even as the revival of Hebrew has been a huge success in many ways, the language is still subject (as are most others, of course) to extensive borrowing from English and other languages. For instance, as a result of the popularity of Spanish-language *telenovelas* in Israel, many young Israelis often "drop words like '*muy*' into their speech" (Collins, 2010, p. 22).

Although the cases of Hebrew and Irish are the most common instances of language revival and revitalization, they are not really the most interesting examples of language revitalization. Far more interesting, and more important from a global perspective, are the examples of language revival and revitalization concerned with endangered languages. The issue of language endangerment is a significant one, with serious implications for language planning and language policy studies (see Abley, 2003; Brenzinger, 1992; Crystal, 2000; Dalby, 2002; Evans, 2010; Grenoble & Whaley, 1998a, 1998b; Hagège, 2000, 2009; Hale, 1998; Harrison,

2007; King, Schhilling-Estes, Fogle, Lou, & Soukup, 2008; Krauss, 1992, 2006; Nettle, 1999; Nettle & Romaine, 2000; Newman, 2003; Woodbury, 1998). K. David Harrison writes:

> The accelerating extinction of languages on a global scale has no precedent in human history. And while it is not exactly equivalent to biological extinction of endangered species, it is happening much faster, making species extinction rates look trivial by comparison. Scientists' best estimates show that since the year 1600 the planet lost a full 484 animal species, while 654 plant species were recorded as having gone extinct. Of course, these are underestimates. But even so, they make up less than 7 percent of the total number of identified plant and animal species. Compared to this, the estimated 40 percent of languages that are endangered is a staggering figure. Languages are far more threatened than birds (11% threatened, endangered, or extinct), mammals (18%), fish (5%), or plants (8%). (2007, p. 7)

Language loss is nothing new; indeed, if we assume that human beings have been using languages for somewhere between 50,000 and 100,000 years, or perhaps even longer, as seems likely (see Burling, 2005; Kenneally, 2007; Nichols, 1998), then the overwhelming majority of human languages are not only unknown and unknowable, but more important, long deceased (see McWhorter, 2001, pp. 253–86). John McWhorter describes language loss using the common biological metaphor: "Like biological extinctions, language death has been a regular and unsung occurrence throughout human history" (2009, p. 193). For most of our history, the loss of languages was of little if any concern, except perhaps to the speakers of the languages at issue, and then primarily *only* when their own lives were also at stake. Of the vast majority of languages in pre- and early human history, we know little. By the time of the Roman Empire, such languages as Hittite, Hurrian, Urartian, Akkadian, and Minoan, for instance, had all long ceased to be used, and most were already long-forgotten, only to be rediscovered in the nineteenth and twentieth centuries. As for the Roman Empire itself, the Imperium was one of the most powerful language killers in human history, at least until the rise of modern European colonialism. The Imperium was not merely linguistically bilingual in Latin and Greek, but included lesser-known and lesser-status languages, including Oscan, Umbrian, Venetic, Messapic, Etruscan, Gaulish, Raetic, Punic, Libya, Berber, Aramaic, Thracian, and a host of others (Adams, 2003; Adams, Janse, & Swain, 2002), nearly all of which died under the *Pax Romana*.

The current concern with language loss, though, is quite new. It dates, in large part, to an article published by Michael Krauss in 1992 in the journal *Language*. Krauss, using the Summer Institute of Linguistics's *Ethnologue* database—the largest and most complete linguistic database in existence, with some 6,909 languages identified (although most linguists would argue that this number is almost certainly inflated)—compellingly argues (as quoted in Woodbury, 1998) that "at least 20 percent—and perhaps as many as 50 percent—of the world's 5,000 to 6,000 languages are already *moribund*, that is, no longer spoken by children and hence doomed within a century from now unless learning is revived. Moreover, he estimates that a century from now many more languages will be moribund. This may leave as few as 10 percent of today's languages in genuinely safe condition" (Woodbury, 1998, p. 234). Krauss's call to action has resulted in considerable concern among linguists, and even a certain amount of concern among various activists working with indigenous peoples, although it would be an exaggeration to say that language endangerment is now seen as a major problem by most politicians, policy makers, and other decision makers.

For his part, Krauss (1992) initially suggested that languages fall into four groups: safe languages, endangered languages, moribund languages, and languages that are now dead. The key distinction among these four categories of languages has to do with the extent to which children are learning and using the language (see Figure 2.4). Thus, the safe languages are those with significant numbers of speakers that are being passed on to the next generation, typically both informally in the home and community and formally in the school (1992, p. 7). Endangered languages are those which are, for the moment, still being passed on to the next generation of speakers, but where there is growing likelihood that this process will cease in the upcoming century (1992, p. 6). Moribund languages are those where children have ceased to be taught or to learn the language as a mother tongue (1992, p. 4). Finally, languages are considered to be deceased when they are no longer spoken at all.

In more recent work, Krauss (2006) suggests a slightly more nuanced view of the status of different languages. The "safe" languages are those that have more than 1 million native speakers, or are the official language of a monolingual nation. The number of native speakers alone is not a perfect criterion for linguistic security, but it does provide us with a certain amount of useful information. At the very least, the smaller the language with respect to the number of native speakers, the more

Safe Languages	Definitions vary, from languages with more than 100,000 speakers to languages with more than 1,000,000 speakers. In fact, language endangerment cannot be predicted solely on the basis of the number of speakers of the language alone; even some languages with more than 1,000,000 speakers may ultimately be threatened. The "safe languages" include between 600 and 2,100 of the 6,000 to 8,000 languages spoken in the world today.
Threatened Languages	Languages with fewer than 5,000 speakers are clearly threatened.
Endangered Languages	Endangered languages are those that are still being learned by children as their native language, but which—if present circumstances continue—will cease to be learned by children as native languages within the next century and will become moribund languages.
Moribund Languages	Moribund languages are no longer being passed on to children from their parents. Once this occurs, it is merely a matter of time until they become extinct. At present, somewhere between 20% and 50% of the languages spoken in the world today (that is, in the neighborhood of 1,200 to 3,000 languages) are already moribund.
Extinct Languages	Extinct languages are those that no longer have any native speakers. One can debate precisely when a language actually "dies": since language is by definition a communal activity, it may die either when the last speaker dies, or perhaps when the next to last speaker dies (and the final speaker no longer has anyone with whom to communicate). The vast majority of languages that have ever been spoken by human beings are extinct; in fact, we do not even know about the existence of most of them.

FIGURE 2.4. *Language endangerment*

threatened it is likely to be. This point becomes especially important when one takes into account the geographic nature of language diversity:

> The median number of speakers for all the languages of the world is just 5,000. Crude size is not the only determinant of language viability; a group of 500 could be maintained in Papua New Guinea, but not in Western Europe. None the less, we can use speaker statistics to make some

> ballpark projections . . . If the size required for medium-term safety is taken as 10,000 speakers, then 59.4 per cent of all languages will be lost in the medium term. If it is taken, perhaps more realistically, as 100,000 speakers, 83.8 per cent will die out, including virtually all of those of Australia and the Pacific. Africa and Asia, which have more medium-sized languages, will sustain much more diversity. If the safety level is taken as one million speakers, 95.2 per cent of all languages will be lost, including every single language indigenous to North America, Central America, Australia, New Guinea, and the Pacific, plus almost all of those of South America. (Nettle, 1999, pp. 113–14)

Excluding the "safe" languages, Krauss also identifies the "stable" languages, which are languages that are spoken by their entire speaker community, including children. All other human languages fall into some category of danger, ranging from unstable and eroded (in which only some children speak the language), to definitively endangered (in which the language is spoken only by the parental generation and up), to severely endangered (in which the language is spoken only by the grandparental generation and up), to critically endangered (where the language is spoken only by very few elderly individuals; 2006, p. 1). The final stage is language extinction, in which there are no speakers or hearers of the language left.

Language endangerment is itself incredibly complex, of course, and no single factor or set of factors on their own will be able to predict with any degree of certainty the future of a particular language. Having said this, it is also clear that certain factors are of disproportionate significance in the extent to which a language is endangered, and perhaps most important, beyond merely the number of native speakers of the language, are such concerns as the extent to which the language is passed on to the next generation, the degree to which the language is used in educational settings, and the recognition of specific language rights of the speaker community by the relevant governmental authorities.

There is an underlying question about language endangerment and language loss that needs to be raised here, and that has to do with what actually causes such loss. The answer to this question is a complex one, just as is the process of language endangerment itself. Both human prehistory and history provide us with a generous supply of potential answers to the question of the cause of language loss, though it is important to note that what took place historically is no longer necessarily what is occurring in the context of the twenty-first century. Dixon (1997, pp. 107–15) identifies several distinctive contexts in which language loss can take place: population loss, forced language loss, and involuntary and voluntary language switching (Dixon separates these last two kinds of language switching, but the difference seems more semantic than real, in my view). Although the end result is basically the same, the processes differ socially, culturally, economically, and of course educationally, and are worth briefly considering here.

Dixon begins by discussing what he labels *population loss* (1997, pp. 107–8). Population loss is the most extreme kind of situation in which language loss takes place, and the phrase is at the very least a misnomer, as it can mean one of two things: either the elimination of a people by war or related means, or the achievement of the same result by the introduction of new diseases (see Kunitz, 1994)—or, perhaps most commonly, a mixture of these two methods. In whichever case, language loss is the outcome of the elimination of the speaker population as a living human community. Unlike in other senses of "language loss," in which language functions as a metaphor for the speaker community, in this first instance it is actual living, breathing people who die. Although common throughout the course of human history, the areas in which such population loss has been most obviously, and effectively practiced in recent historical memory are Australia, North America, and Latin America (see Dixon, 1997; Skutnabb-Kangas, 2000). These are the neo-European settler societies, of course, in which the goal of the settlers (albeit not always expressly articulated) was to replace the "native" peoples, (and, needless to say, their languages), either literally or via assimilation and domination.

A second, albeit commonly related, kind of language loss is forced language loss, typically characterized by situations in which children of an indigenous population are removed from the homes of their parents and either fostered out or sent to special schools (either maintained by religious institutions or by governmental bodies). The goals of such a process are clear: to "civilize" the children, and thus, over a generation, eliminate a problematic population. In the United States, the establishment of Indian schools in the western states in the late nineteenth century had as its principal objective the transformation of Native American children into individuals who would be able to function in white society (see, e.g., Wiley, 2002):

> Replacing the use of native languages with English, destroying Indian customs, and teaching allegiance to the U.S. government became the major educational policies of the U.S. government toward Indians during the latter part of the nineteenth century. The boarding school was an important part

> of these educational policies. It was designed to remove children from their families at an early age and thereby isolate them from the language and customs of their parents and tribes. (Spring, 2008, p. 193)

Nor was the replacement of the child's native language a mere afterthought; as the *Indian Peace Commission Report of 1868* observed, "Through sameness of language is produced sameness of sentiment and thought; customs and habits are moulded and assimilated in the same way, and thus in process of time the differences producing trouble [between Native Americans and whites will be] gradually obliterated" (Prucha, 1990, p. 107). The process of assimilation, needless to say, was profoundly successful linguistically if in no other way, although to be sure there were also a host of other pressures working toward transition to English. The result is that today some 80 percent of the [250+] indigenous languages in North America are no longer being learned by children. In the United States, "only five of the native languages . . . have as many as 10,000 to 20,000 speakers, and only two have as many as 40,000 to 50,000. The Navajo language is the only Native language with more than 100,000 speakers" (quoted in Nettle & Romaine, 2000, p. 8).

Voluntary and involuntary language shift, in Dixon's account, are more understandable in social and economic terms than in any other way. He explains the phenomenon of involuntary language shifting this way:

> In any equilibrium situation, bilingualism would generally have been a two-way process—many speakers of language X would also have competence in Y, and many speakers of Y would know a good deal of X. Modern societies are not egalitarian, and when one language has a prestige status (through being spoken by the largest number of people, or being used by the dominant group), bilingualism is likely to be one-way. . . . This type of language loss has happened—or is happening—with the languages of small minority groups (those with less than 10,000 speakers) in every country. (1997, p. 110)

Voluntary language shift similarly depends on decisions made by speakers of the language in question. In essence, voluntary language shift occurs as speakers of a language, typically in an already bilingual setting, select to make use of the language other than their native language, initially in particular domains (e.g., commerce, education, interaction with agents of the government, and so on), and then gradually in all domains. There are normally variations in the role of generational identity in this process, as children begin using increasing amounts of the socially dominant and therefore more useful language (though this can be delayed by sending children to home-language schools, as is sometimes done). This process of voluntary language shift describes a number of cases, including the decline of Irish in the nineteenth century as English became increasingly the de facto dominant language in Ireland (see Hindley, 1990; Ó Riagáin, 1997), as well as the process by which immigrants generally abandon their language within approximately three generations of settlement in a new society, a pattern that is well-documented in a wide array of settings. In short, language loss takes place in a variety of quite distinct ways, for various reasons, and at differing rates. Not all language loss is the result of ill-intentions; often, groups, for reasons that seem to them to be compelling over time, abandon one language in favor of another. Although certainly sad from the perspective of a linguist, such a shift is radically different, both practically and morally, from those cases in which the process of language shift is imposed, all too often with other social and individual costs as well.

This brings us to the question of why language loss really matters. As I have already noted, it is in fact a natural process, and most languages that have been spoken by human beings are already long dead. But from the perspective of virtually all linguists, language loss *does* matter. Typical of the claims of most linguists with respect to language loss is Mithun's assertion that "Language represents the most creative, pervasive aspect of culture, the most intimate side of the mind. The loss of language diversity will mean that we will never even have the opportunity to appreciate the full creative capacities of the human mind" (1998, p. 189). Such arguments are profoundly linguistic in nature. By this I mean that they are, ultimately, intended to focus on the particular linguistic value of language diversity, and that they are most likely to appeal to professional linguists. It is just such an argument that Paul Newman, in an intriguing essay entitled "The Endangered Languages Issue as a Hopeless Cause," accepts as perhaps the primary compelling case to be made for linguists to care about language loss by stressing such concerns:

> My intention . . . is not to raise the question of why languages disappear . . . Nor do I want to get into the sensitive question of whether it makes any sense philosophically or practically to try to renew or revive dying languages . . . Once one leaves the realm of emotional hand twisting by sentimental scholars, the question is much more debatable than appears at first sight. . . . However, I think that professional linguists *can* agree that the disappearance of a language without documentation is a huge scientific loss. Our linguistic scientific

> enterprise depends on the multiplicity of languages and the knowledge of linguistic diversity. It is only through knowledge of diverse languages with different structures and belonging to different language families that we can truly begin to gain an understanding of universal grammar, i.e., the nature of the human language capacity. Similarly, our understanding of linguistic typology and our ability to classify languages accurately and reconstruct protoforms depends on the availability of a wide array of languages. (2003, p. 2)

Although I would not deny the value of languages and language diversity from a purely linguistic perspective, I would argue that such a perspective is perhaps inadequate to make the case for language loss really matter very much, at least insofar as the more general public is concerned. However, there are, as Harrison notes, other, arguably far more important, justifications for being concerned about the disappearance of languages:

> We have seen at least three compelling reasons to safeguard and document vanishing languages. First is the fact that our human knowledge base is rapidly eroding. Most of what humans have learned over the millennia about how to thrive on this planet is encapsulated in threatened languages. If we let them slip away, we may compromise our very ability to survive as our ballooning human population strains earth's ecosystems. A second reason is our rich patrimony of human cultural heritage, including myth and belief systems, wisdom, poetry, songs, and epic tales. Allowing our own history to be erased, we condemn ourselves to a cultural amnesia that may undermine our sense of purpose and our ability to live in peace with diverse peoples. A third reason is the great puzzle of human cognition, and our ability to understand how the mind organizes and processes information. Much of the human mind is still a black box. We cannot discern its inner workings—and we can often only know its thoughts by what comes out of it in the form of speech. Obscure languages hold at least some of the keys to unlocking the mind. For all these reasons, and with the possibility of dire consequences for failure, documenting endangered languages while they may still be heard, and revitalizing tongues that still may be viable, must be viewed as the greatest conservation challenge of our generation. (2007, pp. 19–20)

So, where does this leave us, especially with respect to language planning and language policy? Language policy, together with educational, social, cultural, and economic policy, can play a key role in either protecting or further threatening endangered languages. The problem is fundamentally an educational one, but it is also one grounded, not surprisingly, in poverty (see Harbert, McConnell-Ginet, Miller, & Whitman, 2009). As the nineteenth-century American humorist Mark Twain once observed, "Soap and education are not as sudden as a massacre, but they are more deadly in the long run." This has often been the case in the history of threatened languages, but it need not be. Suzanne Romaine (2008, p. 8) suggests three different ways to confront the loss of language diversity: we can do nothing, we can document endangered languages while they still exist, and/or we can attempt to sustain and revitalize at least some threatened languages. For many languages, we have already made the decision by default: nothing is being done, and given the number of threatened languages, our societies are almost certainly not going to invest in documenting them, let alone in trying to revitalize them. For others, professional linguists are working even as we speak to save what information is still salvageable, though far too few are doing so.

This brings us back to language revitalization efforts, of which there are many that are certainly noteworthy. Threatened languages can be saved, but to do so requires immense effort and commitment. I have tried to argue here that that effort and commitment is worthwhile and valuable. I think that the NGO ActionAid International's motto, with a focus on language as well as poverty, may be relevant here: "Overcoming poverty is not a gesture of charity. It is an act of justice." Human beings have rights, and among these rights are the right to preserve and maintain their language (see Guillorel & Koubi, 1999; Kontra, Phillipson, Skutnabb-Kangags, & Várady, 1999; May, 2005; Patrick, 2005; Phillipson, 2000; Skutnabb-Kangas, 2000; Skutnabb-Kangas & Phillipson, 1995)—perhaps the single most commonly abrogated human right in the world today, a point to which I shall return shortly. In spite of the widespread violation of language rights, though, around the world there are ongoing, and very promising, language revival and revitalization efforts taking place (Tsunoda, 2006). Indeed, a whole new field of sociolinguistics—reversing language shift—has emerged in recent years (see Fishman, 1991, 2006a, 2006b; Tollefson & Tsui, 2004). Such efforts involve support in a variety of social, cultural and economic domains, but none is as important as the educational domain, and language revival and revitalization continue to occur in a variety of settings, often with quite promising results.

In New Zealand, the Maori language, whose history had paralleled that of other indigenous languages in Anglophone settler societies, is an impressive example of what can be accomplished. By 1975, only 5 percent of Maori children could still speak Maori. As a result of a strong revitalization movement, though, in December 1982 the first fifty *Kohanga Reo* ("language nest") Maori-medium preschools opened, and by 1993, there were 809 of these centers serving some 14,514 students (Skutnabb-Kangas, 2000, pp. 603–4). As of July 2009, the New Zealand Ministry of Education reports a total of more than 25,000 students enrolled in Maori-medium educational programs at a range of educational levels. Maori has become, once again, more than merely a ceremonial language; it is a living language whose future appears to be strong.

As we have seen, the situation for all but a few of the Native American languages in the United States is incredibly grim. And yet, there are a small number of quite promising cases, including the revitalization of the Hawai'ian language in recent decades, though not without considerable debate (see Wong, 1999). Although Hawai'ian language and culture had been mandated as a consequence of the 1978 state constitution, it was not until 1983 that a total immersion preschool for Hawai'ian was established. Hawai'ian-medium immersion programs were then developed in the public schools, and as students moved from one grade to the next, the programs expanded. Finally, in the spring of 1999 the first group of students who had had their entire pre-K–12 schooling in the medium of Hawai'ian graduated from secondary school (McCarty, 2002, pp. 297–98).

Both the cases of Maori and Hawai'ian are, by most accounts, successes, and yet they do serve to remind us of the very real limits of language revitalization. Kaplan and Baldauf note what has happened with Maori:

> Under the present circumstances, given the fact that there are virtually no monolingual speakers of Maori language left, the intergenerational gap has increased; that is, a whole generation has been skipped in language transmission—the best that can now be hoped for is a third generation . . . of more-or-less fluent *second-language* speakers of Maori. While such individuals may be able to use Maori in some limited or reduced number of registers, it is likely that the things to be discussed in Maori will be, at least in part, and perhaps to a significant degree, non-Maori. Even for these proficient second-language speakers of Maori, many important registers will function largely in English, not in Maori (or Maori will constitute a second, weaker, option for the discussion of some registers). (1997, p. 278)

In short, the dominance of a language of wider communication, such as English, in bilingual societies is a permanent threat to effective and truly meaningful language revitalization, and the educational system is not up to the task, as Joshua Fishman reminds us:

> As researchers in an area of specialization that is essentially outside of and broader than education, we tend to be surprisingly mesmerized by schools

> and by schooling . . . All of this would be understandable and harmless enough, were it not for the fact that we tend to make societal extrapolations on this basis—favoring education as the cure-all for sociolinguistic ills—as well. I have noticed this repeatedly. When I was studying reversing language shift, most sociolinguists with whom I discussed my work were convinced that "the schools could turn any language around," oblivious of the fact that exactly this has proven to be impossible in almost every well-documented case. (2006b, p. 137)

Education, then, is a necessary but not sufficient condition for language revival and revitalization.

Turning now from language revival and revitalization, we next come to efforts at *language reform*. Language reform takes place, both formally and informally, in many languages accorded official status in the modern world, and includes lexical and orthographic reform as well as occasional syntactic reform. Language reform as a type of language planning activity is often, therefore, essentially corpus planning. Examples of relatively effective language reform include the reform of written Chinese in the People's Republic of China, in which traditional Chinese characters were simplified to make the acquisition of literacy easier (see Chen, 1999; Tai, 1988); the reforms of Ibo and other indigenous languages in Nigeria, which attempted to correct errors that had been made by missionaries in their early efforts to commit these languages to writing (Emenanjo, 1990; Nwachukwu, 1983); the case of Turkish, in which Atatürk replaced the Arabic script with the Latin script to make it easier to learn and use modern Turkish and to thus increase literacy rates in modern Turkey, as well to replace many words of Arabic origin with terms drawn from European languages (Doğançay-Aktuna, 1995); and the case of Norwegian, one of the earliest efforts at language reform in the modern era, from which two distinct languages emerged, Bokmål and Nynorsk (Haugen, 1966), among others. Indeed, there are relatively few languages in the modern world that are used as official languages that have not been subjected to some sort of deliberate effort at language reform (see Cooper, 1989; Kaplan & Baldauf, 1997; Tollefson, 1991; S. Wright, 2004).

Language standardization involves status planning, when it refers to the selection of a single variety of a language as the standard language; corpus planning, when it refers to the codification of the language in a unified variety; and, of course, attitude planning when it involves changing popular attitudes about the language involved (as it nearly always does). Thus, the selection of Kiunguja, the Zanzibar dialect of Swahili, as the national linguistic norm in Tanzania, would constitute an example of language standardization of the status planning type (see Harries, 1983, pp. 127–28; S. Wright, 2004, pp. 75–82), whereas efforts to create a standardized spelling and grammar for a language would constitute a corpus planning approach to language standardization. Language standardization, it is important to note, can and often does overlap both language reform and language modernization in practice. Further, language standardization is closely tied to the notion of the nation-state:

> The perceived need for a single language runs parallel to the development of the nation-state. As such, standardisation has been a major goal of language planning and policy . . . In some respects, languages are constantly undergoing standardisation. This may occur formally through the work of language planning agencies such as in France or Malaysia, or more informally through the efforts of individuals, as in the English-speaking world. Thus, every time a new dictionary or grammar is published, that publication may be regarded as an additional attempt at standardisation. (Kaplan & Baldauf, 1997, p. 65)

Last, *language modernization* takes place as efforts are made to increase a language's lexicon to allow it to deal with new technological, political, economic, educational, and social developments and concepts. Such efforts are required because "there is often a need for a particular language to expand its capacity to deal with new concepts which have come into use in society more quickly than natural developments can accommodate" (Kaplan & Baldauf, 1997, p. 68). Language modernization therefore constitutes a clear instance of corpus planning, though it also has important implications for both acquisition planning and attitude planning. All languages, of course, from time to time experience what can be termed *lexical gaps*; language modernization refers specifically to controlled and directed attempts to expand a given language's lexicon in a systematic manner (Eastman, 1983, pp. 232–37; Nahir, 1977, p. 117). As Jernudd notes, "A major activity of many language planning agencies . . . be they normal language academies, development boards or language committees, is the development of terminologies, particularly in technical fields" (1977, p. 215). Examples of language modernization abound; indeed, Fodor and Hagège's multivolume *Language Reform: History and Future* includes studies of language modernization efforts in more than sixty different languages (Fodor & Hagège, 1983/4, 1990). While efforts at language modernization are, then, quite common, the extent to which they are effective in mandating language usage can vary quite dramatically from one society to another. With regard to lexical modernization in KiSwahili,

> A serious question that has to be asked, however, is whether external planning, planning from the top, has any effect on actual usage. For example, in the list of astronomical terms, *mchota maji* (literally, "water bearer" from *chota* "dip up" and *maji* "water") is suggested for "Aquarius," but a very popular astrologer in East Africa today uses *ndoo* (literally, "bucket, pail" for that sign; for "Sagittarius" he uses *mshale* (literally, "arrow"), while the suggested list gives *mpiga shaabaha* "shooter of the target" . . . (1979, p. 288)

New lexical items in a language can be created in a number of different ways. Among the most common are:

- new words are created completely *ab initio;*
- words already in the language can be given new meanings;
- words can be borrowed from another language; and
- new words can be created from the existing roots and affixes from the historical base of the language. (see Kaplan & Baldauf, 1997, p. 69)

An example of the first type of lexical creation is not particularly common, apart from the adoption of commercial brand names as more generic lexical items. Examples of the latter, though, are not unusual: Xerox for a photocopy and Kleenex for a facial tissue are both instances of this process. For the case of an old word being "recycled" with a new meaning, consider the verb "to call" in English. Originally refer to calling in the limited sense of "crying out," the term now is far more often used with the meaning of "to telephone." Using words borrowed from other languages is an incredibly common practice in many languages. English has both borrowed extensively and is now borrowed from extensively. For instance, the word *intelligentsia* was borrowed from Russian (интеллигенция), the words *patio* and *tortilla* from Spanish, the word *prestige* directly from French, the words *kindergarten* and *seminar* from German, the words *toboggan, skunk, opossum wigwam*, and *chipmunk* from various Native American languages, and so on. English as a source language has had a huge impact on many languages as a result of the ubiquity of English in the worlds of pop culture and media; as Fromkin, Rodman, and Hyams note, "*jazz, whisky, blue jeans, rock music, supermarket, baseball, picnic*, and *computer* have been borrowed by languages as diverse as Twi, Hungarian, Russian, and Japanese" (2003, p. 514). Finally, the idea of creating new lexical items from the existing word-stock of a language can be seen in practice in the case of the English (and, indeed, relatively international) use of such Latin and Greek-derived terms as *microscope, biosphere, telescope, telephone*, and *telegraph*. The creation of new lexical items is not a value-free, merely technical endeavor, however:

> Technical competence may be enough to create a nomenclature in chemistry, but it is certainly not enough to have the new terms accepted, liked, learned and used. The development of a new lexicon occurs in a sociocultural context where modernization contrasts with tradition, each bearing its own particular ideological weighting, and where there is tension between the imported concept and terms and the indigenous. . . . What is generally wanted in developing societies is not just an adequate terminology, but one that is identified also with the society. (Spolsky, 2004, pp. 35–36)

A particularly interesting contemporary case of both official and more informal language modernization has been taking place in Russia, as that society undergoes massive social, economic, and political changes in the aftermath of the collapse of the Soviet Union. Examples of new terminology in modern Russian abound; the changes that are taking place in society have led to widespread lexical innovation, borrowing, and creation, as new concepts, practices, technologies, and institutions replace those of the Soviet state, which had itself significantly changed the lexicon of Imperial Russian (see Ryazanova-Clarke & Wade, 1999). Examples of such new lexical items in Russian include:

аэробика	*/aerobika/*	"aerobics"
леп-топ	*/lep-top/*	"laptop"
пейджер	*/peidzher/*	"pager"
биг мак	*/big mak/*	"Big Mac"
бойфренд	*/bojfrend/*	"boy friend"
копирайт	*/kopirait/*	"copyright"
маркетинг	*/marketing/*	"marketing"
ток-шоу	*/tok-shou/*	"talk show"

If the Russian case is unusual in that it is largely undirected and driven by speakers rather by particular institutions, this is even more the case for many small languages on the Internet. The United Nations Educational, Scientific and Cultural Organization (UNESCO) Institute for Statistics notes that, "The issue of linguistic diversity on the Internet proves to be central to the debate on the Information Society in a number of unexpected ways" (2005, p. 5), and in a fascinating study of the impact of Wikipedia on the Breton language, Robert Baxter comments:

> Where favourable technological conditions exist, on-line resources such as Wikipedia are potentially useful tools for preserving and developing economically challenged languages by allowing for the production of general as well as technical written material for very limited audiences and in volumes which would be economically unfeasible in hard copy. The terminological pressure exerted on Breton increases in proportion to the speed with which the appeal of on-line open-access resources such as Wikipedia grows and their scope expands. This pressure marks a new terminological turning-point, leading to a methodological return to neologisms created and promoted by individual users as opposed to more recent methods based on collective work, although remaining open to review by other users. (2009, p. 75)

Technological innovation may help not only to preserve smaller languages, but to encourage a democratization of the language planning process.

ORIENTATIONS AND IDEOLOGIES OF LANGUAGE POLICY

Language planning activities and specific language policies not only perform different functions, as we have seen, but also fall into different ideological orientations with respect to their underlying assumptions as well as their social and educational goals and objectives (see, for example, Joseph & Taylor, 1990; Phillipson, 1992; Ruiz, 1984, 1990, 2010; Spolsky & Shohamy, 2000). Richard Ruiz provides one useful way to think about the goals of language planning and language policy; he suggests that there are, broadly speaking, three orientations that one might take with respect to how one views language, especially in bilingual and multilingual settings: language-as-a-problem, language-as-a-right, and language-as-a-resource (Ruiz, 1984, 1990, 2010). The issue he raises is whether language diversity is seen in negative or positive terms—that is, whether linguistic diversity in a society is a problem to be overcome, or involves the recognition of the fundamental human rights of individuals as well as the very real benefits that linguistic diversity can offer a society. The "language-as-a-problem" orientation focuses on the complications and challenges that are created by linguistic diversity, generally in the context of issues of equity and access, education, economics, and so on. The idea that underlies the "language as-a-problem" orientation is that language diversity plays a key role in disempowering groups and individuals, and in promoting ethnic divisiveness and even strife. The "language-as-a-right" orientation focuses on principles of social justice and on the acceptance of the principle that language rights are a fundamental kind of human rights. Finally, the "language-as-a-resource" orientation sees language and linguistic skills as a kind of cultural capital that can and should be developed by society. Although Ruiz does identify these as three distinct orientations, in fact the first stands in contrast to the second and third (Figure 2.5)—a point that Tove Skutnabb-Kangas recognizes: "In several readings of Ruiz, all three have been seen as *competing* views, rather than the last two being complementary (and Ruiz himself does little to prevent this ambivalent interpretation)" (2000, p. 653).

Juan Cobarrubias suggests an alternative way to think about language planning and language policy, identifying four broadly conceived ideologies of language that guide and orient language policies (1983, pp. 63–66). He explains:

> Language ideologies reflect a mode of treatment of one language group with respect to another and ordinarily involve judgments as to what is right or wrong. Also, ideologies involve frames of reference pertaining to an ideal social group that will evolve, at some future time, from the segment of reality to which the ideology is being applied. The ideological aspect related to language status planning is perhaps the most neglected area of language planning, in spite of the fact that ideologies underlie all forms of status planning. It is because ideologies involve value judgments and direct a certain mode of treatment that status decisions raise ethical issues. (1983, p. 63)

The four ideologies of language identified by Cobarrubias are linguistic assimilation, linguistic pluralism, vernacularization, and internationalization, each of which we will now briefly discuss (see Figure 2.6).

Linguistic assimilation as an ideology of language is based on the assumption that linguistic (and, presumably, cultural) unity is at the very least desirable in a society, and may actually be necessary to some extent. Thus, language policies grounded in the ideology of linguistic assimilation tend to favor monolingual models of society. An important component of linguistic assimilation is that advocates of such policies are concerned not merely with individuals and groups acquiring competence in a specific, common language, but also with the rejection and replacement of other languages in the society, at least in the public sphere. The ideology of linguistic assimilation also tends, in practice, to encourage a belief in the superiority of the dominant language in a society, often

Orientation	View of Linguistic Diversity	View of Social Bilingualism / Multilingualism	View of Individual Bilingual / Multilingualism	View of Minority Languages in Society	View of Language Second / Foreign Education
Language-as-a-Problem	Negative	Negative	Negative	Negative	Negative
Language-as-a-Right	Positive	Positive	Positive	Positive	Positive
Language-as-a-Resource	Positive	Positive	Positive	Positive	Positive

FIGURE 2.5. *Orientations in language planning and language policy*

Ideology	Formulation	Explanation	Examples
Linguistic Assimilation	A+B+C+D ==> A	Where A is the dominant language of the society, and members of the society are expected to operate in this language at least for all formal purposes.	The role of French in France is an example of the ideology of linguistic assimilation.
Linguistic Pluralism	A+B+C+D ==> A+B+C+D	Linguistic pluralism takes place when a society opts for a high degree of official multilingualism that reflects, at least to some extent, the linguistic diversity of the society.	Contemporary South Africa's multilingual language policy, in which there are 11 languages that have Constitutional status of "official," is an example of the ideology of linguistic pluralism.
Vernacularization	A+B+C+D ==> C	Where C is an indigenous language, typically in a former colony.	The use of KiSwahili is Tanzania following independence is as example of the ideology of vernacularization.
Internationalization	A+B+C+D ==> E	Where E is a "language of wider communication" (LWC), most often English or French, and is typically the language of the former colonial power.	Examples of the ideology of internationalization abound; in Africa, the division between the Francophone, Anglophone, and Lusophone countries is the result of internationalization.

FIGURE 2.6. *Ideologies of language planning*

resulting in the denial of language rights to speakers of languages other than the dominant language (see Cobarrubias, 1983, pp. 63–64). In the context of the "developing world," language policies based on the ideology of linguistic assimilation were most common during the colonial era; Cobarrubias gives the examples of "Guam, the Philippines under American rule . . . and to some degree Puerto Rico prior to the 1952 Constitution" (1983, p. 64). Educationally, language policies grounded in the ideology of linguistic assimilation most often entail formal schooling in the selected national language, and the exclusion and denigration of other indigenous languages, at least in official settings. Thus, the use of French in Francophone Africa in virtually all educational settings (save, notably, in *Qur'anic* schools) would be an example of the ideology of linguistic assimilation in educational practice (see Ball, 1997; Djité, 1990, 1991; Weinstein, 1980). In such cases, a necessary (and often sufficient) condition for being "educated" is competence in the dominant language.

Unlike the ideology of linguistic assimilation, the ideology of *linguistic pluralism* emphasizes the language rights of minority groups, and in general tends not only to accept, but to support, language diversity in a society. Linguistic pluralism in practice exists in a variety of forms, ranging from relatively weak toleration of diversity to strong support for multiple languages, and often includes the recognition, in some form, of official status for multiple languages in a society. Examples of countries in which some sort of official status abound: countries in which such status is granted to two languages include Belarus (Belarusian and Russian), Botswana (English and Tswana), Cameroon (English and French), Canada (English and French), Chad (French and Arabic), Cyprus (Greek and Turkish), Finland (Finnish and Swedish), Israel (Hebrew and Arabic), Ireland (Irish and English), the Netherlands (Dutch and Frisian), Paraguay (Spanish and Guaraní), and the Philippines (Filipino and English), among many others. A relatively small number of countries are officially trilingual, including Bolivia (Spanish, Aymara, and Quechua), Perú (also Spanish, Aymara, and Quechua), and New Zealand (English, Maori, and New Zealand Sign Language). Countries in which there is a more multilingual official policy include India (with English and Hindi at the national level, and some thirty-four other languages with regional status), Nigeria (with English, Hausa, Ibo, and Yoruba), Switzerland (with French, German, Italian, and Romansh), and, most recently, South Africa (in which the post-apartheid period has seen a shift from official bilingualism in Afrikaans and English to an officially multilingual policy in which there are eleven official languages, including Afrikaans, English, isiZulu, isiXhosa, isiNdebele, Sepedi, Sesotho, Setswana, SiSwati, Tshivenda, and Xitsonga). Although policies of linguistic pluralism are often politically the easiest solution for developing societies because they appear to avoid problems related to the domination of less powerful groups by more powerful ones, such policies entail economic and political trade-offs. This is the case because multilingualism is more expensive than monolingualism (due to the need for interpreters, translations, multiple publications in different languages, lexical development, and a host of other factors), and because such policies can, in fact, encourage the development of insular pluralistic communities within a society. In addition, in settings in which a multilingual policy is adopted, this often in practice means that the former colonial language continues to dominate local languages (see Reagan, 2001b; Wright, 2002).

Also closely related to the ideology of linguistic pluralism is *vernacularization*, which entails the selection of one or more indigenous language(s) in a society to serve in an official capacity. Such selection almost always involves considerable language engineering, as discussed above, and such engineering inevitably focuses on the educational sphere, with the production of textbooks, curricular materials, matriculation examinations, and so on. Further, vernacularization can focus on a single indigenous language, as in the case of KiSwahili in Tanzania, or on multiple languages, as has been the case both historically and at the present in South Africa (albeit for quite different reasons; see Louw, 1983/4; Reagan, 1986b, 1987, 2001b). According to Cobarrubias,

> Vernacularization involves the restoration and/or elaboration of an indigenous language and its adoption as an official language. There are also several processes of vernacularization which include the revival of a dead language (Hebrew in Israel), the restoration of a classical language (the Arabization process in Syria, Egypt, and Morocco), the promotion of an indigenous language to official status and its eventual standardization (Tagalog in the Philippines and Quechua in Peru). (1983, p. 66)

The ideology of *internationalization* involves the selection of a language of wider communication, such as English or French, for use as the society's official language. Such selections have been and continue to be quite common throughout the "developing world" and almost always reflect the colonial past of a country. Thus, the division between Anglophone and Francophone Africa largely reflects differences not only in official languages but also in terms of the colonial past (though other ideologies of language also exist in the African context, especially in Anglophone Africa, as both Nigeria and Tanzania make clear). The ideology of internationalization, although certainly understandable from a pragmatic position, remains highly controversial in many societies, and is certainly tied to concerns about issues of linguistic domination and linguistic imperialism (see Canagarajah, 1999, 2005; Errington, 2008; Hall & Eggington, 2000; Holborow, 1999; Mazrui & Mazrui, 1998; Pennycook, 1994, 1998, 2000, 2001, 2004, 2008; Phillipson, 1992; Skutnabb-Kangas, 2000). It also raises serious questions about matters of equity and access in postcolonial societies.

THE LANGUAGE PLANNING PROCESS

The language planning process can be conceptualized in two very different ways: the traditional, basically positivistic approach, and the critical approach. Both sorts of efforts can be found, though the former are more common. The language planning process as it has traditionally been conceived consists of four interrelated, and to some extent overlapping, components: (1) the initial fact-finding phase; (2) the establishment and articulation of goals, desired outcomes, and the strategies to be employed in achieving these goals and outcomes; (3) the implementation process; and (4) the evaluation of all aspects of the language planning process (see Reagan, 1983; Rubin & Jernudd, 1971). During the first stage of the language planning process, information about the setting in which the language policy is to be implemented is gathered. Clearly, the more information that is available to the language planner, the better. In any event, two sorts of information must be gathered if the language policy is expected to have a significant and positive impact. The first of these is a clear understanding of the sociolinguistic setting in which the language policy is to be implemented; especially important in this context are the common patterns of linguistic usage. The second sort of necessary information is that which would provide a proper understanding of other social, economic, and political processes and developments, not the least of which is the motivation for the language planning activity. It is only with a combination of these two kinds of information that the language planner can gain a realistic perspective on need determination and assessment of needs and wants (see Figure 2.7).

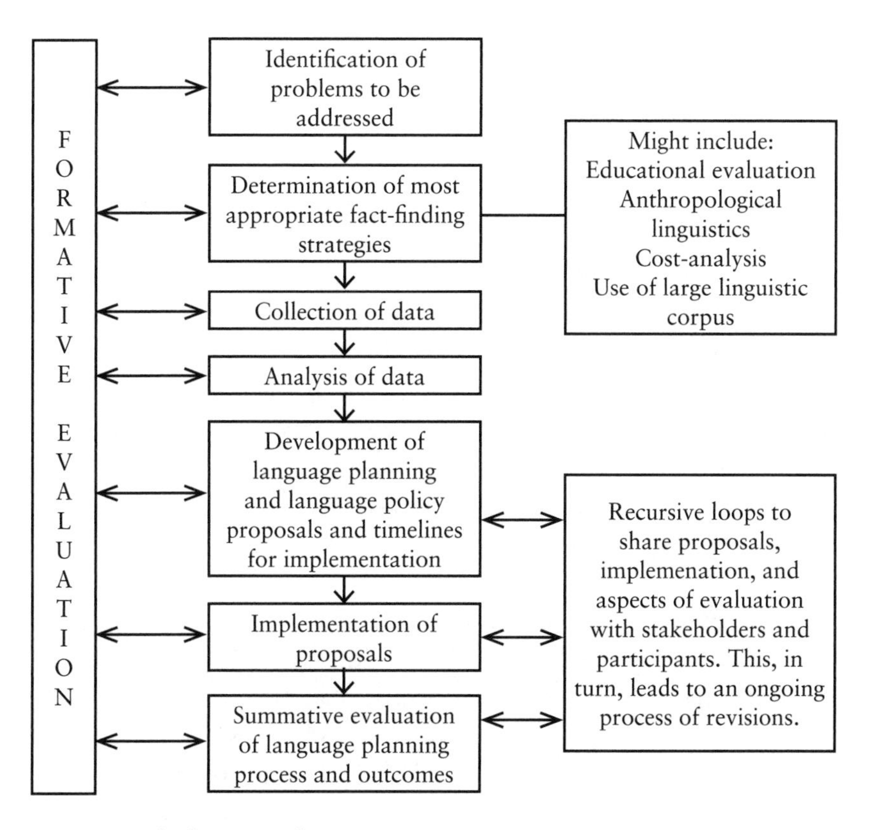

FIGURE 2.7. *The language planning process*

The second step in the language planning process involves the determination and articulation of goals, strategies, and outcomes. This process takes place on several levels and requires a variety of skilled personnel. Goals, both linguistic and extralinguistic, are set based on the assessment of needs and wants determined in the information-gathering phase within the parameters made possible by the political and socioeconomic context. The goals, in turn, will serve to define and delineate the expected (and desired) outcomes of the language policy to be effected. The strategies for achieving these outcomes, which are normally seen as primarily a technical matter, will provide the basis and direction for the implementation of the language policy.

The implementation of the language policy, the third step in the language planning process, is in many ways the central focus of much of the language planning literature. This phase entails the mobilization of resources, general finance and personnel management, motivation and supervision of those concerned both with the management of the language policy program and with its target populations, and preparation, sequencing, and coordination of related aspects of the language policy (such as the development of dictionaries, textbooks, etc.; [Rubin & Jernudd, 1971]).

The last step in the process of language planning, and often in practice the most neglected, is that of evaluation. Evaluation of the language policy should take place in two senses: both as an integral, ongoing component of all phases of the language planning process, and as a final, cumulative examination of the successes and failures of the language policy (mainly, although not exclusively, in terms of the correlation of goals and outcomes). Insofar as the predicted outcomes are still considered valid ones, the actual outcomes ought to be, as a consequence of evaluation, brought continually closer to the articulated goals of the language policy.

The model of the process of language planning presented here is essentially a normative one, which is to say that this is how language planners and policy makers would generally advocate that policies related to language be made. However, such a model does not necessarily actually describe or reflect reality. In fact, language policies and related language planning decisions are frequently made solely or primarily on the basis of short-term political expediency, misguided assumptions and beliefs, and a range of extralinguistic factors. It is also true, however, that language policies and language planning activities are quite often unsuccessful (sometimes spectacularly so), often precisely because of the way in which they were designed and implemented. This is an important topic to which we will return when we discuss the evaluation of language policies.

There is an additional point that needs to be made with respect to the traditional way in which the language planning process is conceptualized, and that has to do with what might be termed the "directionality" of the process. Language planning efforts, and especially the earlier language planning efforts, tended to be "top-down" in nature (see Kaplan & Baldauf, 1997, pp. 196–99). Such policies, although sometimes reflecting the will of the people, often did not do so, and were as a consequence almost doomed from the start. It is clear that language planning efforts, and language policies, like other social policies, are most effective when they are in fact "bottom-up" in nature, directly involving the people whom they are meant to impact most directly, and at all stages of the language planning process.

This leads us to the critical approach to conceptualizing the language planning process. Not only does the critical approach require that we focus on a more "bottom-up" orientation, but it also seeks to move us from an overreliance on ideologically informed "expertise" to a more individual and community-based orientation. In distinguishing between "language planning" and "language policy," Elana Shohamy offers one way to think about this distinction in the planning process:

> While language planning refers to control, it does not leave anything to the individual to decide, as the governing body determines not just what the person will know but also how he or she will arrive there. This is where language planning is combined with practice. Language policy attempts to be less interventionist and to refer mostly to principles with regard to language use. Thus, it may include a statement that a number of languages should be learned in a given country or that indigenous groups should have the right to maintain their language, but it often does not go into which groups or which languages or how this should be implemented. With the increase of less interventionist approaches, the role of planning is subsiding and policy is becoming the bona fide. Yet, it should be noted that the boundaries between planning and policy are far from clear. (2006, p. 49)

In providing a framework for critical policy-making, David Corson (1999) suggests that there are four stages in policy development and implementation, but they are not those of the traditional, positivistic orientation; rather, they can be summarized as follows:

STAGE I: *Identifying the Real Problem(s)*
- The Problem Situation
- The Role of Expert Knowledge
- The Problem(s)

STAGE II: *Trial Policies: The Views of Stakeholders*
- Policy Guidelines
- Controllable Change: Stages in Policy Guidelines

STAGE III: *Testing Policies Against the Views of Participants*
- Testing Policies by Trial Applications
- Testing Policies by Research

STAGE IV: *Policy Implementation and Evaluation*

There are several important points to stress here. The first is the emphasis on the stakeholders in the policy-making setting. The second is the concern with the actual participants in the setting, who may or may not overlap with the stakeholders. The reliance on research is also key here, as is the focus on trial experiments and policies, which must be evaluated by all of those concerned. Such an approach to policy-making is, then, fundamentally distinct from that of the more traditional language planning process.

THE EVALUATION OF LANGUAGE POLICIES

Language policy as an applied sociolinguistic activity has the potential to function either as a tool for empowerment and liberation or as a means of oppression and domination. This is the case, in part, because language planning and language policy activities often involve both implicit and explicit goals and objectives. Further, such activities are fundamentally political and ideological in nature. Indeed, language policy can be used for good or for ill—there are abundant cases of both sorts of uses of language policy and language planning.

Such activities are also profoundly *political* in nature, an important point that was, at least until the 1990s, minimized or overlooked entirely in discussions of language planning (see McKay, 1993; Pennycook, 1994, 1998, 2000; Phillipson, 1992; Shohamy, 2006; Spolsky, 2004; S. Wright, 2004). Language planning involves public decisions about language, its use, status, and development—decisions that have overwhelming social, economic, educational, and political significance for both society and the individual. Language planning cannot be separated from such concerns, nor, indeed, would it be appropriate to try to do so. That language planning efforts are inevitably ideological and political in nature must be taken into account in trying to understand them (see Tollefson, 1991, pp. 22–42).

The philosopher Donna Kerr (1976) suggests four "tests" that any good public policy must pass:

- *The desirability test.* Is the goal of the policy one that the community *as a whole* believes to be desirable?
- *The justness test.* Is the policy *just* and *fair*? That is, does it treat all people in an equitable and appropriate manner?
- *The effectiveness test.* Is the policy *effective*? Does it achieve its objectives?
- *The tolerability test.* Is the policy resource-sensitive? Is it *viable* in the context in which it is to be effected?

These tests are quite useful in evaluating language policies, and they can serve as a working model for analyzing different language planning processes as well, providing us with a series of questions to ask in judging both the process by which different language policies are made and the outcomes of those policies (see Reagan, 2002b).

LANGUAGE PLANNING, LANGUAGE POLICY, AND LANGUAGE RIGHTS

Language planning and policy makers have recently shown increasing interest in language rights. The past century saw not only challenges to and abrogations of human rights, but also a growing awareness and articulation of such rights, and this has been an important facet of both language planning and language policy studies internationally:

> The Second World War involved violations of human rights on an unprecedented scale but its ending saw the dawn of a new era for rights. Following their heyday in the seventeenth century . . . rights played a crucial role in the revolutions of the late eighteenth century. In the nineteenth and early twentieth centuries, however, appeal to rights was eclipsed by movements such as utilitarianism and Marxism which could not, or would not, accommodate them. . . . The contemporary period has seen a further shift in their fortunes and today they provide an accepted international currency for moral and political debate. In many parts of the world, irrespective of cultural or religious traditions, when issues or torture or terrorism, poverty or power are debated, the argument is very often conducted in terms of rights and their violation. (Almond, 1993, p. 259)

Such awareness has been relatively late to develop in the area of language rights, in spite of ongoing and often egregious violations of group and individual rights in the linguistic domain. As recently as 1985, Gomes de Matos could write that, "Although ours has been said to be 'the age of rights' . . . there has not yet been a thorough, well-documented, carefully thought out discussion of the crucial problem of the human being's linguistic rights" (1985, pp. 1–2). Sue Wright notes:

> The right to use one's own language has only recently gained acceptance as a fundamental human right. Until the end of the 20th century, whether or not a language community used its language in the public space depended on its political muscle or the tolerance of the dominant groups among which it lived. Those in power might make it possible to use a language other than their own in the institutions and forums of public life, but such use was not universally accepted as a right. (2007, p. 203)

Given the centrality of language to self-identification and to our sense of who we are and where we fit in the broader world, it is interesting that a concern with language rights has taken so long to emerge. And yet, such concern *has* emerged in recent decades, and the scholarly and political literature dealing with issues of language rights has increased dramatically both quantitatively and qualitatively (see, for instance, Herriman & Burnaby, 1996; Kontra et al., 1999; May, 2005; Paulston, 2003; Phillipson, 2000; Skutnabb-Kangas & Phillipson, 1995). Although it is clear that we have a long way to go in terms of raising consciousness about language rights, and although such rights are far from universally recognized (let alone universally observed or enforced), the fact that the issue itself has been put on the table for discussion and debate is itself promising.

Debates about language and language policy present the fundamental challenge of achieving balance between the competing goods of social unity and access on the one hand and respect for and toleration of diversity on the other (see Cooper, 1989; Kaplan & Baldauf, 1997; Tollefson, 1991). The question that policy makers are trying to address in such debates is the extent to which pluralism, as a necessary condition for a democratic social order, applies to the issue of language. At the heart of this discussion, of course, is the issue of language rights. In other words, to what extent, and in what ways, are *language* rights *human* rights? Do language rights apply only to the individual, or are they "group rights" (rights that apply to a community rather than solely to the members of that community, by virtue of some common, shared feature of the individuals in the community (see Coulombe, 1993; Tollefson, 1991, pp. 167–200)? This is actually a far more complex matter than it might at first seem, since language rights are "preeminently *social*, in that they are only comprehensible in relation to a group of other human beings with whom the language is shared and from which personal and cultural identity is achieved" (MacMillan, 1982, p. 420). In other words, debates about language rights are unique in that, as Kenneth McRae argues, "societies characterized by linguistic pluralism differ from those characterized by racial, religious, class or ideological divisions in one essential respect, which stems from the pervasive nature of language as a general vehicle of communication" (1978, p. 331). This having been said, the concept of "group rights" is itself somewhat problematic, potentially leading to an apartheid-style mandate of ethnic obligation, even as the alternative of linguistic imperialism looms large (see Errington, 2008;

Pennycook, 1994, 1998, 2000, 2001; Phillipson, 1992). The challenge, in short, is a very real one, with very real outcomes.

In working toward a conception of language rights, a good place to begin is with *The United Nations Declaration on the Rights of Persons Belonging to National or Ethnic, Religious and Linguistic Minorities* (18 December 1992), in which the international community attempted to articulate the nature of the human and civil rights that ought to be accorded members of minority groups. This *Declaration* was a follow-up to the *Universal Declaration of Human Rights*, necessitated by the widespread violation of the second article of the *Universal Declaration of Human Rights*, which prohibits discrimination against individuals based on language. Specifically, three articles of the *Declaration* are relevant for our purposes here. First, Article 2.1 prohibits what might be termed active discrimination against members of minority groups:

> Persons belonging to national or ethnic, religious and linguistic minorities (hereinafter referred to as persons belonging to minorities) have the right to enjoy their own culture, to profess and practice their own religion, *and to use their own language, in private and in public, freely and without interference or any form of discrimination.* (Article 2.1, my emphasis)

This, in a sense, is the negative force of the *Declaration*, in that it focuses on simply prohibiting actions and policies that unfairly target minority groups. The *Declaration* goes far beyond this negative constraint, however, and in Articles 4.2 and 4.3 specifies what can be called positive, or proactive, language rights:

> States shall take measures to create favorable conditions to enable persons belonging to minorities to express their characteristics and to develop their culture, language, religion, traditions and customs, except where specific practices are in violation of national and contrary to international standards. (Article 4.2)

> States should take appropriate measures so that, whenever possible, persons belonging to minorities have adequate opportunities to learn their mother tongue or to have instruction in their mother tongue. (Article 4.3)

These explicit statements of both negative and positive aspects of language rights differ in significant ways, of course, from the legal and constitutional provisions governing the issue of language rights in the vast majority of member states of the United Nations, including, notably, the United States. Even more important in this context, though, are the very common gaps between legal and constitutional protections and the reality of daily life in societies around the world. Constitutional guarantees are certainly desirable, but they are by no means *sufficient* to ensure justice.

Violations of language rights occur in a wide variety of contexts and settings and take many forms (see Desai, 1994). Underlying many violations of language rights are assumptions tied to ideologies of linguistic imperialism (Pennycook, 1995, 2001, pp. 59–64). Linguistic imperialism is not language-specific; virtually any linguistic community *could* utilize its language to dominate others and to promote linguistic hegemony. In the real world, though, few language communities have the political, economic, cultural, and military power and status to engage in such linguistic imperialism. The role of English in the contemporary world is often cited as the clearest example of linguistic imperialism. Robert Phillipson, for example, provides a compelling critique of English linguistic imperialism, arguing that it is characterized by situations in which "*the dominance of English is asserted and maintained by the establishment and continuous reconstitution of structural and cultural inequalities between English and other languages*" (1992, p. 47, emphasis in original). There can be little doubt about the increasing dominance of English in the international sphere (see, for example, Crystal, 2003; McArthur, 1998), and in fact it is the very success of English that makes it such a danger and threat to many smaller languages. However, English is by no means alone; the same sort of linguistic imperialism also colors the relations between French and indigenous languages in many parts of the world (see Ball, 1997; Djité, 1990, 1991; Weinstein, 1980) and between Spanish and indigenous American Indian languages in Latin America (see Grinevald, 1998; Hamel, 1995a, 1995b), and, at least historically, it characterized the relationship between Russian and the other languages of the former Soviet Union and the Soviet bloc (see Garibova & Asgarova, 2009; Maurais, 1992; Schlyter, 1998; Sebba, 2006).

The desire for a common language for intercommunication is not itself evidence for linguistic imperialism, of course. Linguistic imperialism goes beyond such needs, as it either explicitly or implicitly encourages linguistic assimilation to the dominant language and involves a complex set of attitudes and beliefs about language and the contexts in which particular languages function. In other words, linguistic imperialism has at its core the exploitation of dominated language communities in favor of the dominant language community. The selection of a language for use in any given setting is associated with a number of factors, but whether the communicative situation is an informal one between two individuals or a matter of government policy, in any context where bi- or multilingualism exists, the selection of a language to be used is at least in part a *political* choice.

Related to linguistic imperialism is a broader kind of social and ideological bias, which has come to be called *linguicism*. Linguicism is essentially the linguistic aspect of racism, sexism, ageism, and so on; the term refers to "ideologies, structures, and practices which are used to legitimate, effectuate, and reproduce an unequal division of power and resources (both material and immaterial) between groups which are defined on the basis of language" (Phillipson, 1992, p. 47). Among the manifestations of linguicism are claims about linguistic legitimacy: that is, debates about what counts as a language (see Reagan, 1997). Debates about linguistic legitimacy are virtually always reflective of differential power relations; one does not come across arguments about whether French or German are legitimate languages, but one *does* find otherwise reasonable people suggesting that sign languages, artificially constructed languages such as Esperanto, and nonmainstream language varieties should not be treated as "real" or "legitimate" languages. The effects of linguistic imperialism and linguicism at their most extreme can be seen in the growing number of languages whose very existence is threatened (see Dorian, 1998). Some scholars, most notably Tove Skutnabb-Kangas, suggest that what actually takes place in many instances is not merely language death, but is in fact linguistic genocide (see Skutnabb-Kangas, 2000). This is a very strong claim, of course, but one for which the evidence in many cases is quite powerful (see, e.g., Bobaljik, Pensalfini, & Storto, 1996; Hernández-Chávez, 1995; Hindley, 1990; Skutnabb-Kangas & Bucak, 1995).

It is important to note here that although the relatively small number of languages of wider communication, and English in particular, are most often identified as the dominating and even oppressing languages in conflicts between language groups, the tables can be quickly turned. As John Edwards observes, "It is natural (and perhaps praiseworthy) for educated minds to support the small, the weak and the downtrodden, but there are often gins and snares. Conor Cruise O'Brien noted . . . "that we ought not to 'idealise minorities, or to forget that today's underdog may be tomorrow's power-crazed bully' and there are, surely, many historical and contemporary contexts which bear him out" (1996, p. 33). The issues of language rights and language oppression apply to all individuals and groups, and they must do so equally if they are to have any meaning at all (see Grin, 2005; Hassanpour, 1999; Phillipson et al., 1995, pp. 3–4).

Our discussion thus far has emphasized language rights and violations of language rights, but this is really only one side of the coin. We can also talk about the language *responsibilities* of both the individual and the society: If the individual has the right to an education in his or her native language, he or she also has a responsibility (or obligation) to learn the socially dominant language of his or her society. Similarly, while a society is certainly within its rights to legislate an official language, it must then recognize that it has the related *obligation* to provide the educational support necessary to ensure that all of its members have access to this language. Thus a fundamental assumption in the discourse about language rights is that such rights are matched by obligations on the part of both the individual and the society—as, indeed, are all human rights.

At the present time, the U.S. Constitution makes no direct reference whatsoever to language or to language rights; such rights are presumed to be inherent in other legal and constitutional protections. Indeed, it is this lack of specific mention of language rights that is, to some extent, at issue in contemporary debates about adopting English as the official language of the United States (see Baron, 1990; Crawford, 1992a, 1992b). With respect to education in the United States, I would argue that language rights (as well as concomitant language responsibilities) are both logically and practically necessary conditions for the provision of fair and equitable education for all children in our society, as well as required by our international commitments to human rights. In practice, this would entail the right of the individual to use his or her language in various contexts, including but certainly not limited to the use of the native language as the medium of instruction as appropriate. At the same time, it would also entail ensuring access to the socially, economically, and politically dominant language of the society. This would thus require educational programs that promote linguistic diversity to at the same time ensure that all students gain competence in the socially dominant language.

Such is not, however, the reality. The numbers of language minority students in the United States are significant, but they take on greater urgency when one considers the demographic and social trends that they represent. Both the percentage and absolute number of limited English proficiency students in the public schools—both those explicitly identified by the schools as nonspeakers of English and those not so identified but nonetheless with English as a nondominant language—will increase dramatically in the years ahead as American society itself continues to become increasingly diverse (see Ager, Muskens, & Wright, 1993; Baker,

2001; Corson, 1993). These children bring with them educational needs that are distinct from their English-speaking classmates, and it is with their educational needs that debates about methodology (bilingual education vs. English as a Second Language, and so on) are most often concerned. If one takes into account *The Declaration on the Rights of Persons Belonging to National or Ethnic, Religious and Linguistic Minorities*, however, then the issue becomes less one of methodology and more one of language rights. Specifically, such children are entitled to both use and learn their mother tongue in school, as well as have the right to acquire the socially dominant language. Thus, traditional subtractive programs in the American context, which have as their principal (and often only) objective the acquisition of English, are simply incompatible with the articulated conceptions of language rights as they apply to minority language children.

Another issue that must be raised here is that of the problem of elitism and language status. In the U.S. context, there is an unarticulated but nonetheless powerful hierarchy of languages and language varieties, with varieties of standard (or mainstream) English at the top of the hierarchy. This hierarchy is important both in terms of the attitudes of educational institutions and educators and with respect to its implications for the perceptions of speakers of languages other than English (see Reagan & Osborn, 2002). For example, Castilian Spanish is generally viewed favorably, while Puerto Rican Spanish is not. This, in turn, leads to radically different views of "bilingualism." For example, a native speaker of English acquiring competence in Spanish is seen as not only positive, but impressive and relatively noteworthy; however, a native speaker of Spanish acquiring competence in English in the U.S. setting is largely taken for granted—and if such a person does *not* acquire competence in English, this is then seen as a deficiency.

One of the most interesting and challenging aspects of dealing with matters of language and language diversity in the U.S. context is that of "ideological monolingualism." In essence, this refers to a set of commonly held beliefs about language among many (perhaps most) English-speakers in our society. Dell Hymes has identified what he takes to be six core, albeit generally tacit, assumptions about language in the United States:

- everyone in the United States speaks only English, or should;
- bilingualism is inherently unstable, probably injurious, and possibly unnatural;

- foreign literary languages can be respectively studied, but not foreign languages in their domestic varieties (it is one thing to study the French spoken in Paris, another to study the French spoken in Louisiana);
- most everyone else in the world is learning English anyway, and that, together with American military and economic power, makes it unnecessary to worry about knowing the language of a country in which one has business, bases, or hostages;
- differences in language are essentially of two kinds, right and wrong; and
- verbal fluency and noticeable style are suspicious, except as entertainment. (1996, pp. 84–85)

Each of these assumptions is fundamentally flawed, and the list as a whole is grounded in a lack of understanding of the nature of language and a confusion of historical mythology with historical fact, and it is replete with both factual and normative errors. Nevertheless, the belief system that undergirds and supports ideological monolingualism is very powerful and has direct implications for matters of language rights as such matters are manifested in U.S. public schools.

LANGUAGE PLANNING AND LANGUAGE POLICY IN EDUCATION

Issues of language policy do not take place only, or at least primarily, at the national and international levels; language policies exist on all levels of society, and one of the places in which they are most powerful is in the context of the school (see, for instance, Corson, 1999; Lambert, 1994). All schools have language policies, although these policies may be implicit or explicit, and all teachers are involved in the implementation of these language policies. As David Corson compellingly explains:

> School language policies are viewed by many in education as an integral and necessary part of the administration and curriculum practice of schools. A language policy . . . identifies areas of the school's scope of operations and program where language problems exist that need the commonly agreed approach offered by a policy. A language policy sets out what the school intends to do about these areas of concern and includes provisions for follow-up, monitoring, and revision of the policy itself . . . (1999, p. 1)

The decision about the language (or languages) to be used as the medium of instruction in the school is a language policy decision, as are decisions about what other languages are to be taught, how language will be taught, the relative significance of different languages in the school context, and so on. For the foreign language educator, this means that our very existence as a profession depends on language policies. The need for students to study a foreign language as a component of their general education is, then, part of the language policy discourse and practice in any school.

Beyond such direct concerns, though, language policy should also be of concern to educators in terms of our efforts to promote *critical language awareness* in students. Among the key concepts that critical language awareness approaches to language and language study seek to convey to students are the following:

- people have the power to shape the conventions that underlie discourse, just as much as any other social practices
- although we tend to accept the way language is, and the way discourses operate, they are changing all the time
- forms of discourse receive their value according to the positions of their users in systems of power relations
- struggles over the control of discourse are the main ways in which power is obtained and exercised in modern societies (Corson, 1999, pp. 143–44)

Further, such concepts are manifested in efforts to promote social awareness of discourse, critical awareness of language variety, and practice for change. In short, language policies can and do serve a variety of quite different ends. Language policies can serve as a tool for empowering groups and individuals, for creating and strengthening national bonds and ties, and for maximizing educational and economic development, but they can also be used (and often have been used) to maintain and perpetuate oppression, social class discrimination, and social and educational inequity (see Fairclough, 1989; Pennycook, 1994, 1998, 2001; Skutnabb-Kangas, 2000). Language policies, if they are to be defensible, must entail the active involvement and participation of those for whom they are intended. Only when emerging in such a context can language policies contribute to the creation of more just, humane and legitimate social and educational policies. As James Tollefson argues quite powerfully, "the foundation for rights is *power* and . . . constant *struggle* is necessary to sustain language rights" (1991, p. 167). It is just such an understanding that we need to promote and encourage in our students.

NOTES

1. Actually, this is precisely the sense in which Chomsky himself would deny that language exists. See Chomsky (1993, p. 43; 2000, p. 181; 1994, p. 159). See also Smith (2002, pp. 100–104) for a detailed discussion of this point and of its implications. My point in the text is not, then, really so much what Chomsky himself would say, but rather, the way in which people who have been influenced by Chomskian linguistic theory tend to talk about "language."

2. Although this aphorism is credited to Weinreich, and while he did publish it in 1945, it was in fact a secondary quote from an audience member at a presentation that he had given.

3. The primary reason for comparing the cases of modern Hebrew and Irish is the disparity between the phenomenal success of the revival of Hebrew and the relative lack of success of Irish. The different outcomes of significant governmental efforts in the two cases demonstrate the importance of the specificity of each language planning and policy effort (see O Laoire, 1995; Wright, 1996).

4. In my view, one of the most interesting aspects of *Language Problems and Language Planning* has been its continuing devotion to publishing in a wide variety of languages. Over the years, articles not only in French, German, Spanish, and Esperanto (a language of particular concern to the journal from its inception) have appeared, but also articles in such languages as Afrikaans, Polish, and Portuguese. Such a commitment to a multilingual approach to scholarly publication offers a serious challenge to the overwhelming dominance of English in academic and scientific publishing in general (see Ammon, 1990, 2003; Sandelin & Sarafoglou, 2004).

Chapter 3

American Sign Language, Language Planning, and Language Policy

The utmost extreme to which tyranny can go when its mailed hand descends upon a conquered people is the proscription of their national language, and with the utmost rigor several generations are required to eradicate it. But all the attempts to suppress signs, wherever tried, have most signally failed. After a hundred years of proscription . . . they still flourish, and will continue to flourish to the end of time. "What heinous crime have the deaf been guilty of that their language should be proscribed?"—Robert P. McGregor, first president of the National Association of the Deaf (Quoted in Lane, 1984, p. xvii)

ASL, as linguistically defined, has nowhere near the power of English for receptive OR expressive purposes. ASL has its own merits, some of them outshining spoken language, but anywhere near as powerful as English for education, commerce, and all-around communication purposes it most certainly is not. (Stewart, 1992, p. 135)

American Sign Language (ASL) emerged at the hands of Laurent Clerc and his students in the first quarter of the nineteenth century in Hartford, Connecticut, at what was then the Connecticut Asylum for the Education and Instruction of Deaf and Dumb Persons, and is today the American School for the Deaf (ASD).[1] Harlan Lane, historically and narratively reconstructing Clerc's life story, has Clerc explain the process as follows:

> I gave lessons in sign language after hours to Reverend Stansbury, to new teachers as they joined us, and, later, to the many hearing teachers who came to the asylum to study with me and then return to their home states to teach the deaf. In these lessons and the classroom I used French Sign Language amended for American practices; for example, I had no signs for various articles of clothing and food unknown in France and these I took

from my pupils. . . . Gradually my sign language underwent expansion and modification in the hands of my American pupils. (Lane, 1984, p. 226)

Given what we know about the early history and evolution of ASL (see Armstrong & Wilcox, 2003; Baynton, 1993, 1996, 2002), such an account seems only too reasonable. In spite of its relatively late beginnings compared to what might be seen as its "mother" language, French Sign Language, as well as to a number of other well-documented natural sign languages, ASL today is arguably among the most socially and educationally well-established, and is definitely the most lexically developed and linguistically studied, natural sign language in the world. In spite of Larry Stewart's claims quoted above, to the contrary, ASL is indeed as powerful as English, if one's concerns are linguistic and communicative in nature. To be sure, if Stewart is simply observing that the vast majority of people in the United States use English in all aspects of their daily lives, and are monolingual native speakers of English, and that this means that users of ASL (and, of course, of all other languages) are therefore at a disadvantage, this is of course perfectly true.[2] However, I do not believe that that is his point at all. Stewart is making a far more powerful claim than that there are power differentials in U.S. society related to language. Rather, he is making what are factual and empirical claims about what can be communicated in ASL, and on these matters, he is simply in error, and there is a half-century of well-conducted research to prove it. ASL serves as both something of a model and a goal for many deaf people around the world when they think about what they would like to achieve for their own sign languages (though as we will see in Chapter 5, this is by no means universally true; some deaf communities around the world are significantly ahead of the U.S. in terms of language rights and many other facets of language policy).

In this chapter, we will examine the specific case of ASL with respect to language planning and language policy. The chapter will begin with an historical overview of language planning and policy efforts related to ASL and will then move to contemporary issues and developments in such efforts.

ASL AND LANGUAGE PLANNING IN THE NINETEENTH CENTURY

Although a number of works deal with ASL in the nineteenth century, and particularly with efforts to suppress it (Baynton, 1993, 1996, 2002; Winefield, 1981, 1987; Reagan, 1989), by far the most thorough and useful study of language planning and language policy related to ASL in the nineteenth century is the Ph.D. dissertation written by Stephen Nover (2000) at the University of Arizona. Nover divides his study into two major historical periods: 1800 to the Civil War, and the Civil War to 1899. Because I am relying fairly extensively on Nover's work, I will for the most part follow his chronological division. The major change that I will make is that with respect to the latter period, I want to deal with the Congress of Milan in 1880 and its aftermath as a separate period, so I will address this period in its own separate section.

The establishment of the Connecticut Asylum for the Education and Instruction of Deaf and Dumb Persons in 1817 actually followed the first major language policy decision related to sign language in the United States. In 1816, the Connecticut legislature, at the prompting of Dr. Mason Cogswell, had appropriated $5,000 for the creation of a school for deaf children. Cogswell was a key figure in the early history of deaf education, not as an educator himself, but rather as the father of a young deaf girl, Alice, who had become deaf at the age of two in 1807. Cogswell was the motivating force behind the efforts to provide adequate and appropriate education for deaf students. It was Cogswell who had convinced Thomas Hopkins Gallaudet to travel to Europe to determine the most effective approach to the education of deaf students, and who raised the money to make such a trip possible. Gallaudet was won over by the sign language-based teaching methods used by the Abbé Roch-Ambroise Sicard at the famous Institution Nationale des Sourds-Muets de Paris, which had been founded by the Abbé Charles-Michel de l'Épée in 1760. He returned to Connecticut not only convinced of the efficacy of using sign language in deaf education, but also accompanied by a young deaf teacher of deaf children, Laurent Clerc, who was himself a graduate of the Institution Nationale des Sourds-Muets de Paris. Gallaudet in turn convinced Cogswell of the value of sign language, and it was Cogswell and his associates who persuaded the Connecticut legislature to fund the new school. Thus, the original and fundamental status planning decision in favor of the use of sign language in the education of deaf students preceded the actual founding of the school (Crouch & Greenwald, 2007, pp. 38–40; Nover, 2000, pp. 43–44).

This decision was not merely one of default. From its inception, the Connecticut Asylum actively promoted the use of sign language. As early as 1819, in the *Third Report to the Directors of the Connecticut Asylum for the Education and Instruction of Deaf and Dumb Persons*, presented to the directors on May 15th, S. T. Terry discussed the "four modes of communication used for instruction," which is, in Nover's words, "the earliest evidence of the use of a 'bilingual approach'" (2000, p. 168). The "four modes" included the use of the natural sign language (that is, the emergent ASL), the use of "methodical signs" (that is, signs modified to accommodate the structure of written English), the use of the manual alphabet, and the use of written communication (see Nover, 2000, pp. 45–46). Perhaps most notable in Terry's report was the rejection of the teaching of articulation altogether. As he explained, "*Articulation* is not taught. It would require more time than the present occasion furnishes, to state the reasons which have induced the Principal of the Asylum and his associates not to waste their labor and that of their pupils upon this comparatively useless branch of the education of the deaf and dumb" (quoted in Nover, 2000, p. 47).

The instructional methodologies developed at the Connecticut Asylum, as well as its educational philosophy with respect to the use of sign language in the education of deaf students, became the model upon which schools for deaf children throughout the country were based. As Nover notes,

> The Connecticut Asylum gave official recognition to the language of signs and became the cornerstone of deaf education by providing leadership for the many American institutions that were later established. Institutions through the U.S. replicated their educational philosophy, curriculum, and bilingual instructional strategies. . . . The manual method dominated deaf education and was the language policy immediately adopted and implemented by all new institutions for the deaf throughout the United States. Thus, the period from 1816 to 1866 can be characterized as the Age of the Manual Method in American deaf education. (2000, pp. 138–39)

Following the end of the Civil War in 1867, this situation changed. Concerned that many deaf people were unable to speak or articulate clearly, and noting that this had been explicitly rejected as an educational goal of the existing schools for deaf children, the Massachusetts legislature, after a series of public hearings, created a new school, the Clarke Institution for Deaf-Mutes, in Northampton, Massachusetts, in which

English alone was to be used as an instructional medium via an "Oral Method." Although oralism would later come to threaten any use of sign language in deaf education in many institutions, initially it appeared to have relatively little effect on most schools for deaf children. Only two schools declared themselves to be strictly oral in nature; in 1867, twenty-five of twenty-seven schools for deaf children claimed to use the "Manual Method." Events in Massachusetts, though, did prove to have a dramatic impact nationally; educators of deaf children felt themselves under sufficient pressure that within a single year, by 1868, only three of twenty-eight schools for deaf children still claimed to be using the Manual Method, two were oral, and twenty-three now claimed to be using the "Combined System" championed by Edward Miner Gallaudet, son of Thomas Hopkins Gallaudet and head of the Columbia Institution for the Instruction of the Deaf and Dumb (now Gallaudet University) in Washington, D.C. (Nover, 2000, p. 87; see also Baynton, 1993, 1996).

As it was originally conceived by Edward Miner Gallaudet, the Combined System was an effort to meet the objections of those concerned with the lack of instruction in articulation in deaf education without fundamentally changing the manual nature of such education. Nover writes:

> Upon his return from Europe in the fall of 1867, E. M. Gallaudet submitted a 46-page report to the Board at the Columbia Institution recommending that the Combined System, a term which he coined, be implemented. The Board agreed to adopt the recommendation that articulation be introduced at the Columbia Institution as an additional program component to the existing manual method so that every deaf child had the opportunity to learn speech. (2000, p. 88)

The basic idea of the Combined System was that the needs of the individual child were to be met in the best and most appropriate educational manner, and that this might mean the inclusion of oral methods in particular circumstances. In May of 1868, the first Conference of Principals of the American Institutions for the Education of the Deaf and Dumb met at the Columbia Institution and by a large majority adopted a resolution approving the use of the Combined System. This resolution read as follows:

> *Resolved*, That in the opinion of this Conference it is the duty of all institutions for the education of the deaf and dumb to provide adequate means for imparting instruction in articulation and lip-reading to such of their pupils as may be able to engage with profit in exercises of this nature.

Resolved, That, while in our judgement it is desirable to give semi-mutes and semi-deaf children every facility for retaining and improving any power of articulate speech they may possess, it is not profitable, except in promising cases, discovered after fair experiment, to carry congenital mutes through a course of instruction in articulation.

Resolved, That, to attain success in this department of instruction, an added force of instructors will be necessary, and this conference hereby recommends to boards of directors of institutions for the deaf and dumb in this country that speedy measures be taken to provide the funds needed for the prosecution of this work. (Quoted in Nover, 2000, pp. 89–90)

This resolution, needless to say, was by no means an overwhelming success for advocates of the Oral Method. It was, at best, a strategic recognition that hard of hearing and deafened students could benefit from instruction in articulation as part of a more general educational program. However, the Combined System (much like "Total Communication" in the twentieth century) was widely misunderstood and misapplied by educators of deaf children, many of whom took it to mean that all deaf children must be taught articulation. As Gallaudet himself, clearly already frustrated with the misapplication of the Combined System, declared,

> It has been stated in recent publication, issued in Boston by the Board of State Charities of Massachusetts, that I am in favor of teaching all deaf-mutes by articulation . . . I have in no sense departed from the views and options that were set forth by my father, and that have been maintained by those who have followed him in the work of teaching the deaf and dumb, down to the present time. And I am not to be claimed as a convert to the system of teaching the deaf and dumb by articulation, which system to a greater or less extent ignores the use of signs. (Quoted in Pratt, 1868, p. 146)

In spite of the efforts of Gallaudet, though, the period 1868 to 1880 did in fact see an increased emphasis on the teaching of articulation, and on the role of English in the curriculum, in many schools for deaf children around the country. In fact, a careful examination of the Combined System leads one to the conclusion that it is more like a component of contemporary ASL/English bilingual education than like Total Communication—a point missed both by many educators of deaf children in the nineteenth century and by some today.

During this same period of time, two noteworthy efforts at corpus planning for ASL took place. The first was proposed by Isaac Peet, the principal of the New York Institution, who suggested that the use of initialized signs might serve two purposes: such signs could, first of all, fill in lexical gaps in ASL, and second, because the initialization would be based on the appropriate English word, such signs would help students to learn English (Nover, 2000, pp. 93–96). Such an approach would allow for the "perfection" of sign language, it was suggested. At the same time, Peet was not naïve about issues of what we have here called attitude planning. He emphasized that "We should not propose to disuse any signs that have been well established and have found general acceptance, but rather, as in the case of a spoken language, to follow out the analogies which have developed themselves, to go as fast as, and no faster than we find that the deaf-mute mind will accept and assimilate our improvements" (quoted in Nover, 2000, p. 95).

The second example of corpus planning in the mid-1870s was the attempt by De Haerne (1875a, 1875b, 1875c) to offer a detailed linguistic analysis of sign language. The basics of such an analysis had been provided earlier, in 1853, by H. P. Peet in an article entitled, "Elements of the Language of Signs," but this had been, at best, a fairly superficial analysis of sign language. De Haerne's work, on the contrary, was remarkably sophisticated. In the first of a series of three articles, he first makes the case for the relevance of the linguistic study of natural sign languages, compares spoken and sign languages, describes the structure of natural sign language (including what he took to be the four distinct classes of signs: imitative, operative, indicative, and expressive), identifies two kinds of natural signs (simple and compound), and finally offers a commentary on the importance of sign language in deaf education. In the second article, De Haerne distinguishes between natural signs and methodical signs and provides further discussion about the acquisition and use of natural sign languages. Finally, in the third article, De Haerne provides an analysis of the development of signs, in which he comments on how compound signs were formed and on the origins of natural sign languages.

By 1880, the field of deaf education in the United States was a vibrant and intellectually challenging one. Although the earlier consensus around the Manual Method was no longer present, the Combined System now clearly dominated deaf education in the United States. Of a total of 55 institutions serving nearly 7,000 deaf students, 9 (with a total enrollment of 417 students) remained officially "manual," 11 (with a total enrollment of 489 students) were officially using the Oral Method, and the vast majority, some 35 institutions serving nearly 6,000 deaf students, used the Combined System (Nover, 2000, p. 105). This was the context of deaf education in the United States in 1880, when the Second International Congress of Instructors of Deaf-Mutes was held in Milan.

THE CONGRESS OF MILAN AND ITS AFTERMATH

The Second International Congress of Instructors of Deaf-Mutes, which was held in Milan in 1880 and is commonly referred to as the Congress of Milan, marks a watershed in the history of deaf education in the United States (see Van Cleve & Crouch, 1989, pp. 120–27). As Katherine Jankowski describes,

> The Milan Congress, comprised of 163 hearing educators and one Deaf educator from several countries, passed almost unanimously (158 to 6) a resolution that only the oral approach should be used as a medium of instruction for Deaf students. The media, particularly the *London Times*, gave positive coverage to the event, pointing to two indicators of the shift to oralism . . . One was the impression that a vast majority of educators from different countries had given their support to the oral approach. Second, an exhibition at the convention had presumably demonstrated the success of oral teaching. Deaf Italian students were able to speak and appeared to be able to speechread and respond accordingly without effort. . . . However, some of the Milan participants described how the Deaf Italian students had begun answering the questions even before the questioner had finished, which led to speculation that the demonstrations had been rehearsed beforehand . . . Further, there was no indication of how much residual hearing the students possessed. Basically, there was no evidence that these students spoke or speechread as a result of receiving oral instruction. (1997, pp. 23–24)

None of this mattered, though; the Congress of Milan had been a huge success for oral educators of deaf children. The common view of the effects of the Congress of Milan on deaf education in the United States is that it resulted in a massive shift to oral education and an increased dominance by hearing "experts" in the field (see, for instance, Jankowski, 1997; Lane, 1984; Lane et al., 1996).

Nover's work, however, suggests a quite different picture. Although the Congress of Milan had a huge impact on the education of deaf students in Europe, its actual impact in the United States seems to have been both more limited and more gradual in nature. It was not until 1926, for example, that the Conference of Superintendents and Principals of American Schools for the Deaf "officially voted to eliminate the language of signs from all departments as a means of instruction," and in fact the preceding half-century had been one in which the Combined System remained largely dominant in American deaf education (Nover, 2000, pp. 140–42). Nor, in spite of common beliefs and claims to the contrary, does it seem that the Congress of Milan resulted in either a purging of deaf instructors in schools for deaf children or an unwillingness to hire such teachers. In fact, according to the data compiled by Nover, the number of deaf teachers in schools for deaf children nearly doubled during this period, increasing from 132 in 1880 to 243 in 1899 (Nover, 2000, p. 140).

At the same time, it is clear that ultimately the oralists did have a significant impact on the education of deaf children. As Van Cleve and Crouch note,

> The efforts of [the oralists] showed steady progress through the 1880s and 1890s and intro the twentieth century, as teachers and school administrators changed their attitudes toward the relative value of sign language and speech. In 1882, for example, only 7.5 percent of the 7,000 pupils in American schools for deaf children were taught orally (that is, without signs or fingerspelling). By 1900 that percentage had increased to 47. The year 1905 marked a watershed—for the first time in American history the majority of deaf students learned without the language bequeathed to them by Clerc and Thomas Hopkins Gallaudet. Speech, speechreading, and writing, rather than sign language and the manual alphabet, were the communication methods used to instruct the majority of deaf students in the United States. By 1919, at the peak of oralism's influence, school reported that nearly 80 percent of deaf students received their instruction and communicated with their teachers without any manual language. Though this figure may have been an exaggeration, for deaf children could not easily be prevented from signing, it was nevertheless true that the pendulum had swung radically against the traditional communication method of American schools for deaf students. (1989, pp. 122–23)

Regardless of its actual immediate impact on education, however, deaf people themselves found the Congress of Milan and its potential results to be clearly unacceptable. Although it took twenty years, there was an effort to turn back the clock. The deaf community prepared for a defense of, if not sign language itself, then of the Combined System. The venue for this action was to be the Fourth International Congress on the Education and Welfare of the Deaf, to be held in Paris in 1900. The deaf community prepared carefully for this Congress, sending over 200 deaf people to attend—in contrast to the slightly more than 100 hearing attendees. Preparations notwithstanding, this new Congress proved a failure in terms of overturning the Milan resolutions. The deaf people involved had, mistakenly, assumed that there would be a fair and level playing field; they did not take the realities of *Realpolitik* into account. Katherine Jankowski relates the events of the Congress:

> [The deaf community's] efforts to build a coalition were thwarted when a decision was reached a year before the conference to hold separate meetings for Deaf and hearing people. At the conference, a proposal was made to combine the two groups. This proposal was ruled out of order by the president, Dr. Ladreit de Lacharriere, a hearing man. His rationale was that the translations between speech and sign would be too confusing and time consuming. . . . However, because the Deaf-to-hearing delegate ratio was large, the possibility of reversing the Milan resolutions remained. Consequently, de Lacharriere ruled that Deaf people would not be allowed to even vote. The Congress rejected the resolutions from the Deaf section. In fact, the Congress rebuffed all recommendations to include the Deaf section in any way. (1997, pp. 27–28)

The Congress of Milan was not the only threat to sign language in the United States in the late nineteenth and early twentieth centuries, however. Just as Edward Miner Gallaudet was the leading proponent for sign language in deaf education, albeit in the form of the Combined System, so Alexander Graham Bell was the leading spokesman for the oralist position. He was the most articulate and dedicated advocate for oralism and among the harshest critics of the use of sign language in any form in the schooling of deaf children (see Baynton, 1996; Reagan, 1989). In terms of language policy, Bell was actively engaged in what might be considered negative status planning with respect to ASL, acquisition planning (negative with respect to ASL, but positive with respect to English), and attitude planning (again, negative with respect to ASL, but positive with respect to English), as we shall see.

Alexander Graham Bell shared a number of biographical characteristics with Edward Miner Gallaudet, although he would ultimately turn out to be his nemesis. Just as the younger Gallaudet had been deeply influenced by his father's involvement in and commitment to the education of deaf children and had followed in his footsteps, so Bell was strongly influenced by his father's (and, indeed, his grandfather's) work in teaching speech and elocution (see Bruce, 1973, pp. 13–16). Bell's father, Alexander Melville Bell, was in fact the model for Professor Pygmalion Higgins in George Bernard Shaw's play *Pygmalion*, more familiarly known today in its film version, *My Fair Lady* (in which Pygmalion Higgins is renamed Henry Higgins). In fact, much of Bell's own work with deaf people was based on his father's system of "Visible Speech," a system by which oral sounds could be accurately represented by written symbols (Bell, 1872; see also Van Cleve & Crouch, 1989, p. 114; Winefield, 1981, pp. 165–78, 1987, pp. 12–14). Both men also had mothers who were hearing impaired, although Edward's mother, Sophia Fowler Gallaudet, was deaf and used ASL whereas Bell's mother Eliza was hard of hearing and apparently had some residual hearing. Eliza Bell used a hearing trumpet on occasion and did not sign but rather relied on speech and lip-reading (Winefield, 1987, p. 12). This maternal model later received reinforcement from Bell's wife Mabel Hubbard Bell, whom he had originally come to know as a pupil. Mabel Bell had become deaf at the age of five and, as a postlingually deaf individual, never lost the ability to speak. These two women provided important and ongoing models of the potentialities that Bell believed were held by oral approaches to the education of deaf children (see Van Cleve & Crouch, 1989, p. 117; Winefield, 1981, pp. 165–78).

Central to Bell's position was his concern with the necessity for deaf people to function in the hearing world as "normally" and to as great an extent as possible. While Gallaudet assumed that competence in English was *one* perfectly appropriate objective in the education of deaf children,[3] Bell saw it as the *only* objective for such education (Lane, 1984, p. 365). Bell believed that sign language actually impeded the development of spoken language and should therefore be rejected completely in the education of deaf children. In a scathing critique of common educational practice in schools for deaf children, he wrote, "The constant practice of the sign language interferes with the mastery of the English language, and it is to be feared that comparatively few of the congenitally deaf are able to read books understandingly unless couched in simple language" (1883, p. 42). Further, for Bell, the very arguments typically used to support the use of signing in education counted rather against its use, because of the risk that English might become "a foreign tongue, and the more [the deaf person] becomes habituated [to the use of sign language] the more he becomes a stranger in his own country" (Bell, 1884, p. 52).

Bell believed that prevailing practices in deaf education served to segregate deaf people, rather than enable them to integrate as fully as possible into the dominant, hearing community. He feared the emergence not only of a different type of language, but, more important, the "formation of a deaf variety of the human race" (Bell, 1883). As he forcefully argued, "If we desired to create a deaf variety of the race, and were to attempt to devise methods which should compel deaf-mutes to marry deaf-mutes, we could not invent more complete or efficient methods than those that actually exist and which have arisen from entirely different and far higher motives" (1883, p. 41).

In Bell's view, the practice of residential schooling for deaf children encouraged the segregation of deaf people (Bell, 1883). By tolerating the use of sign language, by bringing the young deaf people together in residential institutions, and, in adult life, by allowing and even promoting social intercourse among deaf people in state and national organizations devoted to the deaf community and issues of concern to that community, American society was encouraging intermarriage among deaf people (Bell, 1883, pp. 41–42). To prevent this, Bell believed, deaf children had to be taught to identify with the dominant hearing population, and their contacts with other deaf people had to be minimized. This had important implications for the school as well, where Bell wished to see only hearing teachers (Bell, 1883, p. 48). Bell's well-publicized opposition to the creation of a Normal School under Gallaudet's auspices, which led in turn to the breaking out of open hostilities between the two men in the early 1890s, derived from his initial opposition to deaf teachers for deaf children (Winefield, 1981, pp. 51–66).

Bell's fears about the emergence of "a deaf variety of the human race" were not merely a minor facet of his thought; they played a major role in his conception of deafness and his view of how society ought to respond to deafness. Bell would have preferred various types of legislation to prevent intermarriage among deaf people, had such measures been feasible. In 1883, for instance, he argued that "a law forbidding congenitally deaf persons from intermarrying would go a long way towards checking the evil" (1883, p. 45). He recognized, however—for pragmatic rather than humanistic or ethical reasons—that such restrictive approaches were unlikely to be effective, and so rejected them. Instead, Bell supported efforts to encourage intermarriage between deaf and hearing people (Bell, 1914, pp. 1–7).

One unintended outcome of Bell's public condemnations of deaf intermarriage was the practice of sterilizing congenitally deaf children as a way of ensuring that they would not pass their deafness on to the next generation (see Greenwald, 2004, 2007; Murray, 2004), a practice legally sanctioned by a number of state eugenics laws (see Chase, 1980; Haller, 1963). As Harlan Lane describes, "According to the Rector of the All-Angels Mission to the Deaf in Baltimore at the time of Bell's memoir [*Upon the Formation of a Deaf Variety of the Human Race*], news of it spread like wildfire among parents of the deaf, their family physicians, and among surgeons generally throughout the world, and suggested to them a senseless and cruel procedure—the sterilization of children born deaf" (1984, p. 358).

Many such sterilizations took place, and the adult lives of many deaf people were grievously harmed as a result. Deaf people were not the only group to be affected by such practices; a number of "socially inadequate" classes were treated in a like manner (Chase, 1980, p. 16). Furthermore, it is not fair to hold Bell personally or directly accountable for such assaults on deaf children, though many of his deaf contemporaries clearly felt otherwise. As George Veditz, twice the president of the National Association of the Deaf, writes, "[Bell] comes in the guise of a friend, and [is], therefore, the most to be feared enemy of the American deaf, past and present" (quoted in Gannon, 1981, p. 77; see also Van Cleve & Crouch, 1989, p. 114). Finally, as Richard Winefield comments, "[n]owhere . . . not even in his personal papers, does [Bell] reveal concern for the individual 'undesirables' who would be eradicated, sterilized, or prevented from marrying if the extremists had their way" (1981, p. 185).

We should note here that the events that were taking place with respect to deaf people were not unique or even particularly unusual in the context of American thought and life of the period (see Baynton, 1993; 1996, pp. 36–55). In the late nineteenth and early twentieth centuries, eugenics had become a popular, widely accepted, and even intellectually respectable view of how to deal with "undesirable" groups in the overall population:

> For . . . people living in the first half of the twentieth century there was a logical connection between a belief in inherited intelligence and a program of eugenics or controlled human breeding. What better way, they thought, to improve the level of intelligence of the American population than by making it impossible for those with low levels of intelligence to have children. In 1909, California began a program of sterilization of those classified as "mentally impaired or mentally ill." Those institutionalized as "mentally impaired or mentally ill" were often sterilized before being discharged. While sterilization laws were passed in twenty-nine other states, California led the way in the actual numbers of required sterilizations. (Spring, 2008, p. 315)

Such a perspective, whether applied to deaf people, individuals with mental illness, or any other "socially undesirable" population reflected the dominant role of Social Darwinism in nineteenth and early twentieth century American society (see Hawkins, 1997). It was also the intellectual, social, and political rationale that provided a key part of the justification used by the National Socialists in Germany as they began developing the "Final Solution" (*die Endlösung*), which started with precisely such groups (see Kühl, 1994; Schuchman, 2004; for an excellent and powerful discussion of the case of eugenics and sterilization in the case of deaf people in Nazi Germany, see Biesold, 1999).

Returning now to Alexander Graham Bell, we are left with the image of Bell as a man who dedicated his life to trying to help deaf people to overcome their deafness through denial: denial of sign language, denial of the significant cultural differences between the deaf and hearing worlds, denial of intermarriage between deaf people, denial of the value of utilizing deaf teachers in the education of deaf children, denial of the place of the residential school in deaf education, and, ultimately, at least from the perspective of deaf people themselves, denial of the value of the deaf person as a human being. This last point was made by Bell's own wife Mabel, who wrote that "your deaf-mute business is hardly human to you. You are very tender and gentle to the deaf children, but their interest to you lies in their being deaf, not in their humanity" (M. Bell, 1895). For Bell, "the main object of the education of deaf people [was] to fit them to live in the world of hearing-speaking people," (quoted in Lane, 1984, p. 365), and he seems to have been quite literally unable to conceive of any other purpose for it.

The debate between Edward Miner Gallaudet and Alexander Graham Bell exacerbated an already present division among educators of deaf children, between oralists and manualists. Although the Combined System continued to be used in many schools for deaf children, it is clear that, "despite the best efforts of the Deaf community, the oralists prevailed for the next sixty or so years" (Jankowski, 1997, p. 28). It is important to keep in mind, though, that Bell's position also reflected the dominant American view of cultural and linguistic diversity in general during the period. This was, after all, the time of the "new immigration," during which millions of immigrants were arriving in the United States, increasingly from Southern and Eastern Europe, and seemed to many Americans to pose a serious challenge to the unity of the nation. It was a time of Americanization, in which most Americans believed that immigrants needed to assimilate to the Anglo-American mainstream as quickly and as completely as possible. Assimilation, in essence, demands of all groups in the society conformity to the lifestyle, values, and mores of the dominant majority. In the U.S. context, assimilation refers basically to "Anglo-Conformity," and entails the presupposition of the superiority of Anglo-American cultural and linguistic patterns. For educators, assimilation meant, in the words of the educational historian Elwood

P. Cubberley, that "our task is to *break up* their [the immigrants'] groups and settlements, to assimilate or amalgamate these people as part of the American race, and to implant in their children, as far as can be done, the Anglo-Saxon conception of rightiousness [*sic*], law, order, and popular government, and to awaken in them reverence for our democratic institutions and for those things which we as a people hold to be of abiding worth." (1909, p. 16). Americanization, as this view of assimilation was commonly known in the nineteenth and twentieth centuries, was fundamental in nature, involving far more than mere compliance with the norms of the dominant culture. Louis Brandeis wrote:

> What is Americanization? It manifests itself, in a superficial way, when the immigrant adopts the clothes, the manners, and the customs generally prevailing here. Far more important is the manifestation presented when he substitutes for his mother tongue the English language as the common medium of speech. But the adoption of our language, manners and customs is only a small part of the process. To become Americanized the change wrought must be fundamental. However great his outward conformity, the immigrant is not Americanized unless his interests and affections have become deeply rooted here. And we properly demand of the immigrant even more than this—he must be brought into complete harmony with our ideals and aspirations and cooperate with us for their attainment. Only when this has been done will he possess the national consciousness of an American. (1954, pp. 340–41)

For deaf people, the resentment toward difference, aimed primarily at the new immigrants, also had educational consequences, since they, too, were "different." Educational programs should seek to make the deaf child as American as they should seek to make the immigrant child, and that meant, among other things, an emphasis on English and on as great a degree of assimilation to the hearing norms of American society as was possible (see Jankowski, 1997, pp. 25–26; Reagan, 1989, pp. 44–45).

THE BACKGROUND TO THE TWENTIETH CENTURY: THE LEGITIMATION OF ASL

For the first half of the twentieth century, ASL was not thought of as a "legitimate" language at all. Characteristic of the general view of ASL was Myklebust's assertion that "sign language cannot be considered comparable to a verbal symbol system" (1964, p. 158, quoted in Lane,

1992, p. 45), and, more recently, the claim that "the informative power of the natural sign language of the deaf is extremely weak" (van Uden, 1986, p. 89). Such views were not only far from uncommon, they were the norm. Indeed, Myklebust's view about the limits of sign language was even stronger than this might suggest; in the 1957 version of his book *The Psychology of Deafness*, he wrote, "The manual language used by the deaf is an ideographic language . . . it is more pictorial, less symbolic. . . . Ideographic language systems, in comparison with verbal systems, lack precision, subtlety, and flexibility. It is likely that Man cannot achieve his ultimate potential through an Ideographic language . . . The manual sign language must be viewed as inferior to the verbal as a language" (1957, pp. 241–42). As late as 1980 he wrote, "American Sign Language is often described in the following ways: It is a universal language whose grammar is poor compared to that of spoken language; its vocabulary is concrete and iconic; it consists of gestures accompanied by facial expressions" (Markowicz, 1980, p. 1).

As mentioned in passing in Chapter 1, the work of a single individual radically changed all of this. William Stokoe was a junior faculty member in the English Department at Gallaudet College (now Gallaudet University) when he published his monograph *Sign Language Structure* in 1960. I. King Jordan writes about both Stokoe himself and his research:

> To understand how remarkable and unexpected Stokoe's research was, it is necessary to recall that this was a person who had no knowledge of signing at all when he came to Gallaudet. Remember also that in those days, new faculty at the college did not get intensive training in sign language—they were thrust into the classroom and were expected to fend for themselves. Nevertheless, soon after he joined the English Department faculty, Professor Stokoe became intrigued with the communication that was occurring in his classrooms. Because he had an outsider's perspective without all the accepted "baggage" about sign language, he was able to see what others had not. He saw that his students were indeed communicating among themselves about sophisticated ideas. He became fascinated with their fluency and grace, and he soon perceived a contradiction between what he was observing and what he had been told to expect. . . . Puzzled by this paradox, he began to look more carefully at the behavior itself, behavior that he saw happening all around the campus. In doing this, Stokoe was doing something that few, if any, educators or researchers were doing at the time. He simply looked at what deaf people were doing instead of blindly accepting what hearing (and even some deaf) "experts" said. He also asked deaf people what they were doing, and often the answers he received surprised him. Many of the deaf faculty members, people who communicated

easily and fluently with each other and with their students, told him that signing was not language. In fact, when Stokoe argued that sign language *was* a language, many deaf people not only disagreed with him, they criticized him for saying so publically. (2002, p. 3)

Stokoe may well have been criticized, but he was right—and he began a revolution in the study of sign language that continues to the present day. An early reviewer of *Sign Language Structure* wrote at the time:

> It was bound to happen eventually. It was bound to happen—that is, someone would come along to utilize the methods of contemporary scientific linguistic analysis to describe a system of communication distinct from that of ordinary vocal language and its derivative, the writing system, but sufficiently language-like to make the use of these methods possible and fruitful. It is fortunate that the system of communication which came to be described in this way in the present monograph, at least in outline, is the sign language of the American deaf, and that the person who set himself this task was Dr. Stokoe. Not only is this monograph a landmark event in the history of communication studies, it is also a brilliant piece of work and one that holds promise of being helpful in the education of the deaf. (Carroll, 1961, p. 113)

Carroll was correct: Stokoe's work was in fact revolutionary, for linguistics, and for education. It changed the fundamental assumptions that were made about the nature of human language, the nature of sign language, about the role of language in both the DEAF⌒WORLD and deaf education. It also had profound implications for language planning and language policy related to ASL in the United States, and, indirectly, elsewhere in the world.

TWENTIETH-CENTURY LANGUAGE POLICIES AND ASL

Language planning and policy efforts related to ASL in the twentieth century have concentrated on a number of issues and concerns: efforts to achieve official recognition of ASL, issues of language rights related to deafness in general and ASL in particular, matters of corpus planning for ASL (primarily in educational institutions), the rise of ASL-English bilingual/bicultural education programs, and the teaching of ASL as a foreign language in educational institutions. We turn now to a discussion of each of these issues.

Efforts to have ASL recognized and given official status in the United States at both the federal and state levels have had mixed results. The

National Association of the Deaf (NAD) identified the federal recognition of ASL as one of its top twenty priorities for the 2008–2010 period, and the Public Policy Committee has had this priority under review. Specifically, what the NAD is seeking is as follows:

> The NAD shall pursue, as part of its long-range plan, federal legislation recognizing American Sign Language as a natural and legitimate language of deaf Americans. Further, the NAD shall investigate legal precedents, as well as historical reviews of other nations that have enacted legislation with respect to their sign languages. (National Association of the Deaf, 2009)

At the state level, as of 2006 more than forty states had legislation relating to the status of ASL. The legislation differs from state to state and falls into a number of different categories in terms of its concerns and implications. Among the different kinds of legislation currently in place, the most common is legislation that simply recognizes ASL as a language (such as in Arizona, Indiana, Kansas, Maryland, Oklahoma, South Dakota, Tennessee, and Texas), and legislation that recognizes ASL as a *foreign* language (such as in Minnesota, Missouri, Nevada, North Carolina, North Dakota, Ohio, Oregon, Pennsylvania, Vermont, West Virginia, and Wisconsin). Several states recognize ASL for educational purposes alone (such as Florida, Georgia, Hawai'i [though only at the post-K–12 level], Illinois, Kentucky, Louisiana, Massachusetts, Michigan, Montana, South Carolina, Virginia, and Washington).

The problem with such status planning decisions—and it is, in my view, a very significant problem—is that such language planning is fundamentally based on deficit views of ASL. Although such legislation may well be important in increasing the opportunities for students to study ASL as a foreign language, it also sends a powerful message about the need to establish, and to establish by legislative fiat, the legitimacy of ASL as a language. It would simply never occur to anyone, I think, to suggest that we need official legislation to count Spanish, French, German, or Russian—or even less commonly taught languages, like Japanese or Arabic—as foreign languages. Even if we are addressing issues of status and acquisition planning, here there is still a need for attitude planning.

There is, however, a small number of states that have passed legislation that is more appropriate. Perhaps the best example of this is found in Alabama, where the legislation indicates that the "Legislature of Alabama recognizes American Sign Language as the official and native language of Deaf people in Alabama." Maine similarly recognizes ASL as the official state language of the deaf community. In Colorado and Rhode Island, using basically the same legislative language, ASL is recognized "as a fully developed, autonomous, natural language with distinct grammar, syntax and cultural heritage." With the exceptions of Alabama and Maine, of course, all of these pieces of legislation remain deficit-based, but they are at least somewhat more enlightened.

The state legislation that has been passed and is in place, however, despite being based on a deficit model, has nevertheless had a huge impact on the ability and opportunity of hearing students to study ASL. As of the 2004–2005 school year, more than 700 secondary schools in the United States offered ASL, and more than 4,000 individual classes were offered at the secondary level around the country (Rosen, 2008, pp. 17, 21). Furthermore, enrollments in ASL had increased nationally from a total of 56,783 in the 2002–2003 school year to 73,473 in the 2004–2005 school year (see Rosen, 2008, p. 20). Finally, in 2004–2005, these programs employed nearly 725 full-time equivalency teachers (Rosen, 2008, p. 22). Although more recent data on ASL programs is not yet available, anecdotal evidence suggests that these numbers all continue to grow.

Implicit in the efforts to provide some sort of meaningful official recognition of ASL, at either the federal or state level, is really the underlying issue of language rights (see Siegel, 2008). There is a paradox here as well, since most of the current state legislation is not concerned with the language rights of deaf people at all, but rather with the acceptance of the study of ASL to meet foreign language requirements in educational settings—a matter of language rights, perhaps, but one that affects primarily hearing, rather than deaf, people. To be sure, this is not a universal problem: in the case of the Kansas legislation, for example, the relevant statute (72–1120) does read, "The state board of education may provide for the teaching of American Sign Language in accredited schools and all pupils thereof, whether hearing or hearing impaired, may be given instruction in American Sign Language," but this remains a recognition of the right to study ASL as a second/foreign language rather than a right to one's own language as medium of instruction.

More important than legislation that officially recognizes ASL, however, is legislation that ensures that deaf people have access to appropriately trained and skilled ASL interpreters in various settings (see Cokely, 2008). For example, the Department of Justice Analysis of Section 504, 28 C. F. R. Part 42 of the Department of Justice Regulations explicitly states, with respect to law enforcement agencies:

> Law enforcement agencies should provide for the availability of qualified interpreters (certified where possible, by a recognized certification agency) to assist the agencies when dealing with hearing impaired persons. When the hearing impaired person uses American Sign Language for communication, the term "qualified interpreter" would mean an interpreter skilled in communicating in American Sign Language. It is the responsibility of the law enforcement agency to determine whether the hearing impaired person uses American Sign Language. (45 Fed. Reg. 37630 [June 3, 1980])

In educational settings, the picture in terms of interpreters is more complex. Under the Individuals with Disabilities Education Act (IDEA) and Section 504 of the Rehabilitation Act of 1973, it is legally mandatory for the school district to provide a free appropriate public education to all children. All too often, schools have misinterpreted this, and the concomitant obligation to educate every child in the "least restrictive environment," as an obligation to attempt to mainstream the deaf child. This is, of course, not the intent of the legislation at all. The U.S. Department of Education's Office for Civil Rights has explicitly indicated that in developing an Individualized Educational Program (IEP) for a deaf child, among the factors that must be taken into account are:

- communication needs and the child's and family's preferred mode of communication;
- linguistic needs;
- severity of hearing loss and potential for using residual hearing;
- academic level; and
- social, emotional, and cultural needs, including opportunities for peer interactions and communication.

Thus, for many deaf children a mainstream classroom may violate both the letter and the spirit of the law. Even for those children for whom such a placement is appropriate, however, if an interpreter is required, the issue of the competence of the interpreter remains, as does the child's ability to develop fluency in ASL in such a setting. This is a huge matter, since there is a significant shortage of well-trained and certified ASL interpreters available. Both parts of this educational dilemma are also examples of the problems and challenges of implementing language policies, regardless of how good the policies themselves might be. Lawrence Siegel compellingly recommends undertaking two approaches with respect to the language rights of deaf children in the public schools. The first is "to litigate cases for deaf and hard of hearing children based on their First and Fourteenth Amendment rights" (Siegel, 2008, p. 147), recognizing that the issue is not, as is typically assumed by both educators and politicians, either a fiscal or political matter, but rather a constitutional one. The second approach Siegel advocates is to press Congress to pass some kind of "Right to Language and Education Act," which would "recognize that the 'starting point' for any educational system for deaf and hard of hearing students (indeed all students) must be that language and communication access and development drive the system" (Siegel, 2008, p. 149). Finally, where the interpreter chooses or is required to use a manual sign code rather than ASL, there is good reason to believe that the child is even further disadvantaged (see Stack, 2004).

Corpus planning efforts related to ASL have taken place, largely on an informal basis, in educational institutions across the country, ranging from individual (generally residential) schools for deaf students to the National Technical Institute for the Deaf at the Rochester Institute of Technology (RIT) and Gallaudet University. The most extreme sort of corpus planning were the attempts to utilize the Rochester Method, in which each and every letter of each and every word is fingerspelled (we will discuss this particular phenomenon in Chapter 4). More generally, as lexical needs arise, new signs (often initialized signs) are created and put into use. There is no "language academy" or central clearinghouse for such new signs, however, and the extent to which they are actually used and to which they spread depends on a host of factors related to their compatibility with the overall structure of ASL, the degree to which they are seen by deaf users of ASL as appropriate or inappropriate, and so on. Although a number of early dictionaries for ASL had been developed, beginning with that of Stokoe, Casterline, and Croneberg (1976 [1965]) in 1965, they served purposes largely unrelated to corpus planning. The dictionary prepared by Stokoe and his colleagues was essentially a linguistic work aimed at describing the lexicon of ASL. Later dictionaries, such as those of Costello (1994, 2002), Sternberg (1998), and Valli (2005), as well as Bailey and Dolby's (2002) *Canadian Dictionary of ASL*, were basically intended for hearing learners of ASL—a fact made clear by their organizational structures, which are based on alphabetical English word order. Unlike the *Dictionary of British Sign Language / English* (Brien, 1992) or *Auslan: A Dictionary of the Sign Language of the Australian Deaf Community* (Johnston, 1989), which are both truly bilingual in nature and which both use the organizational structure of the natural sign language as their basic organizing premise, common dictionaries of ASL remained limited in their utility as corpus planning instruments because they were unlikely to be used by deaf users of ASL. With the publication in 1998 of Tennant and Brown's *The American Sign Language Handshape Dictionary*, users of ASL did acquire a dictionary of the language that was more truly bilingual in nature. Although this dictionary does seem to be fairly widely used in schools for deaf children, the extent to which it is actually employed by fluent users of ASL is debatable. Perhaps most impressive is the *Multimedia Dictionary of American Sign Language*, which utilizes computer technology to provide a far more useful kind of dictionary for sign language learners and users (see Wilcox, 2003). The most scholarly treatment of the issues involved in the development of an ASL dictionary—and a monolingual one at that—is MJ Bienvenu's (2003) dissertation, *Developing a Prototype for a Monolingual ASL Dictionary*. A number of Internet sites provide English to ASL interpretation, and these are proving to be very valuable especially for students of ASL. Finally, the increase in the numbers of hearing students studying ASL has created a market for good textbooks and supporting materials (videotapes, DVDs, study guides, etc.), and a number have been developed in the last thirty years (see Baker & Cokely, 1980; Baker-Shenk & Cokely, 1981; Cokely & Baker-Shenk, 1980a, 1980b, 1981; Humphries & Padden, 2004; Kettrick, 1984a, 1984b; Lentz, Mikos, & Smith, 1992; Padden, Humphries, & O'Rourke, 1994; Shelly & Schneck, 1998; Smith, Lentz, & Mikos, 1988; Stewart, 1998). The development of such materials is an excellent example of effective corpus planning.

One of the more visible and important developments of the last quarter of the twentieth century, especially for deaf children, has been the development of ASL–English bilingual/bicultural education programs (see Walworth, Moores, & O'Rourke, 1992). Such programs emerged in the 1980s and 1990s as a follow-up to the enormously popular "Total Communication" programs that had spread throughout schools and programs for deaf students after their initial introduction by Roy Holcolmb in 1967. Total Communication, or "TC" as it was commonly known, was originally "defined by whatever works for a particular child, for example, speech, speechreading, audition, signs, print, and so on, as well as combinations of these items" (Paul, 2001, p. 237). In practice, however, TC often became synonymous with Simultaneous Communication ("SimCom"), or the use of some kind of signing together with speech. Thus, what was initially intended to be a statement of educational philosophy became a label for a particular kind of educational practice (see Denton, 1976). As accurately observed by Tom Humphries, "traditionally, the cultural practices of Deaf people and their children have had a covert, unappreciated, and unfulfilled impact on methods of educating Deaf children" (2004, p. 29). The rise of bilingual/bicultural education in the 1980s was an attempt to address this situation, both philosophically and methodologically. In essence, bilingual/bicultural programs aim to produce individuals capable of functioning in both the hearing and deaf worlds, using both ASL and English as instructional media and as educational outcomes (see Allen, 2008; DeLuca & Napoli, 2008; Erting, Bailes, Erting, Thumann-Prezioso, & Kuntze, 2006; Gibson, 2006; Grosjean, 1992; Johnson, Liddell, & Erting, 1989; Ramsey, 2004; Reagan, 1990b, 1995a, 2005b [1985]; Strong, 1988; Tomkins, 2004; Wilbur, 2008).

From a language planning perspective, one of the more interesting concepts to have emerged in the context of ASL-English bilingual/bicultural education is one suggested by Stephen Nover, director of the Center for ASL/English Bilingual Education and Research at Gallaudet University. According to Nover, language policy in the educational sphere has been traditionally concerned with two matters: *oracy*, or the ability to use effectively listening and speaking skills in a language, and *literacy*, the ability to read and write (both concepts are far more complex, but their actual complexity is not relevant for Nover's argument). In the context of deafness and ASL (or, indeed, any natural sign language), Nover compellingly advocates for a third sort of linguistic competence, which he calls *signacy* (Nover, 2005, personal communication). Nover defines signacy as the ability to use a sign language effectively; the concept can be expanded to refer to a kind of metalinguistic understanding of sign language in general, and of the specific natural sign language at issue in particular. Nover argues that the order of significance and emphasis of these three kinds of language skill must, in the case of the deaf child, be signacy, literacy, and oracy (i.e., S-L-O), rather than the more traditional focus on oracy, literacy, and then (if at all) something akin to signacy (e.g., O-L-S).

The rise of ASL programs as foreign language programs in K–12 and university settings in the United States is another aspect of twentieth century language policy related to ASL (see Hayes & Dilka, 1995; Reagan, 2000, 2002a, 2005a, 2009; Wilcox, 1988; Wilcox & Wilcox, 1997). We have already mentioned the legislative side of these developments, but the matter is in fact far more complex, and controversial, than the legislation alone might suggest. The study of ASL by hearing individuals has been increasing quite dramatically around the country over the past few decades, and this is promising for a number of reasons. Wilcox and Wilcox (1997,

p. 51) report an increase in enrollment in ASL courses at the post-secondary level of 181 percent over a five-year period in the 1980s, and enrollments have continued to rise since that time (see Miller, 2008; Mitchell, Young, Bachleda, & Karchmer, 2006). In fact, Sherman Wilcox, a faculty member at the University of New Mexico, maintains a list of universities around the country that accept ASL in fulfillment of their foreign language requirements, and the list currently includes more than 160 institutions, including such top-rate institutions as Ohio State University, Stanford University, the University of Chicago, the University of Michigan, Yale University, and a host of others. At the same time, however, there has been a powerful backlash to such developments, seen most clearly in the resistance among many educators (and especially many foreign language educators) to the inclusion of ASL as a foreign language option in both secondary schools and universities. Perhaps among the more intriguing of these objections is that offered by Howard Mancing, head of the foreign language department at Purdue University: "In no way do I impugn the integrity of ASL as a legitimate academic subject or as a well-developed, intellectual, emotional, subtle, sophisticated language . . . It is all of that, but since it is American Sign Language it is not foreign by definition" (quoted in "Sign Language: A Way to Talk, But Is It Foreign?" a *New York Times* article published in 1992). The issue raised by Professor Mancing is one of definition, and what he has essentially done is to employ a programmatic definition as if it were a reportive definition in order to exclude ASL (see Hamm 1989, pp. 10–15; Scheffler 1960, pp. 11–35). The obvious ordinary language sense of *foreign* in the term *foreign language* is that the language is *foreign to the learner*. To employ Professor Mancing's definition would require that we also exclude Native American languages, such as Navajo, Hawai'ian, Mohawk, and so on, and even perhaps Spanish, which is arguably as indigenous to North America as English and is certainly widely spoken as a native language in the United States. In short, although the argument that ASL is not foreign may initially appear to be compelling, this is in fact far from the case. The extent to which a particular language is foreign has to do with the extent to which it is new or different to the learner.

The second critique of the place of ASL in the foreign language curriculum has to do with the role of ASL in meeting a cultural component in liberal education. Traditional defenses for the study of foreign languages as a part of a liberal education often rely on the close connection of language and culture. It is argued that only through the study of a people's language can their culture be properly understood, and such study can provide an essential international or global component in a student's education. Critics of the acceptance of ASL as a foreign language have suggested that ASL does not meet this aspect of foreign language education on two counts: first, because the culture taught is that of the United States, and second, because the terms *language* and *culture*, when applied to ASL and the culture of the deaf community, are used metaphorically rather than literally. As for the first, I believe that we have already addressed this concern: a culture need not be a non-American one to count as a new one for the student. With respect to the second claim, the challenge has been best put by Thomas Kerth, chairman of the German and Slavic Languages Department at the State University of New York, Stony Brook: "I think these people who talk about deaf culture and foreignness are using it in a metaphorical way, not literally, and when you get into the realm of metaphor the meaning gets obscured. Most would read a foreign language as one not spoken by Americans" (quoted in "Sign Language," 1992). This is a serious distortion of what writers on that culture have actually said and seem to have meant. There are many works devoted to the history, sociology, and anthropology of the cultural community of the American deaf, written by both deaf and hearing scholars. These writings do not suggest that the concept of "cultural Deafness" is to be understood metaphorically; indeed, the overwhelming sense the reader gets from these works is that the term is used in an absolutely literal sense, as we saw in Chapter 1.

With respect to both the teaching and learning of ASL in U.S. secondary schools, and the development of ASL textbooks, one area that was until recently problematic was the gap between common practice in the teaching of ASL and common practice in the teaching of other foreign languages, even other less commonly taught languages. This was especially true with respect to the *Standards for Foreign Language Learning* of the American Council on the Teaching of Foreign Languages (ACTFL; see American Council on the Teaching of Foreign Languages, 1996, 2006). The *Standards for Foreign Language Learning* (see Figure 3.1) provide the fundamental framework for how the teaching and learning of foreign languages is conceptualized, and they have important implications for teaching methodologies, curriculum, and assessment. The *Standards* exist in two forms: a generic, non-language-specific version (see ACTFL, 1996), and language-specific frameworks for Arabic, Chinese, Classical Languages (Greek and Latin), French, German, Italian, Japanese, Portuguese, Russian, and Spanish (see ACTFL, 2006), and there is a separately developed and published version

COMMUNICATION	Communicate in Languages Other Than English
Standard 1.1	Students engage in conversations, provide and obtain information, express feelings and emotions, and exchange opinions.
Standard 1.2	Students understand and interpret written and spoken language on a variety of topics.
Standard 1.3	Students present information, concepts, and ideas to an audience of listeners or readers on a variety of topics.
CULTURES	Gain Knowledge and Understanding of Other Cultures
Standard 2.1	Students demonstrate an understanding of the relationship between the practices and perspectives of the culture studied.
Standard 2.2	Students demonstrate an understanding of the relationship between the products and perspectives of the culture studied.
CONNECTIONS	Connect with Other Disciplines and Acquire Information
Standard 3.1	Students reinforce and further their knowledge of other disciplines through the foreign language.
Standard 3.2	Students acquire information and recognize the distinctive viewpoints that are only available through the foreign language and its cultures.
COMPARISONS	Develop Insight into the Nature of Language and Culture
Standard 4.1	Students demonstrate understanding of the nature of language through comparisons of the language studied and their own.
Standard 4.2	Students demonstrate understanding of the concept of culture through comparisons of the cultures studied and their own.
COMMUNITIES	Participate in Multilingual Communities at Home & Around the World
Standard 5.1	Students use the language both within and beyond the school setting.
Standard 5.2	Students show evidence of becoming life-long learners by using the language for personal enjoyment and enrichment.

FIGURE 3.1. *ACTFL standards*

also available for Esperanto (see Fonseca-Greber & Reagan, 2008). The *Standards* have been widely adopted in foreign language education and play a key role in both the education of future foreign language teachers and the development of contemporary foreign language textbooks (see, e.g., Lafayette, 1996; Omagio Hadley, 2001; Phillips, 1999; Shrum & Glisan, 2005). Between 2007 and 2009, the American Sign Language Teachers Association (ASLTA), in collaboration with the National Consortium of Interpreter Education Centers, produced a draft version of the *Standards for Learning American Sign Language*, and this draft document will ultimately appear in the fourth and final version of the ACTFL *Standards for Foreign Language Learning*. In the meantime, a number of states (California, New Jersey, New York, North Carolina, and Texas, among others) have already developed ASL standards based on the ACTFL *Standards*.

Recent progress has also been made in the teaching of ASL at the elementary school level. Although some signs have been taught in elementary classrooms (especially songs and, of course, the seemingly ubiquitous I-LOVE-YOU sign), there was not any major effort to conceptualize or to develop an age-specific elementary school curriculum for teaching ASL as a foreign language until Linda Pelletier's doctoral dissertation in 2005, which articulates just such a curriculum. Unfortunately, one of the effects of *No Child Left Behind* has been an overall decline in the teaching of foreign languages in elementary schools (see Rhodes & Pufahl, 2010), so the time has simply not been right for the introduction of ASL at this level.

THE PROMISES AND CONCERNS OF THE FUTURE

And what does the future hold for ASL, and for language planning and policies for ASL? It would be disingenuous to suggest that there are no challenges facing both the DEAF⌒WORLD and ASL in U.S. society. Even as the DEAF⌒WORLD is in many ways more visible and successful than at any time in its history, and even as ASL is not only recognized as a language but is increasingly being studied in public schools, colleges, and universities by hearing people, there are very real risks that need to be recognized. Three major kinds of risks threaten the DEAF⌒WORLD and ASL at the present time: biotechnological and medical risks, educational risks, and social risks. Interestingly, although most people tend to focus on the biotechnological and medical challenges to the DEAF⌒WORLD, and whereas these are not small and should certainly not be minimized, it may be that they are not the most serious or important threats that the deaf community will face.

Biotechnological and medical risks to the DEAF^WORLD and to ASL involve the development of medical innovations that threaten the unity of the deaf community. Many of the technological innovations of the twentieth century have been of incredible help and value to deaf people, and technology is not, ipso facto, a bad thing at all. It becomes a concern only when it is seen as attacking core cultural and linguistic values of the DEAF^WORLD. At present, there are two powerful examples of such biotechnological threats: the increasingly common use of cochlear implants in young children, and developments in genetics and prenatal genetic testing.

The debate about the use of cochlear implants in young children was referred to in Chapter 1. As I noted there, although cochlear implants do not restore hearing, they are able to create the perception of sound which, coupled with effective rehabilitation, can assist some hearing impaired individuals to function more effectively in the hearing world (see Christiansen & Leigh, 2006; Woodcock, 2001 [1993]). Although cochlear implants were not originally intended for young children, it is with this population that the debate has been concerned; no one questions the perfectly legitimate right of a late-deafened adult to pursue whatever medical options can help him or her to function more effectively. For young children, however, the matter raises questions about the extent to which such surgical intervention is appropriate, what such surgery says about the view of the child as a hearing impaired individual, and about the overall view of deafness and the DEAF^WORLD. Many in the deaf community view the use of cochlear implants with young children as nothing less than cultural and linguistic genocide, but attitudes are divided. For example, in October of 2009 the National Association of the Deaf issued a "Position Paper" that read, "The NAD recognizes the rights of parents to make informed choices for their . . . children, respects their choice to use cochlear implants and all other assistive devices, and strongly supports the development of the whole child and of language and literacy" (quoted in Christiansen & Leigh, 2006, p. 367). The key issue for the NAD is that parents of young deaf children, and especially hearing parents, be provided with accurate and balanced information about all of their options, as well as about the DEAF^WORLD and the role of ASL, of which they are likely to be unaware.

Nevertheless, although it is not generally articulated in such a fashion, the bottom line is that early implantation of cochlear implants is indeed an assault on deaf culture and, indirectly, on ASL. Since cochlear implant technology involves extensive follow-up to be effective, this means that there is often a tension created about the use of sign language by the deaf child:

> Cochlear implant programs . . . typically require rehabilitation after surgery to realize the full benefit of an implant device. . . . For those implementing such programs, sign language is seen as detracting from or hampering the development of speech and spoken language. Some programs will communicate in subtle ways that whether a child derives full benefit from the cochlear implant will depend on how well parents and caretakers commit fully to the program of rehabilitation, including shielding their children from sign language. (Padden & Humphries, 2005, p. 177)

From the perspective of many deaf people, this sounds like a return to oralism, pure and simple. Cochlear implants may not inevitably rule out membership in the DEAF⁀WORLD or use of ASL, but they do seem to make both considerably less likely.

If cochlear implants have created a challenge for both parents of deaf children and the deaf community, the potential challenges posed by genetic testing are even greater (see Van Cleve, 2004). Teresa Burke provides a powerful summary of just how complex such matters can become, both as ethical dilemmas and as debates of public policy:

> Now that it is possible to identify genes that have been associated with hearing variation, potential parents with a family history of deafness have the option to screen embryos for this genetic trait. Some Deaf people may want to have a Deaf child and will want to use the technology to increase their odds of having such a child; others will use the technology to screen out deafness. Imagine two sets of potential parents who have undergone in vitro fertilization and have learned that some of their fertilized eggs about to be implanted code for deafness, and some of them do not. Do these sets of potential parents have equal freedom of choice regarding which fertilized eggs can be implanted? It is clearly the case that the potential parents who wish to screen out embryos that carry genes associated with deafness will be supported by the mainstream agenda of science and medicine. It is not so clear that this freedom to choose holds for Deaf parents who wish to have a Deaf child that will become a full-fledged member of their community. Yet, if we are to promote the principle of autonomy, with parents having the right to make decisions about the future of their offspring, it seems that both options must be permitted. This is without considering the question of autonomy for the potential person, which adds more complexity to the matter. (2008, p. 73)

Given the demography of deafness in American society, in which only about one in ten deaf individuals is the child of deaf parents, even if the rights of deaf parents to select to have deaf children are recognized, the fact remains that such biotechnology makes possible (and perhaps even probable) a dramatic decrease in the numbers of deaf people in U.S. society. This is, then, a real risk to the DEAF^WORLD, and to the ASL speaker community.

The educational risks to both the DEAF^WORLD and ASL are the result of well-intentioned programs to integrate deaf students into mainstream settings rather than in residential schools for deaf children. This has resulted in a significant decline in enrollment in the traditional residential schools:

> The massive shift toward public schooling of deaf children throughout the 1970s moved deaf children away from schools for the deaf to local school districts. . . . In the early 1970s, one of the largest schools in the country, Indiana School for the Deaf, had nearly 750 students; today it has 321. Utah School for the Deaf has about 40 students, as more students are enrolled in the local schools throughout the state. Despite campaigning by the deaf community, Nebraska School for the Deaf finally closed its doors in 1998 when enrollment dwindled to 28 students. (Padden & Rayman, 2002, pp. 249–50)

The decline in residential schools is significant not just as a reflection of social and educational changes in U.S. society. Traditionally, it has been in just such schools that the culture and language of the DEAF^WORLD have been passed on, largely from student to student with the deaf children of deaf parents serving as the core cultural and linguistic group in the deaf community. A deaf child in a mainstream setting, however, is likely to be the only deaf child in a classroom. This obviously poses serious challenges to both the maintenance of the culture of the DEAF^WORLD and to ASL, and begs the questions of how, where, and by whom the culture and language of the deaf community will be passed on to the next generation of deaf people (see Padden, 2008).

The changes in the educational scene, especially the decline of the residential schools for deaf children, have also contributed to ongoing social and sociological changes in the deaf community. For example:

> The geography of deaf education has changed from sending children off to remote institutions to sending them to their neighborhood schools, in effect fractionating the ways they can meet each other. Deaf communities that developed around deaf schools will no longer have the school to anchor them if the school has closed. Deaf clubs built in those communities in the shadow of deaf

> schools have become curiosities and anachronisms, populated mainly by the old and nostalgic. (Padden & Rayman, 2002, p. 251)

Local deaf communities are no longer geographically fixed, as they once were, but are increasingly "fluid." To be sure, there are strong and vibrant deaf communities in Los Angeles, Washington, D.C., New York, San Francisco, and Chicago, but in many other places, this is becoming less so, and this trend could well continue (see Padden & Rayman, 2002, pp. 252–54). At the same time, it is by no means certain that local deaf communities will not be preserved, perhaps in forms that we cannot yet even imagine:

> The anxieties many of us have at present about holding communities together are valid. In increasingly complex and diverse societies, the fabric of community life appears to be fragile indeed. But, perhaps identities and communities have always been fragile. Their fragility has just been obscured by other stabilities of place and institution. When we look at how different communities, despite lack of geographical cohesion, have managed to maintain and create community, we can see the symbolic work of remembering, rebuilding, and recreating the culture through various practices. (Padden & Rayman, 2002, p. 258)

So, returning now to the particular issue of ASL itself: To what extent might ASL be considered to be an "endangered language"? The question is a legitimate one, because, as we saw in Chapter 2, endangered languages are by far the vast majority of languages in existence in the world today. It is also clear, as Graham Turner (2006) suggests, that the future of many sign languages is indeed threatened, as a result of a variety of medical, social, and educational changes. At the same time, ASL remains the third most widely used language in the United States today, is used extensively in various educational settings, and remains a popular foreign or second language with hearing students. As we have seen in this chapter, ASL has been a target of all aspects of language planning and language policy activities from its very inception. Indeed, ASL may well be among the more planned languages in the world, not in the sense that it is an artificially planned language (which it is not), but in the sense that educators and others have been engaged in developing educational language policies (both positive and negative) related to ASL since the early nineteenth century, to ensure that the language has the necessary lexicon for educational purposes and appropriate and high-quality teaching and that learning materials are available for those wishing to learn it as a foreign or second language.

To be sure, the size of the deaf community may well be reduced in the years ahead, and many changes will be necessary for its culture and for ASL to survive and, perhaps, even to continue to thrive. But there is every reason to expect that this will take place, not least the support of ASL by the members of the deaf community, whose commitment to it as their vernacular language is unquestionable.

NOTES

1. In point of fact, the sign language used in the United States was not actually called "American Sign Language" (ASL) until William Stokoe's work in the mid-twentieth century. This is not to say that the signing used by deaf people prior to that time was not ASL; rather, it is merely to point out that the label that I am employing would not have been one recognized by the users of ASL themselves in earlier times.

2. This is actually a reflection of what I have called "ideological monolingualism" elsewhere. The United States is objectively an incredibly diverse nation linguistically, but most Anglo-Americans are not only monolingual speakers of English, but they see such monolingualism as normative (see Reagan 2005a, 2009).

3. E. M. Gallaudet was in fact ambiguous about the relationship between English and ASL. As educational goals for deaf students changed and oralism rose, so did his position, as can be seen in his advocacy for the "Combined System." It is not unreasonable, however, to suspect that this advocacy was his way of trying to protect and maintain the use of sign language in deaf education (see Reagan, 1989).

Chapter 4

The Creation and Use of Manual Sign Codes as Language Planning

There exists today a notable carelessness in the use of the sign language. The old-time masters of the sign language used a clear-cut, carefully chosen style of delivery which was easy to understand and pleasing to see. Today too many deaf are inclined to slur over their spelling and crowd their signs, and in order to understand them, one must strain both one's eyesight and one's mentality. (Byron Burnes, 1950, quoted in Padden & Humphries, 1988, p. 62)

Nowadays, signs are different. Back then, signs were better, you know, more natural, but . . . Nowadays, with IS and all those things, you get these long drawn-out sentences that take forever to sign. It's a waste of time, I tell you. (Charles Krauel, in an interview, quoted in Padden & Humphries, 1988, p. 63)[1]

From the mid-nineteenth century until recently, the education of deaf children was characterized by a deep division between educators favoring an "oral" approach, in which signing was generally forbidden and children were even punished for signing, and those supporting a "manual" approach, in which signing of some sort was allowed generally in conjunction with speech (see Baynton, 1996; Nover, 2000; Reagan, 1989; Winefield, 1987; Van Cleve, 2007); indeed, some educators of deaf children talk about two competing, bipolar educational philosophies in deaf education (see Paul & Jackson, 1993; Paul & Quigley, 1990, pp. 5–7). This dichotomy between oralism and manualism has become less significant in the past few decades, however. Although oralism remains powerfully attractive for some educators of deaf children and for many hearing parents of deaf children, most educational programs serving deaf people today employ signing of some sort, ranging from those using American Sign Language (ASL) itself (increasingly common) to programs utilizing some type of Total Communication (TC)[2] all the way to the use of a "manual sign code" (MSC) for English (also sometimes called "manual coded English," or MCE).

Since the 1960s, and well into the 1980s, there were a number of efforts, both in the United States and elsewhere, to construct artificial sign languages or, more accurately, MSCs, for use in the education of deaf children (see Paul, 2001, pp. 235–93; Reagan, 1986a, 1995b), and many of these MSCs continue to be used in programs for deaf children. Such MSCs are intended to facilitate the learning of a spoken language by children who have limited or no auditory input from that spoken language; thus these artificial MSCs attempt to provide linguistic and communicative input in a modality different from that normally employed (i.e., visually rather than orally). Although the MSCs that have been developed do typically (though not universally) utilize signs drawn from natural sign languages, they nevertheless differ dramatically from natural sign languages. Phonologically, morphologically, lexically, and syntactically, the basis for an MSC is the norms of the target spoken language rather than those of the natural sign language. In other words, artificial MSCs designed to represent English may best be understood as varieties of English that utilize a visual/manual modality, rather than as varieties of either ASL or British Sign Language. In this chapter I explore the nature and development of MSCs as an example of language planning for sign languages, and I examine both the strengths and weaknesses of MSCs as the products of language planning efforts.

FINGERSPELLING: ITS NATURE AND USES

Manual alphabets are used by deaf people around the world, often in conjunction with a natural sign language (Schein & Stewart, 1995, pp. 77–78). These alphabets are used in fingerspelling particular words, especially personal names, place names, and words for which either there is no sign or the sign is not known. Fingerspelling is thus the most basic and fundamental "bridge" between spoken language and sign language. At the same time, fingerspelling plays a relatively minor role in signing, as David Brien notes in the *Dictionary of British Sign Language / English*:

> It appears to be a widely held belief amongst the general public in the U.K. [and elsewhere] that sign language consists entirely of fingerspelling. In fact, fingerspelling accounts for only a small proportion of the lexical content of BSL [British Sign Language, and other sign languages]. Contrary to public perception, fingerspelling can actually be seen as marginal—since it has developed with explicit reference to written English—in comparison with the naturally and independently evolved elements of linguistic behaviour that form the greater part of visual-gestural language interaction. (1992, p. 849)

The manual alphabet used in the United States employs twenty-six letters, many of which also function as phonemes in ASL (e.g., *T, Y, F*, etc.),[3] and which are also used to create initialized signs (e.g., ASSOCIATION, CLASS, GROUP, TEAM, FAMILY, SOCIETY). Although the American Manual Alphabet is widely used internationally, the manual alphabets used in different countries often vary. In some settings, only small differences exist (in South African Sign Language, for instance, only the letter *T* differs from that used in the American Manual Alphabet), while in others the differences are far more extreme (e.g., because of the use of the Cyrillic script in written Russian, Russian Sign Language uses a very different manual alphabet; the same is true for Chinese, Japanese, and Thai, among others). In Britain, as well as Australia, New Zealand, Scotland, and the former Yugoslavia, the situation is a bit more complex, in that there are both two-handed and single-handed manual alphabets. In some national settings, such as Argentina, more than one manual alphabet can coexist. Finally, there is an International Manual Alphabet (IMA), adopted by the World Federation of the Deaf, which is the same as that of the American Manual Alphabet except for the letters *F* and *T* (as in the South African case, the letter *T* varies because the American sign for the letter is an offensive gesture in many societies). See Figures 4.1 and 4.2.

Fingerspelling can be used not merely to support a natural sign language, but to fully represent a spoken language. This is, arguably, the most basic and fundamental kind of MSC, and was used historically as the "Rochester Method" in schools for deaf children (Nover, 1995). The Rochester Method, devised by Zenas Westervelt in 1878 after he opened the Western New York Institute for Deaf-Mutes (today, the Rochester School for the Deaf), consisted of fingerspelling each and every word in a conversation (see Paul, 2001, pp. 248–49; Schein & Stewart, 1995, pp. 77–81). The Rochester Method was used as a teaching method in conjunction with spoken English until Westervelt's death in 1912, though reports of its use in some settings continue until the 1940s, and there are still a very few deaf individuals who can communicate using it. However, as one would imagine, fingerspelling

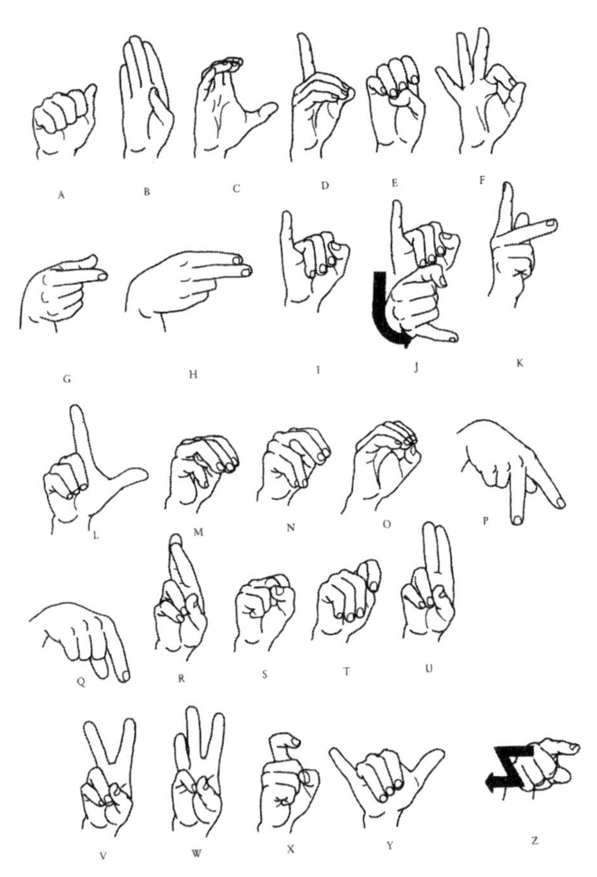

FIGURE 4.1. *American Manual Alphabet. Reproduced from J. Schein & D. Stewart,* Language in Motion: Exploring the Nature of Sign *(Washington, DC: Gallaudet University Press, 1995), p. 64.*

each and every word in a conversation is extremely difficult and taxing, as well as time-consuming. Because of this, the Rochester Method today has virtually no advocates, although it is sometimes used pedagogically to help students improve their fingerspelling skills.

A WORD ABOUT ARTIFICIAL LANGUAGES

In discussing the creation and use of various MSCs, I have used the term *artificial* to describe such language systems. This term is a loaded one; others that might be used in its place include *planned* or *created*. I believe that there are two distinct issues with such terminology and the activities

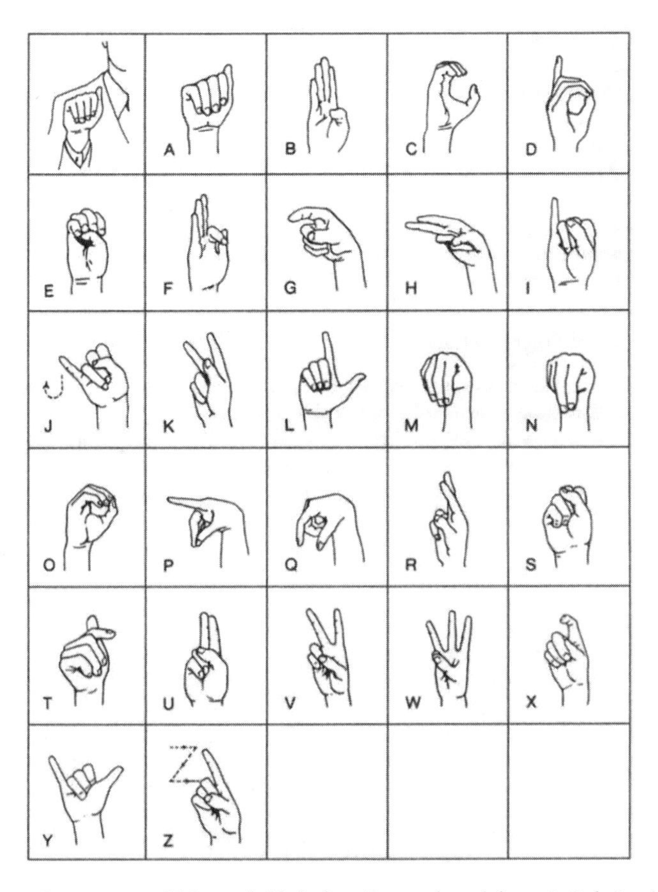

FIGURE 4.2. *International Manual Alphabet. Reproduced from J. Schein & D. Stewart,* Language in Motion: Exploring the Nature of Sign *(Washington, DC: Gallaudet University Press, 1995), p. 79.*

to which they refer that should be discussed here. The first has to do with the deliberate manipulation or creation of a language or language system to accomplish particular ends; the second has to do with attitudes about such efforts. Such terminology is important to consider, because it applies not only to the case of the MSCs, but also to the entire field of interlinguistics (see Aleksandrova, 1989; Blanke, 2003, 2006; Duličenko, 1988, 1989, 2006; Fettes, 2003a, 2003b; Fiedler, 2008; Fiedler & Haitao, 2001; Jansen, 2007, 2008; Kornilov, 1989; Schubert, 1989, 2001; Tonkin, 1997), and to the case of Esperanto in particular (see Auld, 1988; Blanke & Lins, 2010; Eco, 1995; Fonseca-Greber & Reagan, 2008; Forster,

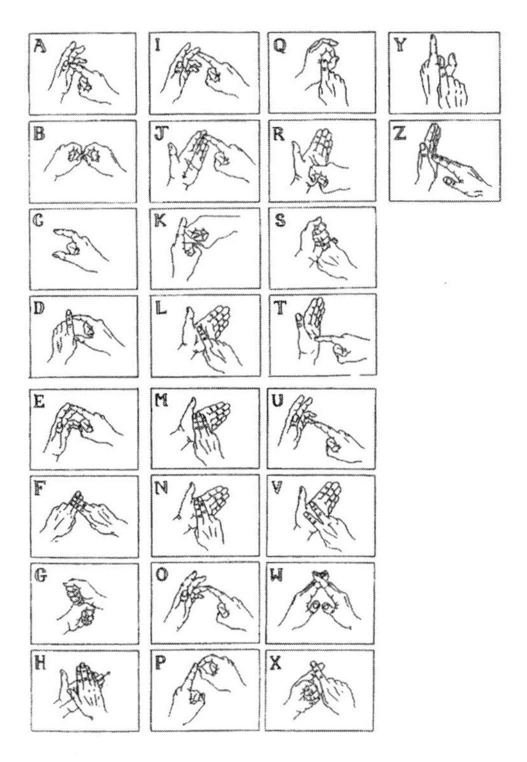

FIGURE 4.3. *British Two-Handed Manual Alphabet. Reproduced from Leila Monaghan, Constanze Schmaling, Karen Nakamura, & Graham H. Turner, eds.,* Many Ways to be Deaf: International Variation in Deaf Communities *(Washington, DC: Gallaudet University Press, 2003), p. 26.*

1982, 1987; Goodman, 1978; Gregor, 1976; Janton, 1993; Large, 1985; Nuessel, 2000; Okrent, 2006, 2009; Sikosek, 2006).

There is nothing wrong with efforts to guide language usage; indeed, such efforts are what language planning and language policy efforts are all about. The creation of a new language is somewhat more complex but not, in and of itself problematic, and there is a substantial literature defending these efforts (see Fantini & Reagan, 1992; Janton, 1993; Nuessel, 2000)—although they do seem to generate quite powerful emotions. Ludwig Wittgenstein, for example, once commented about Esperanto: "Esperanto. The feeling of disgust we get if we utter an invented word with invented derivative syllables. The word is cold, lacking in associations, and yet it plays at being 'language.' A system of purely written signs would not disgust us so much" (1980 [1946], p. 53). Such a view is clearly highly emotional, and, indeed, is simply irrational. This having been said, efforts to create languages do seem to result in such responses all too often.

In the particular case of MSCs, however, the situation is somewhat different from that of other examples of artificial, planned, or created languages. The creation of an MSC is not the creation of a new language, per se; rather, it is simply a systematic manner for an already existing language (that is, a spoken language) to be represented. This means, as we shall see later on, that such efforts are subject to the criticism that they are "neither fish nor fowl"—that is, that they lack the full advantages of both spoken and sign languages.

AN OVERVIEW OF THE DEVELOPMENT OF MANUAL SIGN CODES

Efforts to present oral/aural language in a visual/gestural form are far from new (this point is often ignored in discussions about the development of MSCs but is important to keep in mind). Such efforts almost certainly date back to the earliest literate human civilizations; we know, for example, that some sort of signed communication took place in ancient Egypt, as well as in ancient Israel and in both the Greek and Roman worlds (see Schein & Stewart, 1995, p. 63), not to mention in medieval monastic orders. More recently, we know with a high degree of certainty that the development of education for deaf children in France, first under the Abbé Charles-Michel de l'Epée and then under his successor the Abbé Roch-Ambroise Cururron Sicard, was based not only on the use of sign language in education, but on what were termed "methodical signs"—that is, the use of French Sign Language as the basis for an MSC that could provide "a visual analog to written French" (see Stedt & Moores, 1990, p. 2). It was this sign system that was brought to the United States by Laurent Clerc, and which provided the foundation for the creation of a comparable English-based sign vocabulary that was later to evolve into contemporary ASL (Stedt & Moores, 1990, p. 4).

In the twentieth century, the earliest development of an MSC took place in Britain in the 1930s, by Sir Richard Paget, Lady Grace Paget, and Dr. Pierre Gorman (Paget, 1951; Paget & Gorman, 1976; Sutton-Spence & Woll, 1998, pp. 14–15). The Paget Gorman Sign System was initially designed to be utilized with children with various kinds of speech and communication problems, including hearing impairments. The Paget Gorman Sign System used some thirty-seven basic signs and twenty-one hand postures, which could be combined to create a relatively large English vocabulary. It also included both word endings and verb tense markers. British schools for deaf children widely used the Paget Gorman Sign System (whose signs had no relation to British Sign Language) from the 1960s until the 1980s, when British Sign Language–based Signed English and British Sign Language itself began to be more commonly used.

Although the development of MSCs has been, as the Paget Gorman Sign System demonstrates, an international phenomenon—such systems were developed and used in Australia, Ireland, New Zealand (where the Australian MSC was used), Singapore, and South Africa, among other places, as I will discuss later in this chapter (see, e.g., Kyle, 1987; Penn & Reagan, 1990; Serpell & Mbewe, 1990)—MSCs primarily emerged for educational purposes in the United States. In the U.S. context, several distinct MSCs were developed, though the major systems were closely related, sharing both common historical roots and underlying social and linguistic assumptions. Further, the American MSCs all have as their principal target population deaf children at school, and all of the systems rely on teachers of deaf children and, to a lesser extent, parents of deaf children, for their successful implementation.

The first artificially constructed MSC to be developed in the United States was created by a young deaf immigrant from England, David Anthony, in 1966 (Paul, 2001). This system, initially intended for use with deaf children with developmental delays (Wilbur, 1979, p. 204), was inspired by the Paget Gorman Sign System in use in Britain (see Crystal & Craig, 1978; Paget, 1951; Paget & Gorman, 1976). Anthony's system provided the base for what was eventually to become Seeing Essential English (SEE-1). Beginning in January 1969, groups of deaf and hearing people began meeting in Southern California to develop signs and guidelines for SEE-1. As Gustason and Woodward recount, "a working committee of five [were] elected. Sign classes were taught by these five, and dittoed papers with written descriptions of each sign were utilized in these classes. The papers were mailed to interested persons" (1973, p. v). Furthermore,

> the main concern of the original group was the consistent, logical, rational, and practical development of signs to represent as specifically as possible the basic essentials of the English language. This concern sprang from the experience of all present with the poor English skills of many deaf students, and the desire for an easier, more successful way of developing mastery of English in a far greater number of such students. (Quoted in Paul, 2001, p. 253)

SEE-I, which is also sometimes called the Morphological Sign System (MSS), was distinctive in a number of ways. Some base signs were drawn from ASL, but this was neither a logical nor consistent process. For example, although the ASL sign for BUTTERFLY was recommended, it was also permissible for a child to combine BUTTER + FLY (see Figures 4.4 and 4.5 for the contrast between the ASL and this permitted SEE-I combined sign). In passing, I should note that while this particular example is commonly used in critiques of SEE-I, the criticisms generally ignore the fact that the ASL sign is actually the preferred sign. In addition, SEE-I also used the same sign for different homonyms, as in *sea* and *see*. Many SEE-I signs were initialized, and there were a number of signs for specific English grammatical markers (such as *-ing*). There was a specific sign for the definite article *the* (which does not exist in ASL), and, uniquely, the copula (that is, the verb *to be*) is signed using initialized signs for *am, is*, and *are*. Along similar lines, as a means of best representing English, the verb *to have* was itself initialized, using the "V" handshape.

Disagreements and differences of opinion about certain features of manual signing led to the breakup of this original group in 1971, and as a consequence SEE-1 is no longer found in formal settings. SEE-1 was followed by Signing Exact English (SEE-2), which was developed by Gerilee Gustason and Esther Zawolkow in the early 1970s. SEE-2 makes far better use of ASL signs as base signs, and at least three quarters of the signs used in SEE-2 are either direct borrowings or modified borrowings (often

FIGURE 4.4. *ASL sign* BUTTERFLY . *Reproduced from Clayton Valli, ed.,* The Gallaudet Dictionary of American Sign Language *(Washington, DC: Gallaudet University Press, 2005), p. 66.*

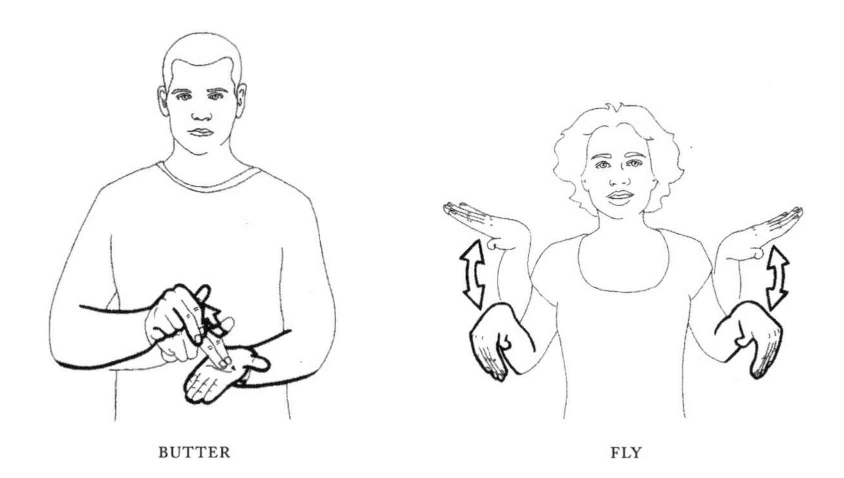

Figure 4.5. *SEE-I combination sign for* BUTTER + FLY. *In David A. Anthony & Associates, eds.,* Seeing Essential English Manual *(Anaheim, CA: Educational Services Division, Anaheim Union High School District, 1971), the ASL sign for* BUTTERFLY *is described but a note underneath reads "Much acrimony and ridicule has centered on 'how to sign* BUTTERFLY.' *The sign given above is a traditional one. Nevertheless if a child signs* BUTTER + FLY *and knows what he is talking about, who are we to censure him?" (p. 495). Reproduced from Clayton Valli, ed.,* The Gallaudet Dictionary of American Sign Language *(Washington, DC: Gallaudet University Press, 2005), pp. 65, 177.*

as initialized signs) from ASL. SEE-2 remains the most commonly used MSC in the United States, and there is a growing research literature on its use in deaf education (see Paul, 2001, pp. 261–65). The underlying principle of SEE-2, though, is a focus on representing spoken and, to a lesser extent, written English. Barbara Luetke-Stahlman argues that SEE-2 is, pure and simple, English in a visual modality:

> English has one combination of sounds for one word. Likewise, one word, one sign: that is Signing Exact English. Signing Exact English differentiates words like electric, electrical, electricity, non-electric, electrician. English itself is not "conceptually accurate," it is riddled with non-literal expressions, and to learn what those groups of words mean, children must be exposed to them in routine ways. How do deaf children understand that a nose doesn't physically run? Just as hearing children do. The expression is directly explained to them or just used in context (for example, "cut that out, stop that, please cut that out"). . . . Parents and teachers simply attend to the child's message and respond with the correct grammar and vocabulary of English. It matters not whether we are speaking or signing to the child. (1993, p. iii).

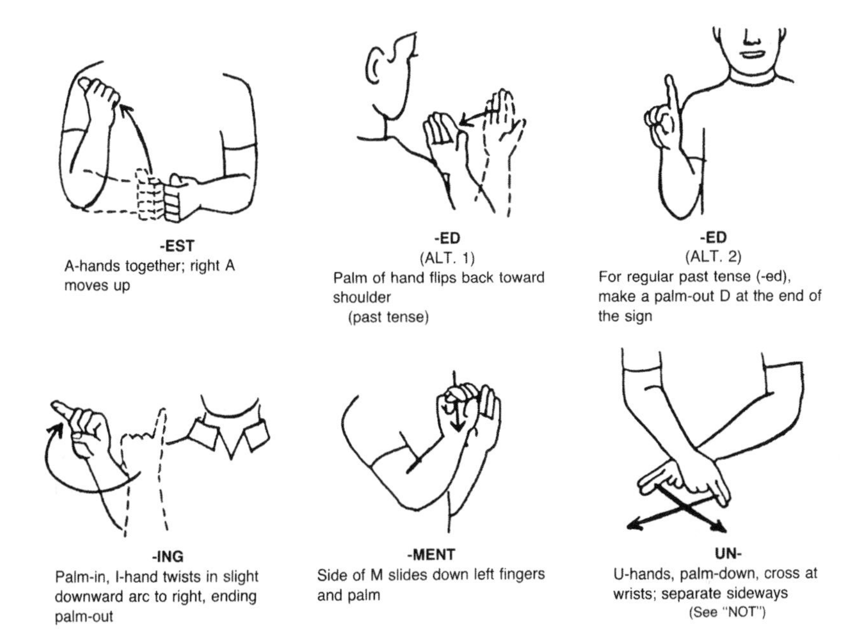

FIGURE 4.6. *SEE-2 affixes. Reproduced from Harry Bornstein, ed.,* Manual Communication: Implications for Education *(Washington, DC: Gallaudet University Press, 1990), p. 114.*

The relationship, or lack of relationship, between SEE-2 and ASL is simply not a particularly relevant concern, which impacts the way that SEE-2 is constructed and implemented. This feature of SEE-2, and of the other MSCs, is seen by supporters of such systems as one of their great strengths, while critics of these systems, such as Ronnie Wilbur, see it as their fundamental flaw:

> [MSCs have] not developed an intonational and rhythmic system that is designed to be seen by the eyes and produced by the hands and face. This evolution has not taken place because the goal of [their] usage is to mimic the lexicon, morphology, and syntax of English. Thus, when [MSCs are] learned by deaf children, [they are] learned with the overriding constraint that [they] must follow English word order. This means that the syntactic structure of [an MSC] cannot adapt over time in the ways that would be suitable for the manual modality. In particular, flexible word order cannot develop. (Wilbur, 2008, p. 130)

Thus, the "Important Principles of Signing Exact English" that appear at the beginning of Gustason and Zawolkow's guide to Signing Exact English include:

- English should be signed in a manner that is as constant as possible with how it is spoken or written in order to constitute a language input for the deaf child that will result in his mastery of English.
- A sign should be translatable to only one English equivalent.
- "Basic words" are words that can have no more taken away and still form a complete word (GIRL, TALK, THE, the noun SAW, etc.).
- "Complex words" are defined as basic words with the addition of an affix or inflection: GIRLS, TALKED, the past tense verb SAW.
- Compound words are two or more basic words put together. If the meaning of the words separately is consistent with the meaning of the words together, then and only then are they signed as the compound words.
- When a sign already exists in ASL that is clear, unambiguous, and commonly translates to one English word, this sign is retained.
- When the first letter is added to a basic sign to create synonyms, the basic sign is retained wherever possible as the most commonly used word.
- When more than one marker is added to a word, middle markers may be dropped if there is no sacrifice of clarity.
- While following the above principles, respect needs to be shown for characteristics of visual-gestural communication. (1993, pp. xiii–xiv)

In short, SEE-2 employs a large number of contractions (-'LL, -'M, -N'T, -'RE, -'S, and–'VE), as well as some seventy different affixes (e.g., -ABLE, ANTI-, -ED, -ING, -FUL, -SHIP, -PRO, -PRE, -UN, etc; see Figure 4.6). Finally, one of the key requirements for the use of SEE-2 is that one speaks in conjunction with speech, thus reinforcing the connection of the signing with English.

In instances in which there are multiple homonyms in English, SEE-2 employs what is called the "two-out-of-three" rule. The basic idea is that one considers the sound, the spelling, and the meaning of the different terms. If at least two of the three are the same, then a single sign is used (see Paul, 2001, p. 254). This is a consequence of the distinctive lexicons of English and ASL. Although it would seem to be obvious, it is important to note explicitly here that signs are conceptual in nature. In other words, there is no one-to-one parallel between ASL signs and English words, any more than there is a one-to-one parallel between Spanish and English words (for example, in Spanish there are two verbs *to be*: *ser* and *estar*, which have different semantic content, whereas in English we have only one verb *to be*). In the case of English and ASL, there are instances in which ASL is more precise than English, and others in which English is more precise than ASL. For example, the English word "manage" can be signed in ASL in a number of different ways depending on its meaning (see Figure 4.7):

It's a good thing that she knows how to *manage* him. (CONTROL)

I don't know how she *manages* to deal with him. (TO-BE-PATIENT)

These employees are under my *management*. (SUPERVISE)

How did she *manage* to climb that mountain? (TO-SUCCEED)

FIGURE 4.7. *Four different ASL glosses for the English word* manage. *Reproduced from Clayton Valli, ed.,* The Gallaudet Dictionary of American Sign Language *(Washington, DC: Gallaudet University Press, 2005), pp. 101, 327, 450, 453.*

On the other hand, the ASL sign CONTROL can mean not only "control," but also "direct," "manage," "administer," "administrate," "govern," or "regulate"—and with a slight change in non-manual features, even "manipulate." In the case of SEE-2, though, the two-out-of-three rule allows a single sign for the word *run* in each of the following sentences, because they sound and are spelled the same way, in spite of the fact that they would be signed using completely different signs in ASL:

The girl hit a home *run*.

There is a *run* in my stocking.

I like to walk rather than *run*.

From the perspective of language planning, one of the especially interesting features of SEE-2 is that it includes specific guidelines for the creation of new signs for English words that do not exist in SEE-2. Among these are:

- Seek an existing sign. Check other sign language texts. Ask skilled signers in your community, especially deaf native signers.
- Modify an existing sign with a similar or related meaning. Generally, this means adding the first letter of the word to a basic sign.
- Consider finger spelling. This depends, of course, on the age and perceptual abilities of the child, and the length and frequency of use of the word in question.
- If all else fails, and you must invent, try to stay as close as possible to ASL principles. (Gustason & Zawolkow, 1993, p. xv)

Although SEE-2 is the most common MSC in the United States, there are others as well, such as Linguistics of Visual English (LOVE), developed by Dennis Wampler, which is similar to SEE-1 in construction. Signed English is also a term that one comes across, and while it is less clearly demarcated, it does exist in practice. In its most common form, Signed English was created by Harry Bornstein and his colleagues, and uses ASL signs in English word order, employing only fourteen essential English grammatical markers (see Bornstein, Saulnier, & Hamilton, 1983). The fundamental idea underlying Signed English is that:

> Signed English is a reasonable manual parallel to English. It is an educational tool meant to be used while you speak and thereby help you communicate with deaf children . . . Here is the basic reason for developing a manual system parallel to speech: Deaf children must depend on what they see to understand what others say to them. (Bornstein, Saulnier, & Hamilton, 1983, p. 20)

In addition to being used in formal educational settings, Signed English has also been used to develop various children's books (among them *Nursery Rhymes from Mother Goose, Goldilocks and the Three Bears*, and *Little Red Riding Hood*; see Bornstein, Saulnier, Peters, & Tom, 1992; Bornstein, Saulnier, & Pomeroy, 1990; Saulnier & Miller, 1980).Various dictionaries of Signed English have been published for use in different settings (see Bornstein, Hamilton, Saulnier, & Roy, 1983).

In recent years, another form of signing—Conceptually Accurate Signed English (CASE)—has appeared, especially in the context of the training and evaluation of sign language interpreters. CASE is occasionally described as a MSC, but it is more commonly viewed as an example of contact sign. For example, the Early Hearing Detection and Intervention Program—a division of the U.S. Department of Health and Human Services, Centers for Disease Control—defines CASE this way:

> Conceptually Accurate Signed English (CASE)—sometimes called Pidgin Signed English (PSE)—is a building block that has developed between people who use American Sign Language (ASL), and people who use Manually Coded English (MCE), using signs based on ASL and MCE. This helps them understand each other.... In CASE, American Sign Language (ASL) and Manually Coded English (MCE) are blended together. CASE is flexible, and can be changed depending on the people using it. . . . Other building blocks can be used with CASE. Often, finger spelling is used in combination with CASE. Finger spelling is used to spell out words that don't have a sign—such as names of people and places.

Others define CASE as the use of contact sign with the affixes of Signed English and greater initialization of signs, while other descriptions are even more vague. It appears that CASE is one of those matters that one knows when one sees it. However, given what are generally taken to be the close ties between CASE and contact sign, it is reasonable to assert that CASE is not really an MSC at least in a strong sense of the term. In any event, CASE is widely used in both interpreter training programs and in mainstream deaf education programs.

Last, there is Cued Speech, a system devised in 1965 and 1966 by R. Orin Cornett, a faculty member at Gallaudet University (Cornett & Daisey, 1992). Cued Speech differs from other MSCs in that it is not an effort to present English in a signed modality, but is rather a supplement for lipreading. The basic idea of Cued Speech is that a small number of handshapes are used near the mouth to represent consonants, while the location around the mouth where they are placed represents vowels (see Figure 4.8). There is a National Cued Speech Association, funded by the U.S. Department of Education, with a website that provides detailed information about Cued Speech (see *www.cuedspeech.org*), as well as a journal dedicated to Cued Speech (the *Cued Speech Journal*).

What is clear, however, is that "in the United States, there exist [a variety of] manual codes of English none of which express the real, authentic perspective of the Deaf community" (Nover, 1995, p. 128). "However well-intentioned," write Padden and Humphries, "[the efforts to devise MSCs] rest on the pervasive belief that sign languages are essentially 'incomplete' systems and amenable to modification for educational purposes. They ignore the fact that individual signs, like words, are inseparable parts of a larger grammatical system" (1988, p. 64).

As we have seen, the various American MSCs are similar in terms of both their philosophical underpinnings and their guiding structural principles. For example, all of the different artificial systems utilize at least some signs borrowed from ASL (though not necessarily with the same semantic space as that identified with the sign in ASL). The different sign codes operate with radically different morphological principles than does ASL, and all require the use of various prefixes and suffixes to convey specific English syntactic information. Further, the different MSCs not only allow the use of fingerspelling, but also employ widespread initialization, though the actual parameters within which such linguistic behaviors are appropriate vary among the different manual code systems. Word order in the different sign codes is nearly always, as a matter of principle, the same as that found in English. Finally, and not terribly surprising given their goal of providing access to English, all MSCs require that one voice and sign simultaneously when communicating. Perhaps especially interesting about the use of MSCs is that, as Brenda Schick observes,

> despite the fact that MCE has been used educationally for about three decades, there has been little systematic study of its acquisition. For children acquiring MCE, the goal is to acquire English as a first and native language, and researchers typically focus on the extent to which children adhere to or deviate from the rules of English, rather than a description of the children's overall communication skills. In addition, children learning MCE are typically learning it from hearing people, who vary widely in their fluency. Therefore, the issue of restricted input is a confound not easily separated from the issue of how well children learn MCE as a system and whether it can function as a true language. (2003, pp. 225–26)

With this background in mind, we now turn to an examination of some of the criticisms that have been targeted at MSCs. I will focus on three sets

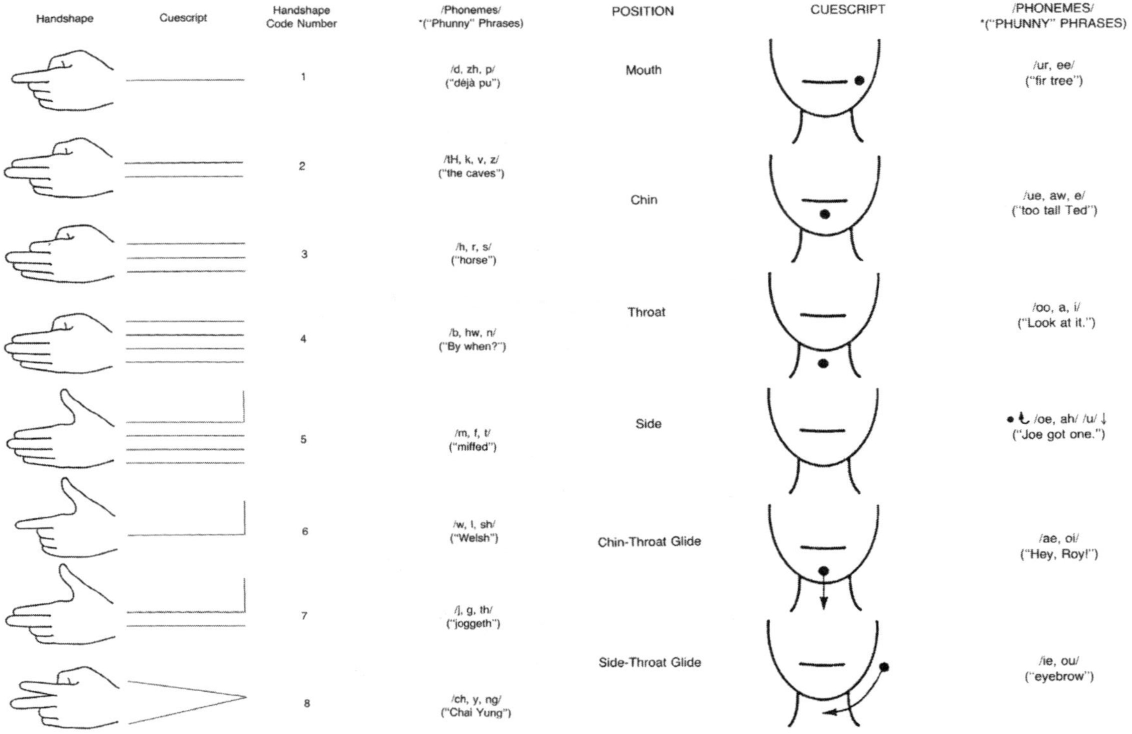

Handshape	Cuescript	Handshape Code Number	/Phonemes/ *("Phunny" Phrases)
		1	/d, zh, p/ ("déjà pu")
		2	/tH, k, v, z/ ("the caves")
		3	/h, r, s/ ("horse")
		4	/b, hw, n/ ("By when?")
		5	/m, f, t/ ("miffed")
		6	/w, l, sh/ ("Welsh")
		7	/j, g, th/ ("joggeth")
		8	/ch, y, ng/ ("Chai Yung")

POSITION	CUESCRIPT	/PHONEMES/ *("PHUNNY" PHRASES)
Mouth		/ur, ee/ ("fir tree")
Chin		/ue, aw, e/ ("too tall Ted")
Throat		/oo, a, i/ ("Look at it.")
Side		• ↲ /oe, ah/ /u/ ↓ ("Joe got one.")
Chin-Throat Glide		/ae, oi/ ("Hey, Roy!")
Side-Throat Glide		/ie, ou/ ("eyebrow")

Figure 4.8. *Cued Speech markers. Reproduced from Harry Bornstein, ed.,* Manual Communication: Implications for Education *(Washington, DC: Gallaudet University Press, 1990), pp. 141–142.*

of critiques: those dealing with the linguistics of MSCs, cultural objections to MSCs, and educational concerns about the effectiveness of the MSCs.

THE LINGUISTIC LIMITATIONS OF MANUAL SIGN CODES

The fundamental objective of those who created the various MSCs, as we have seen, was to represent English in a visual/manual modality. Gustason and Zawolkow explicitly stated that "the most important principle in Signing Exact English is that English should be signed in a manner that is as consistent as possible with how it is spoken or written in order to constitute a language input for the deaf child that will result in his mastery of English" (1993, p. xiii). As Claire Ramsey notes,

> SEE 2 creation occurred in response to a "language problem." Its designers wanted to influence use and choice of language for a set of special purposes: communication in monolingual English-speaking families with deaf children, communication and English instruction in schools with deaf students, and participation in and access to the English-speaking nation. In carrying out their reforms, they followed a standard already operative in the classrooms of the United States, namely, the norms of written English. The goal was to make this variety of English visible to deaf students through signs. In the tradition of language planning in the English-speaking world, the route to this goal of teaching standard English to deaf children was development of a set of norms and publication of a dictionary. (1989, pp. 125–26)

Although widely accepted as a legitimate goal by both teachers of deaf students and hearing parents of deaf children (see Ramsey, 1989, pp. 142–44), such an objective is at best highly questionable from a linguistic perspective. In seeking to represent the lexical items of an oral/aural language in a gestural/visual linguistic context, sign systems such as SEE-1, SEE-2, LOVE, CASE, and Signed English tend to be both awkward and confusing, and they almost inevitably entail violations of the structural and morphological rules and norms of ASL. Ramsey, citing Supalla (1986), points out:

> The related issues of modality and naturalness in signed languages are crucial to understanding both the problems of MCEs and their relation (or lack thereof) to spoken English as well as the failure of MCEs to serve as useable means of communication among those who depend on vision for communication and for learning. Because native monolingual speakers of English can utter an English word and simultaneously produce a sign that have many features of meaning in common with the English word, they are led to believe that the signs they are using actually represent English words and

> that the signed strings they produce are in fact English sentences. Yet given the interaction of modality and linguistic structure found in ASL, there is no deeper way that signs and spoken words could be related. (1989, p. 131)

Insofar as these systems are efforts to represent spoken English visually, of course, this is hardly a problem, especially where they are used with students who are postlingually deaf or with students with a reasonable degree of residual hearing, but for others, this is far from the case. But when the MSCs are contrasted with ASL, the situation is quite different. MSCs are simply not able to make effective use of the most powerful morphosyntactic elements of sign language. MSCs cannot take advantage of simultaneity rather than sequentiality, and hence cannot make use of the layering mechanisms made possible by ASL; they cannot permit phonological and morphological modifications to signs that use the spatial and temporal aspects of ASL; they ignore completely the nonmanual aspects of ASL lexical items; and they fail to allow for the intonational and rhythmic information conveyed by ASL (see Wilbur, 2008, pp. 130–31). Nor is any of this particularly new: the problems, and the underlying lack of "fit" between MSCs and ASL were discussed in considerable detail in the 1970s (see Cokely & Gawlik, 1973; Woodward, 1973).

In short, there are powerful linguistic limitations posed by the development and use of various MSCs. Woodward summarized the problem more than a quarter century ago:

> Normal standardization attempts, not to mention imposition of one language upon another, are considered impossible by many linguists. There are good reasons for this in the history and structure of languages. With the added burden of imposing English (a language with an oral channel) on ASL (a language with a visual channel), one can legitimately question the possibility of success for Manual English systems. (1973, p. 8)

THE CULTURAL LIMITATIONS OF MANUAL SIGN CODES

As we saw in Chapter 1, the single most significant of the various elements of deaf cultural identity in the United States is competence in ASL, the community's vernacular language as well as a powerful marker of "group solidarity" (see Lane et al., 1996; Schein & Stewart, 1995; Valli & Lucas, 2000). It is important to emphasize that this applies *only* to ASL; other types of signing—including the MSCs that are the focus of this chapter—fulfill very different functions and are therefore viewed very differently by the deaf community (see Lane et al., 1996; Lucas, 1989; Lucas & Valli, 1992; Reagan, 1990b, 1995a, 1995b, 2002c, 2005b [1985]; Schein & Stewart, 1995). The cultural problem with the MSCs is essentially that the very existence of MSCs is perceived by members of the DEAF^WORLD as not only an affront to the community's status as a legitimate cultural community, but even more, a rejection of ASL, the community's language. Although the creators of the different MSCs have been careful to distinguish between the nature and purposes of such codes and ASL, and they have often been quite positive about the unique place of ASL in the deaf community, such assurances have rung hollow with most deaf people. As Ramsey has commented, "From the point of introduction, SEE-2 has met with some antagonism, particularly from the deaf community. The goals and values of signing deaf adults are not entirely consistent with those of hearing parents and educators" (1989, pp. 129–30). Without going into unnecessary detail here, suffice it to say that the MSCs are widely rejected by the deaf community not only as awkward efforts to impose the structures of a spoken language on sign, but as efforts at cultural imperialism by the hearing community as well (see Branson & Miller, 1993, 1998, 2002; Gregory & Hartley, 1991; Ramsey, 1989; Reagan, 1995b).

THE EDUCATIONAL LIMITATIONS OF MANUAL SIGN CODES

If one accepts the presence of deaf culture, and the legitimacy of ASL, then the use of MSCs raises a number of fairly important educational implications. Current models and practices in deaf education, by and large, tend to assume a pathological view of deafness, in which deaf people are seen as deficient in significant ways when measured against a hearing norm. The acceptance of deaf culture forces us to reconsider the norm against which deaf people are to be measured, which in turn means reconsidering "appropriate" educational practice. In particular, such a revised view would accord ASL a status and role much different than it has in contemporary practice (see DeLuca & Napoli, 2008; Gutiérrez, 1994; Hoffmeister, 1990, 2008; Johnson, Liddell, & Erting, 1989; Reagan, 2005b [1985]; Stewart, 1992; Woodward, 1982).

There is a substantial literature devoted to making an educational case for the use of ASL in the education of deaf children (see, e.g., Deuchar &

James, 1985; Erting et al., 2006; Gibson, 2006; Gutiérrez, 1994; Gregory, 1992; Johnson et al., 1989; Komesaroff, 2008; Paul, 2001, pp. 427–88; Paul & Quigley, 1987; Reagan, 2000, 2005a, 2009; Stewart, 1992; Strong, 1988). Such arguments focus on the relative ease of acquisition of ASL for deaf children, in contrast to that of either spoken English or MSCs for English; the fact that the acquisition of ASL parallels the normal acquisition of spoken language for the first language learner; the fact that ASL can be used effectively to teach both academic content and literacy skills in the spoken language; and finally, that early language acquisition is essential "for the continual development of cognitive skills and later acquisition of literacy skills in either a first or second language" (Paul, n.d., p. 2). Despite these arguments, at the present time ASL is still relatively rarely used in formal educational settings; most commonly, either contact sign or one of the various MSCs are used (see Bornstein, 1990; Reagan, 1995a, 2005b [1985]).

In an educational environment based on a sociocultural model of deafness, however, instruction would take place through the medium of ASL, and the goal for all students would be functional bilingualism in both ASL and English. Students would study not only the common curriculum shared with their hearing peers, but also the history of deaf culture and deaf communities in other parts of the world. Thus, the goal for such a program would be students who would truly be both bilingual and bicultural, able to function competently and comfortably in the hearing world while still feel at home in the DEAF^WORLD (see DeLuca & Napoli, 2008; Grosjean, 1992; Gutiérrez, 1994; Hoffmeister, 1990; Johnson et al., 1989; Reagan, 2005b [1985]; Stewart, 1992; Woodward, 1982). It is just such a program that was discussed as the ASL-English bilingual/bicultural option in Chapter 3.

Such a program, of course, would almost certainly entail deaf students studying together, in a setting not unlike that provided by residential schools, rather than in mainstreamed settings. This is an important point, since mainstreaming is almost universally seen as a good thing in contemporary American society. The problem is that for deaf students, mainstreaming almost inevitably means a lack of contact with other deaf people. Instead of thinking about appropriate educational placement being based on the least restrictive environment, we might be better off (at least in the case of deaf children) favoring the "most enabling environment"—a subtle distinction, but nevertheless an important one. It is important to note, though, that this does not automatically rule out the inclusion of hearing students in such an educational setting. Such students would be welcome, but only with the clear understanding that such a project rests on the rejection of the dominance of hearing cultural, behavioral, and linguistic norms. Further, an educational program grounded in a cultural model of deafness would actively encourage deaf children to be exposed to a wide variety of deaf adults. In fact, given the importance attached to the use of ASL and familiarity with the DEAF⁀WORLD, such an educational program would generally favor the use of deaf teachers—a radical departure from current educational practice. Finally, control of the educational program would rest, to a significant extent, in the hands of the local deaf community, rather than in the hands of hearing "experts" on deafness and deaf education (see Lane, 1992).

In such an environment, the place and role of MSCs would be severely restricted. At most, such MSCs would be used as pedagogical devices to help students understand the structures of English—but not, importantly, as means of communication themselves. They would, in short, come to be seen not as "languages" in any sense, but rather, as simply a slightly more complex variation on fingerspelling—or, at most, as the visual/manual modality for representing English. This does not mean, of course, that English itself would be minimized in the curriculum; indeed, quite the opposite would be the case. Consideration of how to approach English instruction would be vitally important, as it is in Shannon Allen's invaluable list of preparatory guiding questions for planning and implementing any particular unit in an ASL/English bilingual classroom setting for deaf students:

1. What is the language feature that we want to teach?
2. How will we teach it in both languages in a structured way?
    a. How is the feature used in ASL?
    b. Do the students already know it and use it?
    c. How is the feature used in English?
    d. What do students already know about it?
    e. Can they understand it if they read it?
    f. Do they use it in their writing?
3. How can we contrast the features of the two languages?
4. How can this structure be highlighted within a meaningful curricular content area and in communicatively interactive ways?
5. Finally, how will students demonstrate their learning and what will they be accountable for and when? (2008, p. 148)

We see here the need for education of deaf children to incorporate the active and serious inclusion of both English and ASL, as well as the study of both the hearing world and its culture and the DEAF^WORLD.

INTERNATIONAL USES OF MANUAL SIGN CODES

The development and use of MSCs, although most commonly associated with efforts in the United States, has hardly been unique to that setting. We have already noted the historical use of "methodological signs" in France, as well as the development of the Paget Gorman Sign System in Britain (Paget, 1951; Paget & Gorman, 1976; Sutton-Spence & Woll, 1998, pp. 14–15). More recently, though, and largely in imitation of the developments in the United States, MSCs have been developed and utilized elsewhere in the world, almost always in educational settings. Among the documented MSCs for spoken languages are Signed Afrikaans, Signed Danish (see Hansen, 1987), Signed Dutch (Nederlands Met Gebaren; see De Vriendt & Moierman, 1987; Koenen, Bloem, Janssen, & Van de Ven, 1993, pp. 118–19; Schermer, Fortgens, Harder, & de Noble, 1991, pp. 48–50), Signed Finnish (see Rissanen, 1987), Signed French (see Charlier, Capouillez, & Périer, 1987), Signed German (Lautsprachbegleitende Gebärden, or LBG; see Maye, Ringli, & Boyes-Braem, 1987; Prillwitz 1987), Signed Hebrew (Meir & Sandler, 2008, pp. 203–7), Signed Indonesian (Sistem Isyarat Bahasa Indonesia; Branson, Miller, & Marsaja, 1996), Signed Italian (Italiano Segnato; Caselli, 1987), Signed Mandarin (Ann, Smith, & Chiangsheng Yu, 2007), Signed Polish (System Językowo-Migowy, which is actually based directly on SEE-1), Signed Russian (Yoel, 2007; Zaitseva, 1987), Signed Spanish (Marchesi, 1987; Oviedo, 2004, pp. 15–16), and Signed Urdu (Zeshan, 2000, pp. 5–6), and these are a almost certainly only a small sample of the MSCs that have been created. What unites them is their problematic relationship with the natural sign language of the surrounding deaf community. As Meir and Sandler note about the distinction between Signed Hebrew and Israeli Sign Language,

> While the use of sign language in the schools was warmly welcomed by the Deaf community, it must be said that the signing system that was introduced into the schools was not Israeli Sign Language. Instead, teachers used Signed Hebrew with their pupils. At the time that sign language was first introduced into the schools, [Israeli Sign Language] was nicknamed "the language of the deaf" or "Deafese" in addition to "hand language," and

was considered by many educators, hearing and deaf alike, to be an inferior system consisting of simple gestures and pantomime and therefore not appropriate for education. The system used instead—Signed Hebrew—is a form of communication that makes use of two channels of communications simultaneously: spoken and signed. Its speakers speak Hebrew and accompany their speech with signs from the vocabulary of [Israeli Sign Language]. The result is a hybrid communication system, one that may help hearing and deaf people communicate with each other, but a system that is also cumbersome and contrived, and falls short of providing a natural language in the school. (2008, p. 203)

The problems with MSCs in the U.S. context are by no means unique; precisely the same problems and challenges face them in other settings as well.

CONCLUSION

As we have seen in earlier chapters, language planning as an applied sociolinguistic activity has the potential to function either as a tool for empowerment and liberation or as a means of oppression and domination (see Canagarajah, 2005; Cooper, 1989; Ferguson, 2006; Kaplan & Baldauf, 1997; Reagan, 1991; Shohamy, 2006; Spolsky, 2004; Tollefson, 1991; S. Wright, 2004). The development of artificial MSCs for use in deaf education provides us with a interesting case in which language planning activities can be argued to promote both an explicit agenda (i.e., the teaching of English to deaf children) and an implicit agenda (i.e., the devaluation of natural sign languages and continued hearing hegemony in deaf education; Komesaroff, 2008; Johnson et al., 1989; Ramsey, 1989; Reagan, 1995, 2000, 2002). In addition to the promotion of these two agendas, the development of MSCs for spoken languages can also be argued to support social and ideological positions related to the nature of deafness and the status and role of the deaf community in deaf education (see, e.g., Lane, 1992; Padden & Humphries, 1988, 2005; Sacks, 1989; Schein, 1989; Woodward, 1982).

Central to the ideological and political positions about deafness and deaf people that seem to be embedded in the efforts to create the various MSCs has been a tacit rejection of what has been called the sociocultural paradigm of deafness (see Johnson et al., 1989; Lane, 1992; Paul & Jackson, 1993; Reagan, 1990b, 1995a, 2002c, 2005b [1985]; Woodward, 1982). Rather than conceptualizing deaf people as a distinctive cultural and linguistic community, advocates of the various MSCs in effect adopt the medical, or pathological, view of deafness (though, to be fair, few do so explicitly, and some claim to accept elements of the sociocultural paradigm). Thus deaf children's acquisition of English is not only pragmatically appropriate, but ideologically legitimized; the educator's role is to teach deaf children not a second language but their own language—to give deaf children access to their own culture. The problem with such a view, in essence, is that it can be taken to delegitimize the presence and status of the deaf cultural community, as well as the language of that community.

The construction of artificial MSCs can thus be credibly argued to constitute a series of efforts to impose language on a dominated and oppressed cultural and linguistic minority group. Efforts to encourage the use of various MSCs in deaf education can, on such an account, be seen as attempts to reinforce the subservient role of deaf people even in the matters most important to them and their survival as a community. Further, the creation of artificial sign codes to allow spoken languages to be presented in a visual/manual modality not only suggests assumptions about the superiority of spoken languages, but also demonstrates the continued pattern of hearing hegemony found in the education of deaf children. In short, the development, presence, and use of MSCs in the education of deaf children can be seen as a typical pattern of colonial oppression, in which the dominant group (in this case, the hearing culture) utilizes language and language policy as a tool to maintain its cultural and linguistic dominance, all in the name of doing good for the oppressed, and presumably disadvantaged, group (see Branson & Miller, 1993, 1998, 2002; Gregory, 1992; Johnson et al., 1989; Lane, 1992; Reagan, 1990b, 1995a, 2002c, 2005b [1985]; Woodward, 1982).

Of course, the creators and advocates of MSCs have undoubtedly been sincere in their efforts to help deaf children; it is toward this end that they have undertaken such language planning activities. However, they have failed to take into account the complexity of the issue surrounding the language rights of deaf people (however one defines such rights), and to recognize that both of the communities to which the language planning activities are directed—that is, members of the deaf cultural community *and* the parents of deaf children—must be involved in that language planning activity (see Annamalai, 1986). The problem, in a nutshell, is that "the solution offered by MCEs serves the symbolic needs of the hearing society much better than it does the linguistic and educational needs of deaf children" (Ramsey, 1989, p. 146). This is an important lesson not only for those working with deaf people, but also for those engaged in other types of language planning activities for historically oppressed and dominated populations. Language planning efforts, if they are to be defensible, must entail the active involvement and participation of those for whom they are intended. Only when emerging in such a context can language planning efforts contribute to the creation of more just, humane, and legitimate social and educational policies.

NOTES

1. The "IS" in this quote refers to the use of signed markers for the verb "to be," which would not exist in ASL.

2. *Total Communication* is a widely used term that is problematic because it can be used to refer to a wide array of different, and sometimes conflicting, educational approaches. Originally, the term was "defined by whatever works for a particular child, for example, speech, speechreading, audition, signs, print, and so on, as well as combinations of these items" (Paul, 2001, p. 237). In contemporary practice, however, the phrase has commonly taken on the meaning of Simultaneous Communication (SimCom), or the use of some kind of signing together with speech. Thus, what was initially intended to be a statement of educational philosophy has become a description of a particular kind of educational practice. For a detailed discussion of Total Communication as an educational philosophy, see Denton (1976).

3. The term *phonology* is used in contemporary sign language linguistics to describe the same area of linguistics that it refers to in spoken language studies, i.e., the study of the basic units of the language, in this case handshape, location, palm orientation, movement, and facial expressions.

Chapter 5

International Perspectives on Sign Language, Language Planning, and Language Policy

[The key issue within] the political demands and requests—formulated in unequivocal terms—by the Deaf community (and their interest groups) in the 1990s . . . has been the request for linguistic rights, which one might even call linguistic human *rights. . . . In many . . . countries, because of missing language rights, schooling is still done in a mode that deaf children cannot access, the general level of education is low, and access to higher education is often not provided . . . Participation in public life, the media, politics, and so on is therefore rather difficult. It is not that deaf people cannot participate because they have an auditory problem; rather, it is because the majority are unfamiliar with the language that deaf people use and interpreters are rarely provided. In the field of social and political work, deafness-related issues are generally dealt with in the confined area of "disabilities," which ignores the important linguistic question of the status and rights of sign languages.* (Krausneker, 2000, p. 142)

The assertion of Deaf cultural identity, minority rights and indigenous self-determination in recent decades has created a platform from which Deaf people of ethnic minority family heritage have begun to voice their multilayered experiences of cultural socialization and identity . . . In those places where an indigenous minority is engaged in cultural revitalization . . . a zone of contact exists between the respective empowerment agendas of hearing and deaf members of that minority. These agendas, in which the validation of a minority language plays both instrumental and symbolic roles, may converge in some respects and compete in others . . . (McKee, McKee, Smiler, & Pointon, 2007, p. 31)

These two quotations provide an appropriate opening for this chapter, which deals with the international aspects of language planning and language policy for sign languages. The first quote raises both the question of the status of sign languages and, as a closely related matter, the issue of the rights of users of sign languages, while the second addresses the fascinating situation in which a group of deaf people may also be members of a dominated cultural and linguistic group of hearing—that is, they may be simultaneously members of two oppressed groups, but only partial members of one of them (i.e., the hearing minority group). Both of these excerpts are from discussions of language planning efforts around the world, where, just as with American Sign Language (ASL), we find that all four of the major types of language planning activity occur. In addition, as Krausnecker (2000) observes, a great deal of language planning and language policy activity that takes place internationally with respect to sign languages and their users focuses on issues and matters of language rights. In this chapter, we will begin by examining in broad terms examples of each of the four types of language planning that are taking place for sign languages around the world, and will then move on to a discussion of the role of language rights in these activities. We will examine the case of the development of Gestuno as an example of language planning activity, and, finally, we will look at the recent case of language planning and language policy for South African Sign Language (SASL) in post-apartheid South Africa as an example of a moderately successful language planning effort.

LANGUAGE PLANNING ACTIVITIES FOR SIGN LANGUAGES

As we saw in Chapter 2, there are four major types of language planning activities: status planning, corpus planning, acquisition planning, and attitude planning. In Chapter 3, we also saw that all four of these kinds of language planning activity took place with respect to ASL in the nineteenth century, and these activities continued through the twentieth century up to the present day. The same is true internationally; not only can we find we evidence of language planning and language policy in the nineteenth century, but starting in the twentieth century and continuing in the twenty-first we see a veritable explosion of different kinds of language planning activities for sign languages around the world.

Status Planning

Status planning is without a question the most visible kind of language planning for sign languages. Typical here are efforts of deaf people in various countries to achieve official recognition of their sign language, and an increasing number of countries are granting just such recognition. The nature of official recognition of sign languages varies from one country and setting to another, as does the relative strength of the legislation involved (that is, some kinds of official "recognition" are much stronger in terms of their potential impact than are others). Most commonly, the gaining of official status for a sign language serves three purposes: a symbolic (but nevertheless important) recognition of the legitimate status of the sign language as the vernacular language of the national deaf community; a guarantee of the linguistic rights of sign language users, both in the judicial and legal process and in other social service contexts (e.g., ensuring the provision of sign language interpreters); and finally, a commitment to the use of sign language in the educational domain. Although not all instances of official recognition include all three of these purposes, they are the most typical. It is also important to note that the second and third purposes are often met prior to the official recognition of a sign language—that is, as a result of more disability-oriented thought and legislation—and these purposes remain in place in addition to the symbolic recognition of the sign language as an officially recognized language. Thus, we can see that the recognition of a sign language as an official language, although intended by its advocates to promote the sociocultural view of deaf people and the DEAF^WORLD, may also often involve the continuation of elements drawn from a medical or pathological view of deaf people.

Many of the countries of the European Union (EU) have been at the forefront of the move to officially recognize national sign languages (see Juaristi, Reagan, & Tonkin, 2008; Timmermans, 2005; see Figure 5.1). Finland is often cited as the first country to officially recognize its sign language, and at present, there are a number of countries in the EU that include constitutional recognition of their national sign language, including Austria (BGBI.I Nr. 81/2005), the Czech Republic (*Zákon o znakové* řeči 155/1998 Sb), Finland (Constitution, Section 17), Portugal (Constitution, Article 74, 2[h]), and Slovakia (*Zákon o posunkovej reči* neprčujúcich osob 149/1995 Sb). In most other EU countries, the recognition of the national sign language, while not constitutional, is

Country	Sign Language Legislation
Belgium	Decree on the Right to Sign Language Interpretation (1995), Decree on Basic Education (1988), Decree on the Recognition of Sign Language (2003).
Czech Republic	Sign Language Act (1988), Czech Television Act, Act on Radio and Television Broadcasting.
Denmark	Education Act (1991).
Finland	Law on Administrative Procedure (1982), Criminal Investigations Act (1987), Services and Assistance for the Disabled Act (1987), Support and Assistance for the Disabled Act (1987), Acts on the Positions and Rights of Patients and Clients in the Social and Health Sectors (1992, 2000), Law on the Research Institute for the Languages of Finland (1996), Decree on the Research Institute for the Languages of Finland (1966), Law on Basic Education (1998), Law on Upper Secondary School (1988), Law on Vocational Education (1998), Act on Broadcasting Yleisradio Oy (1998), Law on the Position and Rights of the Social Welfare Client (2000), Nationality Act (2003), Language Act (2003), Adminstrative Procedure Act (2003), and the Administrative Judicial Procedure Act (2003).
France	Law on Equal Rights and Opportunities, Participation and Citizenship of People with Disabilities (2004).
Germany	Code of Social Law (2001), Act on Equal Opportunities for Disabled Persons (2002).
Greece	Law on Special Education (2000).
Hungary	Act I on Radio and Television (1996), ACT XXVI Rights and Equal Opportunities of Disabled People (1998), Act CXXV on Equal Treatment and Promoting Equal Opportunity (2003), Decree No. 28 on Equal Opportunities, Non-Discrimination, and Universal Access for Persons with Disabilities (2003).
Ireland	Education Act (1998).
Italy	Law No. 104 (1992), Law No. 17 (1997, as amended 1999).
Lithuania	Law of Social Integration of the Disabled (1991), Act Concerning the Proclamation of 1996 as the Year of the Disabled (1995).
Norway	Primary Education Act (1997), Education Act (1998, as amended 1999).
Poland	Act on Vocational and Social Rehabilitation and Employment of Disabled Persons (1997).
Portugal	Act No. 31 (1998, as amended 2002), Law No. 380 (1999).
Slovak Republic	Act on Sign Language of the Deaf (1995).
Slovenia	Use of Slovenian Sign Language Act (2002).

(continued on next page)

Figure 5.1. *Status of sign languages in the European Union*

Country	Sign Language Legislation
Spain	Royal Decree 20/60 (1995), Royal Decree 696 (1995), Act on Equal Opportunities, Non-Discrimination and Universal Access for Persons with Disabilities (2003).
Sweden	Comprehensive Schools Act (1997), Education Act (1998, as amended, 1999), Health and Medical Service Act (1982, as amended).
Switzerland	Federal Law on Involuntary Insurance (1959, as amended 2002).
United Kingdom	Police and Criminal Evidence Act (1984), Justice of the Peace Act (1979), National Health Service and Community Care Act (1990), Broadcasting Act (1996), Disability Discrimination Act (1995), Representation of the People Act (2000), Draft Disability Discrimination Bill (2003).

*Based on Timmermans, 2003, 2005.

FIGURE 5.1. *Status of sign languages in the European Union* (continued)

nevertheless largely in place through other kinds of legislation. This is the case in Cyprus, Denmark, Germany, Greece, Hungary, Ireland, Latvia, Lithuania, Norway, Slovakia, Slovenia, Sweden, and the United Kingdom, among others. Perhaps the strongest recognition to be found in the EU at present is the Decreet Houdende de Erkenning van de Vlaamse Gebarentaal [Decree on the Recognition of the Flemish Sign Language] passed on April 26, 2006 (Struk 729 [2005–2006]—Nr. 1), by the Flemish Parliament, which calls for the symbolic recognition of Flemish Sign Language, creates a commission for advising the government in matters related to Flemish Sign Language, and establishes mechanisms for funding for the research and development of Flemish Sign Language. Further, the Decreet explicitly states:

> Cultural recognition entails that the Flemish Government recognises the Flemish Sign Language as the Deaf Community in Flanders. This "recognition" encompasses the following three meanings: (1) the Flemish Government acknowledges the correctness of the fact that the Flemish Sign Language is the language of the Deaf Community in Flanders, (2) the Flemish Government also accepts the language in the judicial domain and treats her accordingly and (3) the Flemish Government expresses her respect for this language.

In addition, the European Parliament passed a "Resolution on Sign Languages" on June 17, 1988 (and reaffirmed it in 1998), which recognizes the legitimacy and importance of sign languages, specifically asks member states to remove "any remaining obstacles to the use of sign language" and calls on the European Commission "to make a proposal . . . concerning official recognition of the sign language used by deaf people in each Member State," as well as to ensure the proper provision of sign language interpreters for the deaf (see Appendix I).

Although the EU has played an important role in status planning for sign languages, it has not been alone in such endeavors. In Europe outside of the EU, legislation exists in Belarus, Iceland, Romania, Russia, and Switzerland. For example, in the Icelandic case, although Icelandic Sign Language does not have constitutional recognition, it does have legal status in educational law. *The National Curriculum Guide for Compulsory School*, published by the Ministry of Education, Science and Culture, notes:

> Deaf children do not learn Icelandic in the same way as children who hear do . . . Sign language is of basic importance for the development of language, personality and thinking of deaf children. For the deaf, sign language is the most important source of knowledge and their route to participation in Icelandic culture and the culture of the deaf. Sign language is of great importance for all school work and for the pupils' life and work. (2004, p. 23)

Elsewhere, constitutional recognition of national sign languages has also been achieved in Ecuador (in the 2008 Constitution), New Zealand (where it became the third official language, along with English and Maori, in 2006), Uganda (in the 1995 revision of the Constitution), and in Venezuela (as of 1999). In a host of other countries, national sign languages are recognized in nonconstitutional ways. According to the website of the World Federation of the Deaf, this is the case in Australia (where Australian Sign Language was recognized as a "community language other than English" in 1987 and again in 1991 [see Dawkins, 1991; LoBianco, 1987]), Canada, China, Columbia, Cuba, Iran, Mauritius, Mozambique, Sri Lanka, Uruguay, and Zimbabwe. Sign languages have also been recognized in some manner in Brazil, for Brazilian Sign Language (commonly known as *Libras*, from *Língua Brasileira de Sinais*), where legislation was passed in April 2002 by the National Congress of Brazil that mandated the use of sign language in education and in the provision of governmental services (Lei Nr. 10.436); in South Africa, where SASL is mentioned in the constitution but not given official status; in Thailand, where Modern Thai Sign Language was recognized as "the national language of deaf people in Thailand" by the Permanent Secretary for Education in a resolution on behalf of the Royal Thai Government in August 1999; and in Turkey, where as of 2005 the Turkish Grand National Assembly mandated the use of Turkish Sign Language in deaf education as well as the provision of sign language interpreting services for deaf people (Disability Law No. 5378).

Typically, recognition of sign languages has taken place as a result of intensive efforts by the local deaf community. However, significant efforts at the international level have also supported such endeavors. In addition to the European Parliament's "Resolution on Sign Languages" (Appendix I), there is also the "Statement on the Recognition of National Sign Languages of the Deaf," passed by the Third European Congress on Sign Language Research in 1989 (see Appendix II), and the World Federation of the Deaf's "Call for the Recognition of Sign Languages" (see Appendix III).

As in the case of the recognition of ASL in various U.S. states, the official recognition of national sign languages around the world remains somewhat problematic, however. Just as the state legislation related to ASL assumes what is ultimately a deficit view of ASL, so too does virtually all national legislation focus simply on the recognition of the *legitimacy* of the sign language, and the *fact* of its use by deaf people. Although this is by no means a small matter, when combined with the concern with legal protections, the provision of interpreters, and educational policy related to the use of the national sign language, we are still nevertheless left with at best a half-hearted recognition of sign language, rather than the full and vibrant recognition for which one might wish. In no case, for instance, is there any explicit discussion of the desirability of (let alone need for) hearing people in the society learning to sign. All of the policies presuppose, at best, that there will be a group of "language brokers" who can interpret between the sign language and the national spoken language. Although discussions and debates about the status of sign languages are generally seen as positive developments, by both deaf people and their advocates and supporters, and although such discussions do have a great deal of positive potential, it is important to note that they are not without risks as well. Perhaps one of the greatest risks is that posed by ASL for other sign languages. Just as English poses a threat to other languages around the world, so too does ASL potentially threaten other sign languages. As Skutnabb-Kangas argues,

> Now when some of the Sign languages slowly start getting some recognition, rights and visibility, others are being replaced (and killed) by . . . recognised, sometimes standardised Sign languages and—surprise surprise—by subtractive spreading of American Sign Language . . . Just like the dominant

> dialects became "languages," and dominant official languages displace and replace other languages nationally, in each country where the Deaf start organising, usually only one Sign language becomes recognised. Hearing people, sometimes Sign language teachers but often teachers with no knowledge of any Sign languages, in most cases dominate these linguicist processes. (2000, p. 227)

Corpus Planning

Corpus planning efforts, as we saw in Chapter 2, "can be defined as those aspects of language planning which are primarily linguistic and hence internal to language. Some of these aspects related to language are: (1) orthographic innovation, including design, harmonisation, change of script, and spelling reform; (2) pronunciation; (3) changes in language structure; (4) vocabulary expansion; (5) simplification of registers; (6) style; and (7) the preparation of language material" (Kaplan & Baldauf, 1997, p. 38). In the case of sign languages, corpus planning efforts fall into five broad categories: lexicography, lexical creation and expansion, textbook production, the creation of manual sign codes, and the development of orthographic systems for representing sign languages. Each of the categories is discussed briefly below.

Lexicography for sign languages has made tremendous strides in recent years (see Armstrong, 2003a, 2003b). The earliest dictionaries of sign languages were generally little more than collections of drawings or pictures of signs, usually in alphabetical word order based on the dominant spoken language. In many instances, these "dictionaries" did not even rely on native informants as sources; rather, they were based on hearing professionals' ideas about how particular words ought to be signed. Although dictionaries of this sort still abound in settings around the world, there are also a number of quite good sign language dictionaries based on very solid linguistic research. Among the best are Brien's *Dictionary of British Sign Language/English* (1992) and Johnston's *AUSLAN Dictionary* (1989) for Australian Sign Language. Other printed dictionaries, of varying quality, exist for Argentine Sign Language (Massone, 1993), Brazilian Sign Language (Oates, 1992), Catalán Sign Language (Perelló & Frigola, 1987), Chilean Sign Language (Pilleux, Cuevas, & Avalos, 1991), Czech Sign Language (Gabrielová, 1988), Danish Sign Language (Petersen & Hansen, 1982), Greek Sign Language (Logiadis, 1985), Irish Sign Language (Foran, 1996),

Italian Sign Language (Angelini, Borgioli, Folchi, & Mastromatteo, 1990; also, Radutzky, 1992), Kenyan Sign Language (Akach, 1991), New Zealand Sign Language (Kennedy, 1997, 2002), Nicaraguan Sign Language (Gómez & Javier, 1997), Portuguese Sign Language (Ferreira & Adalberto, 1991), SASL (Penn, 1992, 1993, 1994a. 1994b, 1994c), Swedish Sign Language (Sveriges Dövas Riksförbund, 1971), and Modern Thai Sign Language (Suwanarat, Reilly, Wrigley, Ratanasint, & Anderson, 1986; Suwanarat, Wrigley, & Anderson, 1990), among others. To be sure, in many instances these "dictionaries" are more accurately described as "word lists" than true dictionaries, but they are evidence of ongoing, and widespread, corpus planning activities for a large and growing number of sign languages.

Online dictionaries of different sign languages, of varying quality, also exist; among the more noteworthy are the following:

- Australian Sign Language
- Austrian Sign Language
- Belgian Sign Language
- Brazilian Sign Language
- British Sign Language
- Croatian Sign Language
- Danish Sign Language
- Finnish Sign Language
- Flemish Sign Language
- French Sign Language
- German Sign Language
- Hungarian Sign Language
- Icelandic Sign Language
- Italian Sign Language
- Japanese Sign Language
- Latvian Sign Language
- New Zealand Sign Language
- Norwegian Sign Language
- Spanish Sign Language
- Sri Lankan Sign Language

That the Internet is being used for such dictionaries is, of course, hardly surprising: it is in many ways an ideal means for storing and providing information about sign languages.[1]

As was the case with ASL, lexical creation efforts for sign languages have generally taken place informally, as new lexical needs arise. The "legitimacy" of new signs depends largely if not entirely on the extent to which they are actually used and accepted by deaf people themselves. Lexical creation and expansion in natural sign languages takes place in five ways: through the compounding of existing signs, through borrowing, through various morphological processes, through the invention of new signs, and through semantic expansion (Reagan, 1990b, pp. 257–58).[2] Compounding occurs when two existing signs are put together to create a new sign with distinctive semantic content. This process, which is quite common in spoken languages (as in English, *breakfast* from *break + fast*), has been documented not only in ASL, but also in British Sign Language, Finnish Sign Language, French Sign Language, Israeli Sign Language, and New Zealand Sign Language, and almost certainly exists in most natural sign languages. Examples in ASL include THINK^MARRY (believe), GIRL^SAME (sister), MOTHER^FATHER (parents), and so on. In Israeli Sign Language, compounding is a very productive process, and we find TEA^FEVER (sick), HEAD^LIE^DOWN (faint), KNOWN^EVERYONE (famous), HEART^OFFER (volunteer), STAND^STRONG (sturdy), EXCURSION^WANDER (field trip), RESPECT^MUTUALITY (tolerance), and a host of others (see Meir & Sandler, 2008, pp. 47–48). In British Sign Language, ICELAND is formed by combining ICE and LAND (i.e., ICE^LAND), just as GREENLAND is formed by combining GREEN and LAND (i.e., GREEN^LAND) (Sutton-Spence & Woll, 1998, p. 221). In Finnish Sign Language, the sign MUSTELMA (bruise) is formed by combining the sign MUSTA (black) with the sign showing the area of the bruise (Vivolin-Karén & Alanne, 2003, p. 42). Finally, in New Zealand Sign Language, we find DOCTOR^ANIMAL (veterinarian) and CAR^BUILDING (garage; Collins-Ahlgren, 1990, p. 295).

Natural sign languages meet new lexical needs by borrowing from other languages, both spoken and sign (see Battison, 1978; Brentari, 2001). Sign languages commonly borrow terminology from spoken languages, generally through fingerspelled loan signs (fingerspelled terms that undergo processes of structural and formational change and become standard signs; this process is also called *lexicalized fingerspelling*). ASL examples of such fingerspelled loan signs include #OR, #TOY, #DOG, #EARLY, and #TOAST.[3] British Sign Language and Australian Sign Language share a number of such lexical items, including both common words such as #BUS, #SON, #LAW, #CLUB, and #JOB, as well as function words such as #HOW, #BUT, #ABOUT, and #FOR (Johnston & Schembri, 2007, p. 182). In both British and Australian Sign Language, lexicalized fingerspelling can involve one letter that is repeated (A-A for "alcohol," D-D for "daughter," K-K for "kitchen," etc.), two letters (A-C for "air conditioning," D-R for "doctor," etc.), and three or four letters (E-M-G for "emergency," S-E-P-T for "September," and so on) (see Johnston & Schembri, 2007, pp. 179–80; Sutton-Spence, 1998, pp. 225–29). In New Zealand Sign Language, a similar process, in which some medial letters are eliminated, also takes place, as in T-S (toys), B-B (club), J-B (job), etc. (Collins-Ahlgren, 1990, p. 303). In Finnish Sign Language, the sign WC (toilet) is fingerspelled, and the sign TAKSI (taxi) is formed by using the T and X letters of the old two-handed alphabet that is no longer used (Vivolin-Karén & Alanne, 2003, p. 44). Some sign languages, including ASL, British Sign Language, Israeli Sign Language, and New Zealand Sign Language also utilize initialized signs (that is, signs that have embedded in them the first letter of the word they represent). Initialized signs allow the creation of groups of related signs based on a single common sign: for instance, in ASL, the signs FAMILY, GROUP, ASSOCIATION, and TEAM are distinguished only by the letter used in the handshape formation (see Figure 5.2). Similarly, in Israeli Sign Language, the basic sign BETTER can be initialized to create PREFERABLE (Meir & Sandler, 2008, p. 52).

Sign languages also increasingly borrow signs from other sign languages; most often, ASL is the source sign language because of its relatively large and technically well-developed lexicon, although ASL also borrows from other sign languages (this has been especially true in recent years with respect to the names of countries and other foreign place names, as in AUSTRALIA, CHINA, GERMANY, ITALY, JAPAN, KOREA, PAKISTAN, SINGAPORE, and so on). British Sign Language has borrowed extensively from a number of different sign languages. There are currently two signs for LANGUAGE in British Sign Language, one borrowed from Swedish Sign Language and the other from ASL; ATTITUDE is a sign borrowed from Danish Sign Language (Sutton-Spence & Woll 1998, p. 220). Interestingly, in the case of Australian Sign Language, despite its historical links with British Sign Language, borrowed signs have come overwhelmingly from ASL (Johnston & Schembri, 2007, p. 185). As Johnston and Schembri explain,

> The amount of borrowing from modern BSL [British Sign Language], however, remains small compared with the number of ASL loan signs. Loan signs from ASL appear to have come from a number of sources. During the last few decades, a small number of influential members of the Australian

FIGURE 5.2. *ASL signs for* FAMILY, GROUP, ASSOCIATION, *and* TEAM. *Reproduced from Clayton Valli, ed.,* The Gallaudet Dictionary of American Sign Language *(Washington, DC: Gallaudet University Press, 2005), p. 66.*

> deaf community were or are themselves of American origin, while others are Australian graduates of Gallaudet University or the National Technical Institute for the Deaf in Rochester, New York. Many other Australian deaf people have worked or lived for periods in the USA or Canada. Partly for these reasons, many ASL signs (including signs originally from artificial sign systems used in American deaf education) have entered Auslan [Australian Sign Language], such as COLLEGE, PHILOSOPHY, THEORY, MARKETING and INTERVIEW. This is particularly true of signs in the area of language teaching, such as CURRICULUM, SUBJECT, TEST, COURSE and EVALUATE. (2007, pp. 185–86)

Two additional morphological processes are sometimes used to create new signs. The first results in what can be termed a "derivational sign"; here, for example, one begins with a verb and by changing the nature of the movement, a corresponding noun is created. Thus, the ASL verb BLOW^DRY^HAIR, when made with a short, repeated action, becomes the noun for BLOW^DRYER. The second morphological process that is used is to combine classifier morphemes, as in using the classifier for "a large flat object" together with the classifier for "a two-legged person" to form the sign HANG^GLIDING. In Finnish Sign Language, the sign KÄNNYKKÄ (cell phone) is formed in this manner (Vivolin-Karén & Alanne, 2003, p. 41). Technical signs are often created to meet user needs, especially in educational settings. Such signs are especially common in such areas as computer science, medicine, engineering, and so on. In the ASL case, the National Technical Institute for the Deaf (NTID) and Gallaudet University have both been important contributors to the creation of new lexical items. In British Sign Language, examples of new signs that have been created include FAX, LASER, INJECTION, and AIDS (see Sutton-Spence & Woll, 1999, p. 32). Finally, semantic expansion occurs when an existing sign takes on new or additional meanings. In ASL, for example, the sign FULL has also come to mean "fed up," while in British Sign Language the sign ENOUGH performs the same function. Also in British Sign Language, the sign for PULL^THINGS^OFF^A^WALL has undergone semantic expansion, and is now used to entail any sort of decorating or redecorating. One area in which semantic expansion has taken place in recent years in both spoken and sign languages is in the area of new technologies; in Australian Sign Language, for example, one uses the signs WINDOW, CLOSE, OPEN, and SAVE in exactly the same way that English employs these words to express computer-related concepts (Johnston & Schembri, 2007, p. 125).

Textbook production has been an important arena of corpus planning for sign languages. The first sign language textbooks consisted of little more than vocabulary lists, with little (if any) information about the syntax and structure of natural sign language. In fact, it is clear that sign language teaching has been focused primarily on teaching hearing students to communicate in some sort of contact sign language with the deaf, and so in a very real sense, students were not studying a natural sign language at all. As we saw in Chapter 3, recent efforts in the United States to develop textbooks, curricula, and qualified teachers for ASL have made important strides in correcting this, and there are now a number of quite good textbooks that are, in reality as well as in name, textbooks of ASL. In other settings, textbook development has generally not been as successful, for a variety of reasons. For most sign languages, textbooks, where they exist at all, remain in the vocabulary list phase. There are some exceptions to this, of course; for instance, *British Sign Language for Dummies* (City Lit Centre for the Deaf, 2008) is now available for British Sign Language, and is a very good text. There is also a plethora of online courses for various sign languages, although these tend to have the same problems as published materials.

The creation and use of manual sign codes for spoken language is the fourth type of corpus planning involving sign languages. Although the development of MSCs is an international phenomenon, the emergence and educational implementation of MSCs has taken place primarily in the United States. Both the U.S. and international experience with the creation of MSCs were discussed in detail earlier in Chapter 4, so we need not discuss them further here.

An especially problematic kind of corpus planning for sign languages that has emerged in a number of different settings in which there are multiple indigenous sign languages is the attempt to create a unified (and often "purified) sign language for use in deaf education and by deaf people. An excellent example of such an undertaking is currently taking place in the Arab world. In various parts of the Arabic-speaking world, deaf people and deaf communities use a number of different indigenous sign languages. Although some of these are related, many are not. The Arab Federation of Organizations Working with the Deaf (AFOOD) has been at the forefront of a multiyear process to create a prescriptive dictionary for "Arab Sign Language" (see World Federation of the Deaf, 2009). Although AFOOD has denied that its goal is the creation of a single, unified Arabic Sign Language, governmental representatives from a number of Arab governments, as well as the chief expert on the dictionary and sign language interpretation for Al Jazeera (the satellite television channel), have consistently and emphatically stressed that the goal is indeed "a unified Arabic Sign Language that parallels spoken Arabic" (quoted in World Federation of the Deaf, 2009)—and thus more of a manual sign code than a full and complete sign language. This effort, and others like it, although well intentioned, are based on profound misunderstandings of the nature of language in general and the nature of sign language in particular. They also reflect an extremely audiocentric worldview, and a lack of understanding of the DEAF⁀WORLD:

> The WFD is very concerned about such activities because they reflect persistent lack of understanding of local/national Sign Languages. Such activities suggest directly and indirectly that local/national sign languages are backwards, complicated, weak and lacking. . . . The WFD asserts that such beliefs impair and block deaf people's path to opportunities. Not their Sign Languages, but poor teacher training and the lack of interpreter certification in local/national Sign Languages have kept deaf Arabs marginalized. . . . In place of such unification activities, the WFD strongly believes that resources are better spent on preserving and promoting local/national sign languages through documentation and linguistic, historical, and cultural study. (World Federation of the Deaf, 2009)

Indeed, efforts to unify different sign languages involve the violation of the linguistic rights of deaf people. As the WFD Board states, "any forcible purification or unification of Sign Languages, conducted by governments, professionals working with Deaf people, and organizations for or of the Deaf, is a violation of the UN and UNESCO treaties, declarations and other policies, including the recent UN Convention on the Rights of Persons with Disabilities" (World Federation of the Deaf, 2007).

The final sort of corpus planning involving sign languages consists of the efforts to development orthographic systems for representing such languages in written form. These "sign writing systems" have become increasingly common and viable in recent years as a consequence of developments in computer science. Such efforts, although interesting (see Hutchins, Poizner, McIntire, & Newkirk, 1990; Papaspyrou & Zienert, 1990; Prillwitz & Zienert, 1990), have not thus far gained much support from the signing community, which universally uses the surrounding hearing community's written language as its own. Nevertheless, these efforts are useful in the linguistic descriptions of sign languages and may have a great deal of potential for both dictionaries and sign language textbooks. The three most common methods currently in use for representing sign language in a written form are the Stokoe System, the Hamburg Notation System, and SignWriting. The Stokoe System is that created by William Stokoe, although it has been significantly modified by others in the years since the publication of *Sign Language Structure*. In its original form, the Stokoe System consisted of 55 symbols, divided into three groups to allow for the representation of location, handshape, and movement. Later, palm orientation was added. The Hamburg Notation System (HamNoSys) was designed for research purposes at the University of Hamburg in the later 1980s, and includes about 200 symbols that can be used to represent any sign language (see Prillwitz & Zienert, 1990). Finally, SignWriting was developed by Valerie Sutton, and computer programs are available for using SignWriter (the original SignWriter program has now been replaced with SignPuddle and SignBank). Although in some ways the most "user friendly" system, SignWriter is based on body movement and facial expression rather than the actual linguistic features of sign language.

Acquisition Planning

Acquisition planning in the case of sign languages refers to two distinct matters: first, the education of deaf children in settings in which they will acquire the sign language of the surrounding deaf community, and second, the study of the sign language by hearing people. Understandably, the focus in deaf communities around the world has been on achieving the former goal. The right of the deaf child to an education in which sign language is employed is a common concern, and one that is increasingly (although by no means universally) recognized around the world. In fact, recent years have witnessed growing calls in many countries for bilingual/bicultural education programs for deaf children along the lines of those advocated for in the United States (see Ahlgren, 1990; Bergmann, 1994; Bouvet, 1990; Hansen, 1987, 1990; Mas, 1994; Penn & Reagan, 1991, 1995, 2001; Quintela, Ramirez, Robertson, & Pérez, 1997; Skutnabb-Kangas, 2008). Such calls, ultimately, have to do with the reality of the "deaf experience." As Danielle Bouvet comments,

> All deaf children are . . . destined to become bilingual and bicultural. They become *bicultural* in that they belong to two different communities—deaf and hearing—each of which has its own culture, that is, its own way of seeing things and its own values to live by. While not making value judgments about either culture, we must nonetheless recognize their existence as two distinct sociological realities. One of the most striking cultural differences between the two communities is their respective modes of linguistic communication. For deaf children being bicultural means being *bilingual*. They must be able to wield different languages depending on the situation they find themselves in. (1990, pp. 133–34)

In spite of this, as Markku Jokinen observes, "Only a very small fraction of Deaf children today have access to bilingual deaf education where their national sign language is both the language of teaching and learning and a mother tongue subject in the curriculum (the Nordic countries, parts of USA, some countries in South America and very few others)" (2000, p. 2007).

Opportunities for hearing people to learn to sign are also important, of course, but they are necessarily secondary in nature to the need to ensure appropriate educational environments for deaf children. As for hearing people learning to sign, we have already mentioned the development of textbooks and other teaching materials in many settings. In addition, there is always the possibility of introducing sign language into the regular school curriculum. Although this would have a number of valuable advantages, it should not lead us to miss the larger point here:

> Before envisioning the possible benefits of Sign Language to hearing children, however, it is vital to recognize the necessity of this language in the education of *deaf* children. Deaf children must no longer be left without verbal communication during the first crucial years of their lives . . . The moment deafness is diagnosed, parents must be informed that a visual language *does* exist. This would change their whole way of receiving their child. They would perceive their child as an *infant*—a little human being who *will* speak, provided that he or she is spoken to. (1990, p. 236)

Perhaps the most important example of acquisition planning for sign languages, though, is in the preparation of sign language interpreters—"language brokers" who can mediate between the deaf community and the hearing world. The training of sign language interpreters has played an important role in the empowerment of deaf people in many societies.

Attitude Planning

Attitude planning, the last of the four major types of language planning activity, has also played an important role with respect to sign languages. In essence, deaf communities around the world have been, and continue to be, engaged in active efforts to reject and counter misinformation both about sign languages in general and about specific national sign languages. Such efforts parallel those of the American deaf community and basically involve the same beliefs about signing and sign language: that sign language is not a "real" language, that sign language lacks a real grammar, that signing is nothing more than gesturing and fingerspelling, that there is a single universal sign language that is shared by all deaf people, that sign language interferes with a deaf child's learning to speak and lipread, and so on. All of these beliefs are false, but this does not mean that they are not widely accepted. In some countries, the situation is made more complex by the acceptance of ASL as a "real" language but the rejection of any local sign language as "real." Nor, it should be pointed out, is such language planning focused solely on hearing people; all too often, deaf people themselves also have hostile attitudes about sign language and hold misinformed beliefs (see Hill, forthcoming; Kannapell, 1985).

We see, then, that all four of the major types of language planning activity are taking place in various international settings. Beyond this, it is important to note that the four types of activity, in the sign language context as in the context of spoken language, clearly overlap and interact in a number of ways.

SIGN LANGUAGES AND LANGUAGE RIGHTS

In Chapter 2, we explored the broad issue of language rights in general terms, and then in Chapter 3 discussed some of the implications of the concept of language rights for users of ASL in the United States. We turn now to an examination of the place of language rights for deaf individuals and groups internationally, which has been and remains an important facet of language planning and language policy for sign languages in many parts of the world. As in other cases—both for spoken languages and ASL—what we will find is that language rights are far more often violated than respected, and further, that in addressing language rights, we are largely concerned with studying *calls* for language rights rather than the *reality* of language rights (see Haualand & Allen, 2009; Jokinen, 2000; Muzsnai, 1999; Siegel, 2008; Skutnabb-Kangas, 1994, 2000, 2008).

The human rights of deaf people are violated in many ways in different countries around the world. Indeed, in a 2009 survey conducted by the World Federation of the Deaf in conjunction with the Danish Deaf Association, the Finnish Association of the Deaf, the Norwegian Association of the Deaf, and the Swedish National Association of the Deaf, the findings with respect to the human rights of deaf people in the ninety-three countries surveyed indicates a very depressing overall situation. In some countries, deaf people cannot vote (for instance, in Egypt), while in others (one third of those responding, in fact) they are not allowed to drive. Sometimes this is the result of explicit legislation, but more often it is an outcome of traditional practice and assumptions about deaf people (see Haualand & Allen, 2009, p. 21). In at least eight of the countries surveyed, deaf people are forbidden to adopt children (Haualand & Allen, 2009, p. 22).

If there is considerable variation in the extent to which the human rights of deaf people are honored and respected or rejected in different countries, then the situation with respect to *linguistic* human rights is even more complex:

> Most of the literature on Deaf children focuses on their education, perhaps the most controversial and most frequently discussed area through the centuries. But in spite of Deaf people's long struggle for equal human rights, particularly educational language rights, there is still little research on how most Deaf children are the victims of linguistic genocide every day, every moment, all over the world. Having a sign language accepted as a mother tongue already from birth is the most important human right for Deaf children because sign language is the only language they can acquire spontaneously and naturally without teaching, provided they have exposure to it. Still it is denied to them all over the world. (Jokinen, 2000, p. 203)

The phrase "linguistic genocide" may strike some readers as extreme, but it is a phrase that widely appears in the literature that deals with the language rights of the deaf. As Tove Skutnabb-Kangas suggests,

> Most school systems in Europe and Europeanized countries commit *linguistic genocide* vis-à-vis most immigrated and refugee minority children, and to some extent also towards indigenous and even national minority children. The Deaf Community should be considered a national linguistic minority in every country in the world. While European states have started ratifying the new *European Charter of Regional or Minority Languages* (accepted 22 June 1992), not one of them has so far . . . designated the Deaf Community as a national minority that the Charter should apply to. I leave it up to you to decide, to what extent what happens to deaf children and adults in different countries can be defined as linguistic genocide. I would also like to add, that linguistic genocide, or *linguicide* is the extreme form of a language-based form of racism, *linguicism*. (1994, pp. 151–52)

The failure to recognize or allow the use of sign languages in education and other settings is the major challenge about which this passage seems to be concerned, but it is not the only one. The increasingly common use of cochlear implants, especially when implemented in educational settings in the deliberate absence of sign language (as they most typically are), is an additional concern (see Skutnabb-Kangas, 2008, p. 77).

Beyond these concerns, though, there is an additional, and quite puzzling, paradox involving the language rights of deaf people. In essence, this paradox is that even if deaf people are recognized as a distinct cultural and linguistic minority group in a country, and even if sign language is given official status and the rights of sign language users are protected, this will almost inevitably apply to a *single* sign language, in spite of the fact that in many settings there are actually multiple sign languages in use. As Tove Skutnabb-Kangas notes,

> If/when Sign language users, especially Deaf users, and their languages, start gaining Linguistic Human rights . . . for instance, the right to use a Sign language in some official contexts, these rights have so far always been given to one Sign language in each state. In most states, Deaf people have, because of their relative isolation from each other, developed many Sign languages and dialects. When Deaf people have started organizing, they have often been told that they have to standardize one Sign language that everybody understands (even if some dialectal variation may be allowed). The literature talks about The American Sign language, The Swedish Sign language, The Australian Sign language, The Japanese Sign language, even if I am sure there are or at least have been many Sign languages in each of those countries. . . . That means that all the other Sign languages in the country will often disappear when some rights are achieved. (2008, pp. 76–77)

This passage is reminiscent of the quotation at the beginning of this chapter that addresses the issue of double minority identity for individuals who are both deaf and members of oppressed linguistic or cultural communities. In a sense, this dilemma brings us full-circle, from the issue of language rights to the issue of language endangerment, since it means that the vast majority of sign languages in the world are likely to disappear just as the vast majority of spoken languages will disappear, as we saw in Chapter 2. When combined with other factors that impact the future of the deaf community, we are presented with a complex but not particularly positive outcome, as Graham Turner writes in an article entitled "Why Protect Heritage Sign Languages?":

> The social and hence linguistic contexts of signing Deaf communities differ markedly around the world . . . Nevertheless, between these three sets of arguments—that sign languages may be subject to powerful forces generating linguistic "shifts" away from heritage forms; that access to an exclusively oral education may prevent signing communities from taking shape by denying children access to the language *ab initio;* and that the linguistic vitality of signing communities may be radically undermined by medical and demographic factors—it is hard, if not impossible, to imagine a country anywhere that cannot expect its signing Deaf community to be overshadowed by one or more forms of linguistic threat. (2006, p. 410)

Such concerns, of course, in no way diminish the strong and compelling case that has been offered for the linguistic rights of the deaf; on the contrary, they underscore the complexity of the issue. Such rights do not depend on the existence of a unified sign language, nor do they depend on the relative size of the deaf population in a particular society. They do have implications, though, for education, as well as for the ability of the deaf community to organize itself and to play a central role in decision-making about matters that directly affect deaf people.

THE ODD CASE OF GESTUNO

Gestuno was intended to be an international auxiliary language for sign language users at international conferences and other kinds of events. In fact, prior to the creation of Gestuno in the 1950s, 1960s, and 1970s, an informal international sign language, known as International Sign, existed (see Supalla & Webb, 1995, pp. 334–35). The development of Gestuno was, however, a specific case of corpus planning that needs to be discussed here.

The need for such an international auxiliary sign language was raised initially at the first World Deaf Congress in 1951, and a commission (the Unification of Signs Commission) was created. The Commission ultimately published three books, the first two in 1959 and 1965. The third, published in 1975, contained a list of almost 1,500 signs (British Deaf Association, 1975). This third book, entitled *Gestuno: International Sign Language of the Deaf*, was intended to replace the earlier volumes, and was to some extent seen as the final product of the Commission. As Francesco Rubino, the Commission's president, notes in the book's preface,

> This book was originally planned as the third of a series by the World Federation of the Deaf toward unification of sign languages used by deaf people. However, as it contains over 800 new signs, together with the 614 already printed in the previous two books, (total 1,470), it is in effect the new revised book of international signs adopted by the World Federation of the Deaf and replaces the first two books. . . . It should be noted that some signs printed in the original books have been changed. This was done during compilation in order to avoid possible confusion between one sign and another and not because they were incorrect or mistaken.

The signs of Gestuno were largely derived from the lexicons of major Western sign languages, and were, for the most part, highly iconic in nature. In addition, although the grammar of Gestuno, and indeed of International Sign in general, seems to be fairly complex, the lexicon is relatively small in nature (see Rosenstock, 2004; Supalla & Webb, 1995). Interestingly, when Gestuno was first used at the World Federation of the Deaf Congress in Bulgaria in 1976, many of the deaf participants found it unintelligible (Rosenstock, 2004), and this continues to be a problem. Today, one rarely hears about Gestuno; rather, the older label International Sign is used, and it appears that in international settings, when International Sign is used, relatively few recognizable Gestuno signs are employed. The World Federation of the Deaf still carries out its deliberations in International Sign, and its written work in English, but has found it necessary to offer a "1-day, preassembly orientation and training session that includes a crash course on International Signs used for meetings. These signs include concepts such as government, approve and not approve, funds, people, terms of time, various action verbs, parliamentary procedures, human rights, and labels for officers and participants" (Rosen, 2009, p. 381). Although at both the 2003 and 2007 General Assemblies of the World Federation of the Deaf there were discussions about changing the label "International Sign" to "International Sign Language," such efforts have thus far been unsuccessful.

A CASE STUDY OF LANGUAGE PLANNING FOR SIGN LANGUAGE: POST-APARTHEID SOUTH AFRICA

Language planning and language policy have a long and complex history in South Africa, and the end of the apartheid regime and establishment of a democratic government radically changed both the discourse and practice of language planning in the country. Not quite a decade after the establishment of democracy, Heugh commented:

> Language-policy developments in South Africa have undergone dramatic changes over the last decade. Explicit statements of policy have shifted away from the segregationist mould of the previous apartheid government with the widely divergent roles and functions it ascribed to the various languages of the country. There is now a move toward principles that espouse the equal promotion of respect for, and use of, other languages. The extraordinary circumstances surrounding the political negotiations that led to a sharing of power after the country's first democratic elections of 1994 created the opportunity for "proposals from below" (from civil society), to take root

> in a manner which has never before been possible in South Africa. Many of the proposals for new language policy have been accepted on an official level and an encouraging, optimistic environment seemed, in the early years of the new government of national unity, to promise a vibrant future for language development and multilingualism. (2002, p. 449)

Although there is an extensive and growing literature that addresses issues related to most aspects of language-in-education policy in contemporary South Africa, one area in which the literature remains fairly sparse has been that of the implications of current government policy for SASL. My goal here is to present an overview of the complex issues presented by the case of SASL as an example of language planning activity for sign language, especially with respect to language-in-education policy. I believe that the South African case has a great deal to teach us about such matters more generally.

In the years following the end of apartheid, SASL has to some extent been recognized constitutionally and legally in ways that would appear to indicate cognizance of the language rights of deaf people in South Africa, although it is also important to note that such rights are all too often not yet manifested in practice (see Reagan, 2007; Reagan, Penn, & Ogilvy, 2006, pp. 187–208). The *Constitution of the Republic of South Africa* (Republic of South Africa, 1996a) identifies a total of eleven official languages: Afrikaans, English, isiNdebele, Sepedi, Sesotho, Setswana, SiSwati, Tshivenda, Xitsonga, isiXhosa, and isiZulu. Although SASL is not among the eleven official languages, it is nevertheless directly mentioned in the Constitution. In Chapter 1 (6) 5, the Constitution created the Pan-South African Language Board (PANSALB), which is empowered to "promote, and create conditions for, the development and use of (i) all official languages; (ii) the Khoi, Nama and San languages; and (iii) sign language" (see also the "Pan-South African Language Board Act" [Republic of South Africa, 1995]). Under the auspices of PANSALB, a specific National Language Board has been created for each of the official languages as well as for the Khoe and San languages (Pan-South African Language Board, 2005, p. 15). In 2001, a National Language Board was created for SASL as well, with two specific objectives: (1) initiating and implementing strategic projects aimed at creating awareness, identifying needs, and promoting SASL, and (2) identifying and funding projects aimed at developing SASL (Pan-South African Language Board, 2005, p. 15). The *National Language Policy Framework*, issued by the Department of Arts and Culture (Republic of South Africa, 2002), similarly includes mention of

SASL. In the educational sphere, the *South African Schools Act* (Republic of South Africa, 1996b) also includes specific mention of SASL in the section devoted to language policy in government schools. The Constitution, in Chapter 2 (the "Bill of Rights") guarantees that, "Everyone has the right to receive education in the official language or languages of their choice in public educational institutions where that education is reasonably practicable" (29[2]). The *South African Schools Act* takes this right further, noting that "a recognised Sign Language has the status of an official language for purposes of learning at a public school" (Chapter 2, 6[4]). This point is further elucidated and reinforced in the Department of Education's *Language in Education Policy* (Republic of South Africa, 1997), which is remarkably sympathetic to issues of the deaf community in South Africa and to SASL. It begins with a "Preamble," which is intended to set the stage for the national approach to educational language policy:

> This Language-in-Education Policy Document should be seen as part of a continuous process by which policy for language in education is being developed as part of a national language plan encompassing all sectors of society, *including the deaf community*. . . . In terms of the new Constitution of the Republic of South Africa, the government . . . recognises that our cultural diversity is a valuable national asset and hence is tasked . . . to promote multilingualism, the development of the official languages, and respect for all languages used in the country, *including South African Sign Language* . . . (emphasis added)

In other words, at least at a rhetorical level, the rights of the deaf community, especially with respect to SASL, are both constitutionally and legally protected in the South African context. Although not an official language of the Republic, SASL would appear to have virtually the same rights as an official language.

NOTES

1. Rather than provide specific URL sites in the text, which may well have changed by the time of the publication of this book, I am simply identifying sign languages for which on-line dictionaries exist at the time of writing. These and others should be easily able to be found and accessed by any search engine.

2. Vivolin-Karén and Alanne (2003, pp. 41–44) offer a far more complex treatment of lexical creation in sign language. Using the case of Finnish Sign Language, they argue that a total of eleven different processes can be employed to create

new signs: (1) polysynthetic signs using classifier formations; (2) conversion of an existing sign to add a new meaning; (3) derivation from an existing sign; (4) incorporation, which refers to the creation of compound signs; (5) borrowing, either from other sign languages (see also Brentari, 2001) or from spoken language, typically Finnish; (6) abbreviation; (7) terming, which refers to borrowing a sign from the standard language that in turn becomes a professional term; (8) enlarging the meaning of an existing sign; (9) paraphrasing an explanation into a sign; (10) fingerspelling; and (11) newly created signs. I believe that all of these different processes are in fact included in the far simpler model provided in my text.

3. The # indicates that the sign is a fingerspelled loan sign.

Chapter 6

Conclusion:

The DEAF^WORLD, Language, and Power

> *Language planning in toto and each of its subparts individually are much too complex and much too dictated by history to be independently or jointed predicted with any comforting degree of accuracy. The total process neither necessarily starts with nor ends with any particular subpart, handy metaphors to the contrary notwithstanding. Where it starts, when it starts, and in which way it develops is determined by the context—political, economic, cultural—in which it develops . . . Cultures differ widely throughout the world. They stress different values, priorities and goals vis-à-vis language . . . as well as everyday life. If there is any parsimony to understanding language planning, it exists within the certainty that it corresponds in many crucial ways to the state of the culture that elicits and nurtures it.* (Fishman, 2006a, p. 17)

> *[My] purpose . . . is to explore the relationship between language policy and language education with a particular emphasis on power and inequality. A key aim . . . is to link ideology and the analysis of power relations to language policy in education.* (Tollefson, 1995, p. 1)

The complexity of language planning referred to by Joshua Fishman is not true only in the case of spoken languages; where sign languages are concerned, the complexity is far greater. Sign languages are not merely minority languages, although they certainly *are* minority languages. Nor are deaf communities merely subcultures surrounded by dominant cultures, although they certainly are distinctive cultural communities. Both sign languages and deaf communities are unique in that they are based in part on physiological difference that inevitably makes deaf people different from hearing people. Assimilation into the dominant society and into that society's spoken language is rarely a viable or reasonable option for deaf people, and it is this difference that makes sign language and the deaf culture unlike other minority linguistic and cultural groups. I do not want to disparage the very real linguistic and cultural rights of all minority groups, but I maintain that the case of deaf people is quite special and needs to be recognized and addressed as such. Such sentiment could all too easily lead to precisely the kind of paternalism that has long dominated approaches to deaf education and other matters affecting deaf people, which is why I include the epigraph from James Tollefson, as a warning about the relationship of language and inequality.

Deaf people are not only a special case, but they are a case in which those most concerned—deaf people themselves—have historically been largely ignored in policy decisions, and this includes decisions about sign language. A great deal of language planning activity related to sign languages remains largely controlled by and in the hands of hearing people, most often hearing educators of deaf children. The concern, then, with the potential for "hearing hegemony" in such efforts is both real and substantial, and needs to be taken into account (see Eichmann, 2009; Turner, 2009). Insofar as language planning activities and language policies for sign languages are to have any credibility with the deaf community toward which they are targeted, that community must have ownership of the activities and policies. This means that deaf people themselves must be key players in the development of both language planning efforts and language policies that impact them. This, in turn, brings us to the different orientations in language policies related to sign languages around the world. There can be no doubt that much, perhaps even most, of the language policy efforts addressing sign languages and their users remain firmly grounded in the "language-as-a-problem" orientation, and only a smaller number of examples rely on the "language-as-a-right" orientation. Further, in many of the cases where there is a "language-as-a-right" orientation with respect to the rights of users of sign languages, there is also a concomitant tendency for the same kind of paternalism that exists with respect to the "language-as-a-problem" orientation. The "language-as-a-resource" orientation is virtually absent from the discourse on language planning and language policy for sign languages altogether, perhaps in large part because of the hegemony of hearing people in controlling so many aspects of deaf education and other services for deaf people. The recognition that sign language might well have unique and useful advantages for learners (both deaf and hearing) seems to be consistently overlooked or ignored.

Furthermore, deaf people pose a very interesting challenge with respect to how human rights in general, and language rights in particular, are conceived. In Chapter 2, I mentioned that such rights can be thought of either as individual rights (as they typically are), or sometimes, perhaps, as group rights. In the case of language in general, there is a tension here because language is fundamentally social in nature. In the case of deaf people, this tension is even greater, as we try to determine who speaks, first, for the DEAF^WORLD, and second, for the deaf child. The former question is relatively easy: the deaf community itself, through its formal and informal institutions, can more than adequately articulate its concerns and desires, and these concerns and desires need to be listened to and taken seriously. For the deaf child, however, the picture is somewhat more complex, making the general claim that minority-language parents should make the decisions regarding their children's education a problematic one. Adrian Blackledge, for example, argues that

> rather than producing relations of power in which minority groups are marginalised and silenced, schools can create structures which enable minority-language parents to decide what is best for their children's schooling and to take an active part in developing policy and practice accordingly. (2000, p. 145)

The deaf child's parents are the ultimate decision makers for the child, of course, but it is reasonable to expect that, in the case of hearing parents, they have been provided with sufficient information, including exposure to both the DEAF^WORLD and deaf adults, to make an informed decision for their child. Unfortunately, in many instances this is not the case, and such decisions are guided entirely by hearing professionals, whose knowledge of the DEAF^WORLD may be based on misinformation, misunderstanding, or outright error. In the case of deaf children, there are actually multiple constituent communities that should have a say in such policy and practice matters: members of the DEAF^WORLD, deaf parents of deaf children, hearing parents of deaf children, and educators of deaf children (both hearing and deaf educators). Finally, as deaf children become older and more aware of their situation, they should become the primary, if not exclusive, decision makers with respect to what kind of education, and what sort of language medium, are most appropriate and meaningful for them.

The issue at heart here is power, and how power—and differences in power—impact both language attitudes and language policy. Skutnabb-Kangas argues:

> For most . . . Deaf people worldwide, political, economic and social rights are extremely important. They are weak or lacking today. Their achievement often seems to be the first priority. It might seem for some that linguistic human rights [LHRs] and other cultural rights come only AFTER basic material needs have been satisfied, at least to some extent. The two types of rights are often, erroneously, seen as exclusive. . . . In fact, LHRs are a necessary prerequisite for both demanding and enjoying all the other rights. Understanding and analyzing the connections between language, culture, identity, social and political structures and philosophy of life, presupposes language—one's own language, as well as other languages. (2008, p. 80)

In short, in order to empower deaf people it is essential that they control the status and destiny of their own languages. This has, of course, significant implications for education, not the least of which involve the language of instruction, who should be engaged in teaching deaf children and what their qualifications (both linguistic and otherwise) should be, how and in what language deaf children should be assessed, what the role of a spoken and written language in deaf education ought to be, and so on. Michael Strong notes that such changes, although far from complete, are currently underway in the United States:

> In an environment where hearing administrators and teachers have traditionally been in control of the education of the deaf, it is not surprising that decisions about language are often viewed, rightly or wrongly, as a means of exercising power. However, as the nation was made aware during the time of the successful student protest and strike at Gallaudet University (when Elizabeth Zinser, a hearing woman was elected president of the university over three deaf candidates, and subsequently was forced to step down in favor of a deaf president, I. King Jordan), deaf people are taking more control of their language, and hence of their lives. Evidence of this is all around. There is an increase in the number of deaf teachers receiving credentials; deaf researchers are studying the linguistics of ASL, ASL acquisition, and ASL testing; more and more courses in ASL are being offered, usually taught by deaf persons . . . (1999, p. 201)

My own concern is that deaf people as individuals, and the DEAF^WORLD as a community, *become* empowered. This is by no means the same as talking about *empowering* deaf people. I have on occasion used the term *empowerment* in this book, and it is widely used in both the literature in critical pedagogy (see Irwin, 1996; Shor, 1992) and the literature that has emerged from and is concerned with advocating for the DEAF⁀WORLD and its worldview (see Branson & Miller, 2002; Jankowski, 1997; Komesaroff, 2008). Although this use is well intentioned, it is potentially problematic when used by hearing people (or other individuals in a socially, economically, and politically "dominant" group). Like the term *toleration* (see Pratte, 1988, pp. 71–72), *empowerment* suggests a "giving of power" from those who have power to those who do not—again, a highly paternalistic, and, indeed, insulting conception of what actually needs to take place, which is the *taking* of power to which one is legitimately entitled (see Edwards, 2010, pp. 195–200). Interestingly, the ASL sign for empowerment clearly suggests the "giving of power" view of the concept. As articulated by South African Archbishop Desmond Tutu, "I am not interested in picking up crumbs of compassion thrown from the table of someone who considers himself my master. I want the full menu of rights" (1983, p. xx). This is a broader discussion that needs to take place, of course, and it concerns other disempowered groups as well, but it is one that, in my view much needs to be put on our agenda.

Matters of language and power are inextricably linked. Language policies can serve oppressive and linguicist ends, they can serve progressive and liberating ones, or they can accomplish anything in between. In most contexts and settings, language policy functions in a complex manner that achieves both good things and less good things, and this is the case with respect to sign languages as well. At the heart of questions of whether particular language policies and practices are progressive or regressive much of the time is the actual process by which they are created and implemented. What is essential in this regard is that policies are developed not in a top-down fashion, as has typically been the case with respect to language policy and planning for sign languages, but rather that they be grassroots efforts. Further, it is important that the people most involved—the deaf community itself—take ownership of the language policies. Until that takes place, such policies will inevitably be perceived to be yet more evidence of hearing hegemony and colonialism directed toward deaf people, the DEAF⁀WORLD, and, most importantly, deaf children.

Language planning is planning society, and it has implications for virtually all aspects of society. Typically, language policies impact the language or languages of government, the police and judiciary, the military, cultural institutions, commercial endeavors, the media, and, often most significantly, education. Language planning and language policies for sign languages are more restricted in nature than those for most spoken languages: they rarely involve more than the right to an interpreter in judicial settings, captioning or interpretation for media, and decisions about language and the medium of instruction for deaf children in educational settings (as well as decisions about whether sign languages "count" as foreign languages for hearing students). These are not, of course, small matters, but they do not actually constitute real, meaningful equality in terms of language policy for the deaf. Archbishop Tutu once said about apartheid in South Africa that "at present nobody is really free; nobody will be really free until Blacks are free. Freedom is indivisible" (1983, p. 45). Along the same line of thought is Dr. Martin Luther King Jr.'s observation: "Injustice anywhere is a threat to justice everywhere. We are caught in an inescapable network of mutuality, tied in a single garment of destiny. Whatever affects one directly, affects all indirectly." Precisely the same is true for deaf people: Language policy for deaf people, both in the United States and in most parts of the world, does not yet reflect equality or social justice, and this colors language rights everywhere and for everyone.

Appendix I

European Parliament Resolution on Sign Languages 1988

The following text is the first "Resolution of the European Parliament on Sign Languages." It was adopted on June 17, 1988.

A. Whereas there are half a million profoundly deaf people and many times that number of partially hearing and deafened people in the Community,

B. Whereas most deaf people can never become proficient in spoken language,

C. Whereas sign language, which can be properly be regarded as a language in its own right, is the preferred or only language of most deaf people,

D. Recognising that sign language and sign language interpreters are one of the means by which the deaf gain access to information needed for everyday life as well as reading and television,

E. Wishing to promote the integration of deaf people into hearing society on terms fair to the deaf,

F. Recognising the major contribution of the World Federation of the Deaf (WFD) over the past decades to improving the lot of deaf people, and welcoming its creation of a Regional Secretariat covering the countries of the European Community,

1. Welcomes the concern expressed and the support provided to date by the Commission to organisations representing deaf people in the Community;

RECOGNITION OF AND RIGHT TO USE A SIGN LANGUAGE

2. Calls on the Commission to make a proposal to the Council concerning official recognition of the sign language used by deaf people in each Member State;

3. Calls upon the Member States to abolish any remaining obstacles to the use of sign language;

SIGN LANGUAGE INTERPRETATION

4. Stresses the importance of recognising sign language interpreting as a profession and of establishing a full time sign language interpreter training and employment programmes in each Member State under the responsibility of the national associations for the deaf;

5. Urges Member States, in consultation with the European Regional Secretariat of the World Federation of the Deaf (WFD), to submit projects for the training of sufficient numbers of sign language tutors, assessors and interpreters, for support under the European Social Fund;

6. Calls upon Community institutions to set an example by making provision, as a matter of principle for sign language interpretation at meetings organised under their auspices and attended by deaf people;

SIGN LANGUAGE AND TELEVISION

7. Calls upon broadcasting authorities to include translation into sign language, or at least subtitles, of television news programmes, those of political interest and, to the extent possible, of a selection of cultural ad general interest programmes; also urges broadcasting authorities, in consultation with the European Regional Secretariat for the Deaf and the European Broadcasting Union, to determine minimum levels of provision of sign language interpretation or subtitling for programmes aimed at adults and children respectively, as well as teletext provision;

8. Urges Member States to ensure that all relevant government circulars on welfare benefits, health and employment are produced using sign language on video for the use of the deaf community;

9. Calls upon the Commission to support research in the area of television services for the deaf;

TEACHING SIGN LANGUAGE TO THE HEARING

10. Calls upon Member States, in cooperation with the Commission, to support pilot projects aimed at teaching sign language to hearing children and adults, using deaf people trained for the purpose and to back research in this area;

SIGN LANGUAGE DICTIONARIES

11. Urges Member States to support research into and publication of up-to-date dictionaries of their respective national sign languages; invites the Commission to foster such activities and in due course, to promote development of multilingual dictionaries of the sign languages in use within the Community;

SIGN LANGUAGE EXCHANGES

12. Invites the Commission to consider how, at a suitable juncture, Community level exchanges might best be brought about between those proficient in their respective countries' sign languages and cultures;

INSTITUTIONAL AND FUNDING ASPECTS

13. Considers it essential that the deaf be fully involved in determining policy for the non-hearing at national and Community level, notably through the European Regional Secretariat of the WFD;

14. Calls for more generous funding under the Community budget for development of devices for deaf people in the Member States;

15. Instructs its President to forward this resolution to the Commission, the Council, the Member States, the European Regional Secretariat of the World Federation of the Deaf, and the European Broadcasting Union.

Appendix II

Statement on the Recognition of the National Sign Languages of the Deaf

The Third European Congress on Sign Language Research took place in Hamburg, Germany, from July 26–29, 1989. This international linguistic congress was arranged by the International Sign Language Association (ISLA); about 200 professionals from twenty-one countries were in attendance.

In the closing session the participants unanimously declared sign languages to be full and equal languages. They strongly demanded that the national sign languages of the deaf be recognized by society.

In this context, the following statement was, again unanimously, agreed on. It could serve as the basis for another international resolution to be worked out by ISLA and the World Federation of the Deaf.

Prejudices and attitudes towards sign language rooted in educational philosophy have deeply influenced the living conditions of deaf people and their chances of personal development. Due to the grave consequences that negative perception of sign language have in deaf people's lives, we consider it our duty to go beyond the realm of scientific discourse and with this resolution bring to the public's attention the social and political implications of our research.

EARLIER OPINIONS OF SIGN LANGUAGE

In Milan, 1880, the hearing participants of the International Congress of Educators of the Deaf approved a resolution in which sign language was officially banned and virtually eliminated from deaf education. Sign language was no longer recognized as the language of deaf people but was seen, at best, as suitable only for the most elementary communication needs, as a mixture of simple pantomime and primitive gesturing incapable of conveying abstract concepts and complex ideas, as a form more closely related to subhuman forms of communication.

RECENT SCIENTIFIC RESEARCH ON SIGN LANGUAGE

In recent years, there has been a dramatic change in how sign language has been perceived. Scientific investigations of a number of national sign languages over the past 30 years have produced ample evidence that sign languages are full and complex language systems equivalent to spoken languages in functional and structural respects. These studies have demonstrated that sign languages possess sophisticated grammars and large vocabularies; linguists have described the basic linguistic structures, rules, and functions of these languages.

Sign languages, however, are more than just abstract linguistic systems. Psychological, psycholinguistic and sociolinguistic studies have also shown that the use of sign language promotes emotional, social, and mental development in deaf children. Early use of sign language facilities concept formation, developmentally appropriate acquisition of knowledge, of social values and norms of behavior, and a high degree of overall communicative competence. There is evidence that even acquisition of the spoken and written language may be strengthened by the early acquisition of sign language. In general, early and consistent use of sign language by deaf children results in more effective learning both in and out of school.

THE DEAF AS A LINGUISTIC COMMUNITY

For the deaf adult, sign language is a prerequisite to social integration. It is not physical disability but sign language which unites deaf people in a social community that exhibits all the traits of a language community. The sign language community is the deaf person's safeguard against the fate of living isolated in a hearing world; the deaf community is a guarantee for the individual's social and psychological well-being.

PUBLIC RECOGNITION OF THE DEAF COMMUNITY AND THEIR LANGUAGE

The society should recognize the sign language of the deaf and the community of the deaf. Deaf people must be able to decide themselves all questions directly concerning themselves and their community.

In particular, the policy-making agencies must no longer ignore deaf people's demand for bilingual education, which explicitly recognizes the importance of sign language and the deaf community for the deaf person.

Sign language is also a means of meaningful integration of the deaf into hearing society. Through provision of adequate, qualified interpreting services, deaf people can benefit from all existing sources of information as well as make themselves heard within the larger society.

WE DEMAND THE FOLLOWING POLITICAL ACTION NECESSARY TO ALTER CURRENT SITUATION:

- **Recognition of sign languages and recognition of the deaf as a language minority** by national parliaments in accordance with the resolution unanimously passed by the European Parliament on 12 June 1988.
  - Translation into action of this decision through appropriate legislative and administrative measures.
- **Public financing of interpreting services** and all ensuing costs including interpreter training. Elimination of discrimination against deaf persons by making academic instruction and vocational training for the deaf more available through the provision of qualified interpreters.
  - Increased use of interpreters in public institutions and on television.
- **Support of a sign language environment for the deaf baby and young deaf child,** to begin from the time when deafness is first diagnosed, by supporting the study and use of sign language within the family, as well as outside of the family (play groups, day-care centers, kindergartens), by making possible regular contact by developing sign language materials for this age group.
- **Introduction of a bilingual curriculum** in cultural and educational institutions for the deaf by creation of appropriate prerequisites (e.g. training of qualified deaf teachers and educators; further training of existing hearing staff; production of suitable teaching materials).
- **Support of autonomous cultural activities of the deaf** through support for sign language courses and development of appropriate teaching methods; access to visual media; production of television programs by and for deaf people.
- **Support for further basic theoretical and applies research** towards the attainment of these goals.

Appendix III

World Federation of the Deaf "Call for Recognition of Sign Languages," 1991

The World Federation of the Deaf (WFD) Commission on Sign Language puts forward the following recommendations:

1. We recommend that the WFD call for the recognition of sign languages and of the right to use sign languages around the world.
   A. This calls on every government to propose (if not already implemented) official recognition of the sign languages(s) used by deaf people in their country as one of the country's indigenous languages.
   B. This calls on every government to abolish any remaining obstacles to the use of sign language as the primary and everyday language of deaf people.
2. We recommend that the WFD call for the right of deaf children to have full early exposure to sign language, and to be educated as bilinguals or multilinguals with regard to reading and writing.
   A. A sign language should be recognized and treated as the first language of a deaf child.
      a) The sign language in question must be the national sign language, that is, the natural sign language of the adult Deaf community in that region.
      b) In order for the deaf children to acquire their first language early and with full fluency, they must be guaranteed the right to be exposed to sign language early in life, in a environment which includes highly skilled signers.
   B. Deaf children have the right to be educated, particularly with regard to reading and writing, in a bilingual (or multilingual) environment.
      a) The national sign language should be the language of instruction for most academic subjects.

b) Instruction in the national spoken and written language should occur separately but in parallel, as is common in bilingual/multilingual educational programs for other languages.

C. Sign language teaching programs should be established and further developed for parents and personnel working with deaf children.

D. Teachers of the deaf must be expected to learn and use the accepted natural sign language as the primary language of instruction.

E. In order to achieve A.–D. above, the national sign language must be included as an academic subject in the curriculum of programs for the deaf, including both the programs which deaf students attend and the programs which train teachers of the deaf.

3. We recommend that the WFD call for substantially increased government support for research on the native sign languages, with fluent deaf users of sign language prominently included at every level.

A. Research on sign language must be established at universities, research institutes, and educational institutions in every country.

B. Because deaf individuals are the primary fluent users of sign language, Deaf individuals and national Deaf associations must be closely involved with the research and its dissemination.

a) Deaf individuals who are fluent native users of their national sign language should be recognized as the legitimate arbiters in the correct usage of the indigenous sign language and should hold significant positions in research efforts.

b) Funds must be provided for advanced training of deaf individuals in sign language research, so that adequate numbers of Deaf researchers are available.

c) Deaf individuals should be encouraged to attend meetings concerning sign language in national and international settings.

C. Research findings should be disseminated to deaf people around the world, through the national Deaf associations, as well as through other means which will inform Deaf people about research on their languages.

D. Research findings on sign language should be used to guide the teaching of sign language, the training of interpreters, and the training of parents and professionals. Training and teaching programs established for these purposes should be encouraged to combine research with training and teaching.

4. We recommend that the WFD call for massive expansion of sign language instruction in every country.

   A. Programs offering sign language instruction must be available to all of the following groups:
      a) Relatives and friends of deaf children.
      b) All professionals working with deaf children and adults.
      c) Deaf people with no prior knowledge of sign language.
      d) Deafened and severely hard of hearing individuals with poor lip-reading skills.

   B. Programs offering broader training in sign language studies must be available to the above groups, as well as to all deaf children, deaf adults, and teachers of the deaf. Sign language studies curricula should include training in the structure of natural sign languages, as well as in the culture of the Deaf communities in which these sign languages are used.

   C. Training programs must be available for sign language instructors, including both training in language instruction and broader academic training in sign language studies.

   D. Specialized programs must be offered for those dealing with deaf-blind individuals.

   E. All of the above programs should be initially established in cooperation with the national organization of the Deaf to maximize the academic quality of the program. This cooperation and supervision should occur with governmental or non-governmental organizations according to the traditions each country.

5. We recommend that the WFD call for the right of all deaf individuals to have access to high quality interpreting between the spoken language of the hearing community and the sign language of the Deaf community. This in turn requires the establishment of qualified interpreter training programs, and

the establishment of mechanisms in every country for making professional interpreters widely available to deaf individuals.

A. It must be recognized that sign language interpreters are the principal means by which deaf individuals gain access to the facilities, services, and information of the larger communities in which they live. Sign language interpreters are thus a crucial mechanism by which deaf individuals obtain equal access and opportunities as the hearing individual in any society.

B. Interpreting between sign language and spoken language must involve full translation between two different languages.

C. In order to fulfill A. and B. above, sign language interpreting must be recognized as a highly skilled profession requiring both extensive training and extensive well-funded employment mechanisms. (See the recommendations from the Commission on Interpreting for further details.)

6. We recommend that the WFD call for Government support of widespread availability of the media through sign language.

   A. Broadcasting authorities must include translation into sign language of TV news programs, programs of political interest, and to the extent possible, a selection of programs of cultural or general interest.

   B. Broadcasting authorities must include sign language programs for deaf adults and children, and sign language teaching programs for the general public.

   C. Written materials of the same types as described in A. and B. (e.g. newspapers, news or political documents and information) should be translated into sign language and made available in video form.

   D. Support should be provided for the expansion of TV, video, film and books which are developed in sign language (e.g. materials to inform the Deaf communities about their sign languages or materials to be used in teaching sign language).

Bibliography

Aarons, D., & Akach, P. (1998). South African Sign Language—One language or many? A sociolinguistic question. *Stellenbosch Papers in Linguistics, 31*, 1–28.

Aarons, D., & Akach, P. (2002). South African Sign Language: One language or many? In R. Mesthrie (Ed.), *Language in South Africa* (pp. 127–47). Cambridge, England: Cambridge University Press.

Aarons, D., & Reynolds, L. (2003). South African Sign Language: Changing policies and practice. In L. Monaghan, C. Schmaling, K. Nakamura, & G. Turner (Eds.), *Many ways to be deaf: International variation in deaf communities* (pp. 194–210). Washington, DC: Gallaudet University Press.

Abley, M. (2003). *Spoken here: Travels among threatened languages*. Boston, MA: Houghton Mifflin.

Adams, J. (2003). *Bilingualism and the Latin language*. Cambridge, England: Cambridge University Press.

Adams, J., Janse, M., & Swain, S. (Eds.). (2002). *Bilingualism in ancient society: Language contact and the written word*. Oxford, England: Oxford University Press.

Ager, D., Muskens, G., & Wright, S. (Eds.). (1993). *Language education for intercultural communication*. Clevedon, England: Multilingual Matters.

Ahlgren, I. (1990). Swedish conditions: Sign language in deaf education. In S. Prillwitz & T. Vollhaber (Eds.), *Sign language research and application: Proceedings of the International Congress on Sign Language Research and Application* (pp. 91–94). Hamburg, Germany: Signum.

Aiello, P., & Aiella, M. (2001). Cochlear implants and deaf identity. In L. Bragg (Ed.), *DEAF-WORLD: A historical reader and primary sourcebook* (pp. 406–7). New York, NY: New York University Press. (Original work published 1999)

Akach, P. (1991). *Kenyan Sign Language dictionary*. Nairobi, Kenya: Kenyan National Association of the Deaf.

Akinnaso, F. (1989). One nation, four hundred languages: Unity and diversity in Nigeria's language policy. *Language Problems and Language Planning, 13*, 133–46.

Aleksandrova, O. (1989). Единство интерлингвиститической семиотики и семиолгических основ естественного человеческого языкфю [The unity of interlinguistic semiotics and of the semiological bases of the nature of human language]. *Interlinguistica Tartuensis*, 6, 50–56.

Alexander, N. (2004). The politics of language planning in post-apartheid South Africa. *Language Problems and Language Planning, 28*, 113–30.

Allen, S. (2008). English and ASL: Classroom activities to shed some light on the use of two languages. In K. Lindgren, D. DeLuca, & D. Napoli (Eds.), *Signs and voices: Deaf culture, identity, language, and arts* (pp. 139–49). Washington, DC: Gallaudet University Press.

Almond, B. (1993). Rights. In P. Singer (Ed.), *A companion to ethics* (pp. 259–69). Oxford, England: Basil Blackwell.

Altbach, P. (1984). The distribution of knowledge in the third world: A case study in neocolonialism. In P. Altbach & G. Kelly (Eds.), *Education and the colonial experience* (2nd rev. ed., pp. 229–51). New Brunswick, NJ: Transaction.

American Council on the Teaching of Foreign Languages (ACTFL). (1996). *Standards for foreign language learning: Preparing for the 21st century.* Lawrence, KS: Allen Press.

American Council on the Teaching of Foreign Languages (ACTFL). (2006). *Standards for foreign language learning in the 21st century: Including Arabic, Chinese, Classical Languages, French, German, Italian, Portuguese, Russian, and Spanish* (3rd ed.). Lawrence, KS: Allen Press.

Ammon, U. (1990). German or English? The problems of language choice experienced by German-speaking scientists. In P. Nelde (Ed.), *Language conflict and minorities* (pp. 33–51). Bonn, Germany: Dümmler.

Ammon, U. (2003). Global English and the non-native speaker: Overcoming disadvantage. In H. Tonkin & T. Reagan (Eds.), *Language in the 21st century* (pp. 23–34). Amsterdam, The Netherlands: John Benjamins.

Andersson, Y. (1990). The deaf world as a linguistic minority. In S. Prillwitz & T. Vollhaber (Eds.), *Sign language research and application* (pp. 155–61). Hamburg, Germany: Signum.

Andersson, Y. (1994). Deaf people as a linguistic minority. In I. Ahlgren & K. Hyltenstan (Eds.), *Bilingualism in deaf education* (pp. 9–13). Hamburg, Germany: Signum.

Angelini, N., Borgioli, R., Folchi, A., & Mastromatteo, M. (1991). *Piccolo dizionario della Lingua Italiana dei Segni per comunicare con i sordi* [The small dictionary of Italian Sign Language for communicating with the deaf]. Florence, Italy: La Nuova Italia.

Ann, J., Smith, W., & Chiangsheng Yu. (Ed.). (2007). The sign language of mainland China at the Ch'iying School in Taiwan. In D. Quinto-Pozos (Ed.), *Sign languages in contact* (pp. 235–58). Washington, DC: Gallaudet University Press.

Annamalai, E. (1986). Language rights and language planning. *New Language Planning Newsletter 1*, 1–3.

Armstrong, D. (Ed.). (2003a). Special Issue on Dictionaries and Lexicography, Part I. *Sign Language Studies, 3*(3), entire issue.

Armstrong, D. (Ed.). (2003b). Special Issue on Dictionaries and Lexicography, Part II. *Sign Language Studies, 3*(4), entire issue.

Armstrong, D., & Wilcox, S. (2003). Origins of sign languages. In M. Marschark & P. Spencer (Eds.), *The Oxford handbook of deaf studies, language, and education* (pp. 305–18). Oxford, England: Oxford University Press.

Audi, R. (1998). *Epistemology: A contemporary introduction to the theory of knowledge.* London, England: Routledge.

August, D., & Hakuta, K. (Eds.). (1998). *Educating language-minority children.* Washington, DC: National Academy Press.

Auld, W. (1988). *La fenomeno Esperanto* [The Esperanto phenomenon]. Rotterdam, The Netherlands: Universala Esperanto-Asocio.

Baai, Z. (1992). Towards a more communicative approach to the teaching of African languages, particularly Xhosa, as second languages. *Southern African Journal of Applied Language Studies, 1*, 60–68.

Bahan, B. (1992). American Sign Language literature: Inside the story. In *Deaf Studies: What's up?—Conference Proceedings* (pp. 153–64). Washington, DC: College for Continuing Education, Gallaudet University.

Bailey, C., & Dolby, K. (Eds.). (2002). *The Canadian dictionary of ASL.* Alberta, Canada: The University of Alberta Press.

Baker, Charlotte. (1999). Sign language and the deaf community. In J. Fishman (Ed.), *Handbook of language and ethnic identity* (pp. 122–39). New York, NY: Oxford University Press.

Baker, Charlotte, & Battison, R. (Eds.). (1980). *Sign language and the deaf community.* Silver Spring, MD: National Association of the Deaf.

Baker, Charlotte, & Cokely, D. (1980). *American Sign Language: A teacher's resource text on grammar and culture.* Silver Spring, MD: T. J. Publishers.

Baker, Colin. (2001). *Foundations of bilingual education and bilingualism* (3rd ed.). Clevedon, England: Multilingual Matters.

Baker, Colin, & Hornberger, N. (Eds.). (2001). *An introductory reader to the writings of Jim Cummins.* Clevedon, England: Multilingual Matters.

Baker-Shenk, C., & Cokely, D. (1981). *American Sign Language: A student text, units 10–18.* Washington, DC: Gallaudet University Press.

Ball, R. (1997). *The French-speaking world: A practical introduction to sociolinguistic issues.* London, England: Routledge.

Bamgbose, A., Banjo, A., & Thomas, A. (Eds.). (1997). *New Englishes: A West African perspective.* Trenton, NJ: Africa World Press.

Barakat, R. (1975a). On ambiguity in Cistercian Sign Language. *Sign Language Studies, 4*, 275–89.

Barakat, R. (1975b). *The Cistercian Sign Language: A study in non-verbal communication* (Cistercian Study Series, No. 7). Kalamazoo, MI: Cistercian Publications.

Barbour, S., & Stevenson, P. (1990). *Variation in German: A critical approach to German sociolinguistics*. Cambridge, England: Cambridge University Press.

Barley, N. (1974). Two Anglo-Saxon sign systems compared. *Semiotica, 12*, 227–37.

Baron, D. (1981). *Going native: The regeneration of Saxon English* (American Dialect Society, No. 69). Tuscaloosa, AL: University of Alabama Press.

Baron, D. (1990). *The English-only question: An official language for Americans?* New Haven, CT: Yale University Press.

Barton, L. (1997). Blaming the victims: The political oppression of disabled people. In R. Farnen & H. Sünker (Eds.), *The politics, sociology and economics of education: Interdisciplinary and comparative perspectives* (pp. 63–72). Houndsmills, Hampshire, England: Macmillan Press.

Baskan, Ö. (1986). Turkish language reform. In G. Redna & C. Kortepeter (Eds.), *The transformation of Turkish culture: The Atatürk legacy* (pp. 95–111). Princeton, NJ: Kingston Press.

Batterbury, S., Ladd, P., & Gulliver, M. (2007). Sign language peoples as indigenous minorities: Implications for research and policy. *Environment and Planning, 39*, 2899–915.

Battison, R. (1978). *Lexical borrowing in American Sign Language*. Silver Spring, MD: Linstok Press.

Bauman, H. (2004). Audism: Exploring the metaphysics of oppression. *Journal of Deaf Studies and Deaf Education, 9*, 239–46.

Bauman, H. (2008a). Body/text: Sign language poetics and spatial form in literature. In K. Lindgren, D. DeLuca, & D. Napoli (Eds.), *Signs and voices: Deaf culture, identity, language, and arts* (pp. 163–76). Washington, DC: Gallaudet University Press.

Bauman, H. (Ed.). (2008b). *Open your eyes: Deaf Studies talking*. Minneapolis, MN: University of Minnesota Press.

Baxter, R. (2009). New technologies and terminological pressure in lesser-used languages: The Breton Wikipedia, from terminology consumer to potential terminology provided. *Language Problems and Language Planning, 33*, 60–80.

Baynton, D. (1993). "Savages and deaf-mutes": Evolutionary theory and the campaign against sign language. In J. Van Cleve (Ed.), *Deaf history unveiled: Interpretations from the new scholarship* (pp. 92–112). Washington, DC: Gallaudet University Press.

Baynton, D. (1996). *Forbidden signs: American culture and the campaign against sign language*. Chicago, IL: University of Chicago Press.

Baynton, D. (2002). The curious death of sign language studies in the nineteenth century. In D. Armstrong, M. Karchmer, & J. Van Cleve (Eds.), *The study of signed languages: Essays in honor of William C. Stokoe* (pp. 35–52). Washington, DC: Gallaudet University Press.

Becker, C. (1955). What are historical facts? *Western Political Quarterly, 7*, 327–40.

Bell, A. (1872). Visible Speech as a means of communicating articulation to deaf-mutes. *American Annals of the Deaf and Dumb, 17*, 1–21.

Bell, A. (1883). *Memoir upon the formation of a deaf variety of the human race*. New Haven, CT: National Academy of Science.

Bell, A. (1884). Fallacies concerning the deaf. *American Annals of the Deaf and Dumb, 29*, 32–69.

Bell, A. (1914). How to improve the race. *Journal of Heredity, 5*, 1–7.

Bell, M. (1895). Letter to A. G. Bell, 9 July. Bell Papers, Library of Congress. Washington, DC.

Benvenuto, A. (2005). Bernard Mottez and the sociology of the deaf. *Sign Language Studies, 6*, 4–16.

Bergmann, R. (1994). Teaching sign language as the mother tongue in the education of deaf children in Denmark. In I. Ahlgren & K. Hyltenstan (Eds.), *Bilingualism in deaf education* (pp. 83–90). Hamburg, Germany: Signum.

Berman, D., Bove, L., Bragg, B., Bunge, G., Charlip, R., Flemming, C., . . . National Theatre of the Deaf. (1973). *My third eye* [VHS]. Chicago, IL: WTTW-TV.

Bernstein, L., & Auer, E. (2003). Speech perception and spoken word recognition. In M. Marschark & P. Spencer (Eds.), *Oxford handbook of deaf studies, language and education* (pp. 379–391). Oxford, England: Oxford University Press.

Beukes, A. (1991). The politics of language in formal education: The position of Afrikaans. *Journal for Language Teaching, 25*, 64–77.

Beukes, A. (1996). New horizons in language laws and language rights: Multilingualism in the new South Africa. In *XIV World Congress of the Fédération Internationale des Traducteurs Proceedings*, Vol. 2 (pp. 609–22). Melbourne: The Australian Institute of Interpreters and Translators.

Bienvenu, MJ. (1994). Reflections of deaf culture in deaf humor. In C. Erting, R. Johnson, D. Smith, & B. Snider (Eds.), *The DEAF WAY: Perspectives from the international conference on deaf culture* (pp. 16–23). Washington, DC: Gallaudet University Press.

Bienvenu, M. (2003). *Developing a prototype for a monolingual ASL dictionary*. Unpublished doctoral dissertation, Union Institute and University, Cincinnati, OH.

Biesold, H. (1999). *Crying hands: Eugenics and deaf people in Nazi Germany*. Washington, DC: Gallaudet University Press.

Bishop, M., & Hicks, S. (Eds.) (2008). *Hearing, mother father deaf: Hearing people in deaf families*. Washington, DC: Gallaudet University Press.

Blackledge, A. (2000). *Literacy, power and social justice*. Stoke on Trent, Staffordshire, England: Trentham Books.

Blanke, D. (2003). *Interlinguistic und Esperantologie* [Interlinguistics and Esperantology]. (Esperanto-Dokumente 7). Bamberg, Germany: Deutscher Esperanto-Bund e.V., Geschäftsstelle.

Blanke, D. (2006). *Interlinguistische Beiträge* [Interlinguistic behavior]. Frankfurt am Main, Germany: Peter Lang.

Blanke, D., & Lins, U. (Eds.). (2010). *La arto labori kune: Festlibro por Humphrey Tonkin* [The art of working together: Festschrift for Humphrey Tonkin]. Rotterdam, The Netherlands: Universala Esperanto Asocio.

Blommaert, J. (1996). Language planning as a discourse on language and society: The linguistic ideology of a scholarly tradition. *Language Problems and Language Planning, 20*, 199–222.

Bobajik, J., Pensalfini, R., & Storto, L. (Eds.). (1996). *Papers on language endangerment and the maintenance of linguistic diversity*. Cambridge, MA: MIT Working Papers in Linguistics.

Bornstein, H. (Ed.). (1990). *Manual communication: Implications for education*. Washington, DC: Gallaudet University Press.

Bornstein, H., Hamilton, L., Saulnier, K., & Roy, H. (Eds.). (1975). *The Signed English dictionary for preschool and elementary levels*. Washington, DC: Gallaudet College Press.

Bornstein, H., Saulnier, K., & Hamilton, L. (1983). *The comprehensive Signed English dictionary*. Washington, DC: Gallaudet College Press.

Bornstein, H., Saulnier, K., Peters, P., & Tom, L. (1992). *Nursery rhymes from Mother Goose: Told in Signed English*. Washington, DC: Kendall Green Publications.

Bornstein, H., Saulnier, K., & Pomeroy, B. (1990). *Little Red Riding Hood: Told in Signed English*. Washington, DC: Gallaudet University Press.

Bouchauveau, G. (1994). Deaf humor and culture. In C. Erting, R. Johnson, D. Smith, & B. Snider (Eds.), *The deaf way: Perspectives from the international conference on deaf culture* (pp. 24–30). Washington, DC: Gallaudet University Press.

Bouvet, D. (1990). *The path to language: Bilingual education for deaf children*. Clevedon, England: Multilingual Matters.

Bragg, B. (1996). The past and present of deaf theatres around the world. In M. Garretson (Ed.), *Deafness: Historical perspectives* (pp. 17–20). Silver Spring, MD: National Association of the Deaf.

Bragg, L. (Ed.). (2001). *DEAF-WORLD: A historical reader and primary sourcebook*. New York, NY: New York University Press.

Brandeis, L. (1954). True Americanism. In P. Miller (Ed.), *American thought: Civil War to World War I* (pp. 340–341). New York: Holt, Rinehart and Winston.

Branson, J., & Miller, D. (1993). Sign language, the deaf and the epistemic violence of mainstreaming. *Language and Education, 7*, 21–41.

Branson, J., & Miller, D. (1998). Achieving human rights: Educating deaf immigrant students from non-English-speaking families in Australia. In A. Weisel (Ed.), *Issues unresolved: New perspectives on language and deaf education* (pp. 88–100). Washington, DC: Gallaudet University Press.

Branson, J., & Miller, D. (2002). *Damned for their difference: The cultural construction of deaf people as disabled.* Washington, DC: Gallaudet University Press.

Branson, J., Miller, D., & Maraja, I. (1996). Everyone here speaks sign language, too: A deaf village in Bali, Indonesia. In C. Lucas (Ed.), *Multicultural aspects of sociolinguisticsin deaf communities* (pp. 39–57). Washington, DC: Gallaudet University Press.

Brentari, D. (Ed.). (2001). *Foreign vocabulary in sign languages: A cross-linguistic investigation of word formation.* Mahwah, NJ: Lawrence Erlbaum Associates.

Brien, D. (Ed.). (1992). *Dictionary of British Sign Language/English.* London: Faber & Faber.

Brink, A. (1984). The future of Afrikaans. *Leadership SA, 3*, 29–36.

British Deaf Association. (1975). *Gestuno: International sign language of the deaf.* Carlisle, England: British Deaf Association.

Brown, N. (2007). Status language planning in Belarus: An examination of written discourse in public spheres. *Language Policy, 6*, 281–301.

Bruce, R. (1973). *Bell: Alexander Graham Bell and the conquest of solitude.* Boston, MA: Little, Brown.

Bullard, D. (1986). *Islay.* Silver Spring, MD: T. J. Publishers.

Burch, S. (2000). In a different voice: Sign language preservation and America's deaf community. *Bilingual Research Journal, 24*, 333–54.

Burke, T. (2008). Bioethics and the deaf community. In K. Lindgren, D. DeLuca, & D. Napoli (Eds.), *Signs and voices: Deaf culture, identity, language, and arts* (pp. 63–74). Washington, DC: Gallaudet University Press.

Burling, R. (2005). *The talking ape: How language evolved.* Oxford, England: Oxford University Press.

Burnes, B. (1950). The editor's page. *The Silent Worker, 2*, 2.

Campbell-Makini, Z. (2000). The language of schooling: Deconstructing the myths about African languages. In S. Makoni & N. Kamwangamalu (Eds.), *Language and institutions in Africa* (pp. 111–29). Cape Town, South Africa: Centre for Advanced Studies of African Society.

Canagarajah, A. (1999). *Resisting linguistic imperialism in English teaching.* Oxford, England: Oxford University Press.

Canagarajah, A. (2005). *Reclaiming the local in language policy and practice.* Mahwah, NJ: Lawrence Erlbaum Associates.

Carroll, J. (1961). Review of W. C. Stokoe, Jr., "Sign language structure: An outline of the visual communication systems of the American Deaf." *Exceptional Children, 28,* 113–16.

Caselli, M. (1987). Language acquisition by Italian deaf children. In J. Kyle (Ed.), *Sign and school* (pp. 44–53). Clevedon, England: Multilingual Matters.

Charlier, B., Capouillez, J., & Périer, O. (1987). The use of Signed French and Cued Speech in combination: A flexible approach to Total Communication. In J. Kyle (Ed.), *Sign and school* (pp. 171–180). Clevedon, England: Multilingual Matters.

Charlton, J. (1998). *Nothing about us without us: Disability oppression and empowerment.* Berkeley, CA: University of California Press.

Chase, A. (1980). *The legacy of Malthus: The social costs of the new scientific racism.* Urbana, IL: University of Illinois Press.

Chen, P. (1999). *Modern Chinese: History and sociolinguistics.* Cambridge, England: Cambridge University Press.

Chomsky, N. (1993). Mental constructions and social reality. In E. Reuland & W. Abraham (Eds.), *Knowledge and language: Vol. 1. From Orwell's problem to Plato's problem* (pp. 29–58). Dordrecht, The Netherlands: Kluwer.

Chomsky, N. (1994). Chomsky, Noam. In S. Suttenplan (Ed.), *A companion to the philosophy of mind* (pp. 153–167). Oxford, England: Blackwell.

Chomsky, N. (2000). *New horizons in the study of language and mind.* Cambridge, England: Cambridge University Press.

Christiansen, J., & Leigh, I. (2006). The dilemma of pediatric cochlear implants. In H. Goodstein (Ed.), *The Deaf Way reader II: Perspectives from the Second International Conference on Deafness* (pp. 363–69). Washington, DC: Gallaudet University Press.

Christie, K., & Wilkins, D. (1997). A feast for the eyes: ASL literacy and ASL literature. *Journal of Deaf Studies and Deaf Education, 2,* 57–59.

Ciscel, M. (2007). *The language of the Moldovans: Romania, Russia, and identity in an ex-Soviet republic.* Lanham, MD: Lexington Books.

City Lit Centre for the Deaf. (2008). *British Sign Language for dummies.* Chichester, England: John Wiley.

Cluver, A. (1993a). The decline of Afrikaans. *Language Matters: Studies in the Languages of Southern Africa, 24,* 15–46.

Cluver, A. (1993b). *A dictionary of language planning terms.* Pretoria, South Africa: University of South Africa.

Cobarrubias, J. (1983). Ethical issues in status planning. In J. Cobarrubias & J. Fishman (Eds.), *Progress in language planning* (pp. 41–85). Berlin, Germany: Mouton.

Cobarrubias, J., & Fishman, J. (Eds.). (1983). *Progress in language planning: International perspectives*. Berlin, Germany: Mouton.

Cohen, L. (1994). *Train go sorry: Inside a deaf world*. Boston, MA: Houghton Mifflin.

Cokely, D. (2008). Never our language; never our culture: The importance of deaf community connectedness for interpreters. In C. Bidoli & E. Ochse (Eds.), *English in international deaf communication* (pp. 57–73). Bern, Switzerland: Peter Lang.

Cokely, D., & Baker-Shenk, C. (1980a). *American Sign Language: A student text, units 1–9*. Washington, DC: Gallaudet University Press.

Cokely, D., & Baker-Shenk, C. (1980b). *American Sign Language: A teacher's resource text on curriculum, methods, and evaluation*. Washington, DC: Gallaudet University Press.

Cokely, D., & Baker-Shenk, C. (1981). *American Sign Language: A student text, units 19–27*. Washington, DC: Gallaudet University Press.

Cokely, D., & Gawlik, R. (1973). A position paper on the relationship between manual English and sign. *The Deaf American* (May), 7–11.

Collins, L. (2010, January 22–26). It had to be YOO? The English—or almost English—names given to the country's real-estate projects say a lot about the modern State of Israel. *The International Jerusalem Post*, p. 22.

Collins-Ahlgren, M. (1990). Word formation processes in New Zealand Sign Language. In S. Fischer & P. Siple (Eds.), *Theoretical issues in sign language research: Volume 1. Linguistics* (pp. 279–312). Chicago, IL: University of Chicago Press.

Combrink, J. (1991). Die toekomstige status en funksies van Afrikaans [The future status and funtions of Afrikaans]. *Tydskrif vir Geesteswetenskappe, 31*, 101–12.

Cone-Wesson, B. (2003). Screening and assessment of hearing loss in infants. In M. Marschark & P. Spencer (Eds.), *Oxford handbook of deaf studies, language and education* (pp. 420–33). Oxford, England: Oxford University Press.

Conley, W. (2001). Away from invisibility, toward invincibility: Issues with Deaf theatre artists in America. In L. Bragg (Ed.), *DEAF-WORLD: A historical reader and primary sourcebook* (pp. 51–67). New York, NY: New York University Press.

Cooper, R. (1989). *Language planning and social change*. Cambridge, England: Cambridge University Press.

Cooper, R., Shohamy, E., & Walters, J. (Eds.). (2001). *New perspectives and issues in educational language planning*. Amsterdam, The Netherlands: John Benjamins.

Corina, D., & Singleton, J. (2009). Developmental social cognitive neuroscience: Insights from deafness. *Child Development, 80*, 952–67.

Corker, M. (2000). Disability politics, language planning and inclusive social policy. *Disability and Society, 15*, 445–62.

Cornett, R., & Daisey, M. (1992). *The Cued Speech resource book for parents of deaf children*. Raleigh, NC: National Cued Speech Association.

Corrado, A. (1990). Sign theatre. In S. Prillwitz & T. Vollhaber (Eds.), *Sign language research and application* (pp. 241–50). Hamburg, Germany: Signum.

Corson, D. (1993). *Language, minority education, and gender*. Clevedon, England: Multilingual Matters.

Corson, D. (1999). *Language policy in schools: A resource for teachers and administrators*. Mahwah, NJ: Lawrence Erlbaum Associates.

Corson, D. (2001). *Language diversity and education*. Mahwah, NJ: Lawrence Erlbaum Associates.

Costello, E. (1994). *Random House American Sign Language dictionary*. New York, NY: Random House.

Costello, E. (2002). *Random House Webster's concise American Sign Language dictionary*. New York, NY: Bantam.

Coulombe, P. (1993). Language rights, individual and communal. *Language Problems and Language Planning, 17*, 140–52.

Covington, V. (1976). Problems for a sign language planning agency. *International Journal of the Sociology of Language, 11*, 85–106.

Crawford, J. (1992a). *Hold your tongue: Bilingualism and the politics of "English only."* Reading, MA: Addison-Wesley.

Crawford, J. (Ed.). (1992b). *Language loyalties: A source book on the official English controversy*. Chicago, IL: University of Chicago Press.

Crouch, B., & Greenwald, B. (2007). Hearing with the eye: The rise of deaf education in the United States. In J. Van Cleve (Ed.), *The deaf history reader* (pp. 24–46). Washington, DC: Gallaudet University Press.

Crystal, D. (2000). *Language death*. Cambridge, England: Cambridge University Press.

Crystal, D. (2003). *English as a global language* (2nd ed.). Cambridge, England: Cambridge University Press.

Crystal, D., & Craig, E. (1978). Contrived sign language. In I. M. Schlesinger & L. Namir (Eds.), *Sign language of the deaf: Psychological, linguistic and sociological perspectives* (pp. 141–68). New York, NY: Academic Press.

Cubberley, E. (1909). *Changing conceptions of education*. Boston, MA: Houghton Mifflin.

Cummins, J. (2000). *Language, power and pedagogy: Bilingual children in the crossfire*. Clevedon, England: Multilingual Matters.

Cummins, J. (2009). Pedagogies of choice: Challenging coercive power in classrooms and communities. *International Journal of Bilingual Education and Bilingualism, 12*, 261–71.

Dalby, A. (2002). *Language in danger*. New York, NY: Penguin Books.

Davidson, M. (2008). Tree tangled in tree: Re-sitting poetry through ASL. In K. Lindgren, D. DeLuca, & D. Napoli (Eds.), *Signs and voices: Deaf culture, identity, language, and arts* (pp. 177–88). Washington, DC: Gallaudet University Press.

Davis, J. (2006). A historical linguistic account of sign language among North American Indians. In C. Lucas (Ed.), *Multilingualism and sign languages: From the Great Plains to Australia* (pp. 3–35). Washington, DC: Gallaudet University Press.

Davis, J. (2007). North American Indian signed language varieties: A comparative historical assessment. In D. Quinto-Pozos (Ed.), *Sign languages in contact* (pp. 85–122). Washington, DC: Gallaudet University Press.

Davis, J. (2010). *Hand talk: Sign language among American Indian nations*. Cambridge, England: Cambridge University Press.

Davis, L. (1995). *Enforcing normalcy: Disability, deafness, and the body*. London, England: Verso.

Davis, L. (Ed.). (1997). *The disability studies reader*. New York, NY: Routledge.

Dawkins, J. (1991). *Australia's language: The Australian language and literacy policy*. Canberra, Australia: Australian Government Publishing Service.

De Haerne, M. (1875a). The natural language of signs: I. *American Annals of the Deaf and Dumb, 20*, 73–87.

De Haerne, M. (1875b). The natural language of signs: II. *American Annals of the Deaf and Dumb, 20*, 137–53.

De Haerne, M. (1875c). The natural language of signs: III. *American Annals of the Deaf and Dumb, 20*, 216–28.

DeLuca, D., & Napoli, D. (2008). A bilingual approach to reading. In K. Lindgren, D. DeLuca, & D. Napoli (Eds.), *Signs and voices: Deaf culture, identity, language, and arts* (pp. 150–59). Washington, DC: Gallaudet University Press.

Denton, D. (1976). The philosophy of Total Communication. *Supplement to the British Deaf News*. Carlisle, England: British Deaf Association.

Desai, Z. (1994). *Praat* or *speak* but don't *thetha*: On language rights in South Africa. In D. Barton (Ed.), *Sustaining local literacies* (pp. 19–29). Clevedon, England: Multilingual Matters.

Deuchar, M. (1980). Language planning and treatment of BSL: Problems for research. In I. Ahlgren & B. Bergman (Eds.), *Papers from the First International Symposium on Sign Language Research* (pp. 109–19). Stockholm: Swedish National Association of the Deaf.

Deuchar, M., & James, H. (1985). English as the second language of the deaf. *Language and Communication, 5*, 45–51.

De Vriendt, S., & Moierman, D. (1987). Total Communication in the education of deaf children in Flanders. In J. Kyle (Ed.), *Sign and school* (pp. 120–31). Clevedon, England: Multilingual Matters.

Dixon, R. (1997). *The rise and fall of languages*. Cambridge, England: Cambridge University Press.

Djité, P. (1990). Les langues africaines dans la nouvelle francophonie [The African languages in the new Francophonie]. *Language Problems and Language Planning, 14*, 20–32.

Djité, P. (1991). Langues et développement en Afrique [Languages and development in Africa]. *Language Problems and Language Planning, 15*, 121–38.

Doğançay-Aktuna, S. (1995). An evaluation of the Turkish language reform after 60 years. *Language Problems and Language Planning, 19*, 221–49.

Dolnick, E. (1993). Deafness as culture. *The Atlantic 272*, 37–53.

Dorian, N. (1998). Western language ideologies and small-language prospects. In L. Grenoble & L. Whaley (Eds.), *Endangered languages: Current issues and future prospects* (pp. 3–21). Cambridge, England: Cambridge University Press.

Duličenko, A. (1988). Проекты всеобщих и международных языков [Universal and international language projects]. *Interlinguistica Tartuensis, 5*, 126–62.

Duličenko, A. (1989). Интерлингвстика: Снщность и проблемы [Interlinguistics: Essence and problems]. *Interlinguistica Tartuensis, 6*, 18–42.

Duličenko, A. (2006). *En la serĉado de la mondolingvo* [The search for the world language]. Kaliningrad, Russia: Sezonoj.

Eastman, C. (1983). *Language planning: An introduction*. San Francisco, CA: Chandler & Sharp.

Eastman, G. (1974). *Sign me Alice: A play in sign language*. Washington, DC: Gallaudet College Bookstore.

Eco, U. (1995). *The search for the perfect language*. Oxford, England: Blackwell.

Edwards, J. (1984). Irish: Planning and preservation. *Journal of Multilingual and Multicultural Development, 5*, 267–75.

Edwards, J. (1994). *Multilingualism*. London, England: Routledge.

Edwards, J. (1996). Language and society in a changing world. In T. Hickley & J. Williams (Eds.), *Language, education, and society in a changing world* (pp. 29–37). Dublin, Ireland: Irish Association for Applied Linguistics and Multilingual Matters.

Edwards, J. (2010). *Language diversity in the classroom*. Bristol, England: Multilingual Matters.

Eichmann, H. (2009). Planning sign languages: Promoting hearing hegemony? Conceptualizing sign language standardization. *Current Issues in Language Planning, 10*, 293–307.

Emenanjo, E. (Ed.). (1990). *Multilingualism, minority languages and language policy in Nigeria*. Agbor, Nigeria: Center Books Ltd., in collaboration with the Linguistic Association of Nigeria.

Emmorey, K. (Ed.). (2003). *Perspectives on classifier constructions in sign languages*. Mahwah, NJ: Lawrence Erlbaum Associates.

Emmorey, K., & Reilly, J. (1995). Theoretical issues related language, gesture, and space: An overview. In K. Emmorey & J. Reilly (Eds.), *Language, gesture, and space* (pp. 1–16). Hillsdale, NJ: Lawrence Erlbaum Associates.

Errington, J. (2008). *Linguistics in a colonial world: A story of language, meaning, and power*. Oxford, England: Blackwell.

Erting, C. (1978). Language policy and deaf ethnicity in the United States. *Sign Language Studies, 19*, 139–52.

Erting, C., Bailes, C., Erting, L., Thumann-Prezioso, C., & Kuntze, M. (2006). Signs of literacy: Naturalistic inquiry into ASL/English bilingualism at home and at school. In H. Goodstein (Ed.), *The Deaf Way reader II: Perspectives from the Second International Conference on Deafness* (pp.87–95). Washington, DC: Gallaudet University Press.

Evans, N. (2010). *Dying words: Endangered languages and what they have to tell us*. Oxford, England: Wiley-Blackwell.

Fairclough, N. (1989). *Language and power*. London, England: Longman.

Fakuade, G. (1989). A three-language formula for Nigeria: Problems of implementation. *Language Problems and Language Planning, 13*, 54–59.

Fantini, A., & Reagan, T. (1992). *Esperanto and education: Toward a research agenda*. Washington, DC: Esperantic Studies Foundation.

Fellman, J. (1973). *The revival of a classical tongue: Eliezer Ben Yehuda and the modern Hebrew language*. The Hague, The Netherlands: Mouton.

Ferguson, G. (2006). *Language planning and education*. Edinburgh, Scotland: Edinburgh University Press.

Fernandes, J., & Myers, S. (2010). Inclusive Deaf Studies: Barriers and pathways. *Journal of Deaf Studies and Deaf Education, 15*(1), 17–29.

Ferreira, A., & Adalberto, F. (1991). *Gestuário : Lingua Gestual Portuguesa* [Sign dictionary: Portuguese Sign Langugae]. Porto, Portugal: Orgal.

Fettes, M. (2003a). The geostrategies of interlingualism. In J. Maurais & M. Morris (Eds.), *Languages in a globalising world* (pp. 37–46). Cambridge, England: Cambridge University Press.

Fettes, M. (2003b). Interlingualism: A world-centric approach to language policy and planning. In H. Tonkin & T. Reagan (Eds.), *Language in the twenty-first century* (pp. 47–58). Amsterdam, The Netherlands: John Benjamins.

Fiedler, S. (2008). Interlingvistiko/esperantologio kiel fako en universitatoj: Spertoj el Leipzig [Interlinguistics/Esperantology as a fact in universities: Experiences from Leipzig]. *Informilo Por Interlingvistoj, 65*, 2–25.

Fiedler, S., & Liu Haitao. (Eds.). (2001). *Studoj pri interlingvistiko / Studien zur Interlinguistik: Festschrift für Detlev Blanke zum 60. Geburtstag* [Studies on interlinguistics: Festschrift for Detlev Blanke on his 60th birthday]. Kava-Pech, Czech Republic: Dobřichovice (Praha).

Finchilescu, G., & Nyawose, G. (1998). Talking about language: Zulu students' views on language in the new South Africa. *South African Journal of Psychology, 28*, 53–61.

Fischer, R., & Lane, H. (Eds.). (1993). *Looking back: A reader on the history of deaf communities and their sign languages*. Hamburg, Germany: Signum.

Fischer, S., & Siple, P. (Eds.). (1990). *Theoretical issues in sign language research: Linguistics*. Chicago, IL: University of Chicago Press.

Fishman, J. (Ed.). (1971). *Advances in the sociology of language: I*. The Hague, The Netherlands: Mouton.

Fishman, J. (Ed.). (1972). *Advances in the sociology of language: II*. The Hague, The Netherlands: Mouton.

Fishman, J. (Ed.). (1974). *Advances in language planning*. The Hague, The Netherlands: Mouton.

Fishman, J. (Ed.). (1978). *Advances in the study of societal multilingualism*. The Hague, The Netherlands: Mouton.

Fishman, J. (1991). *Reversing language shift*. Clevedon, England: Multilingual Matters.

Fishman, J. (2006a). *Do not leave your language alone: The hidden status agendas within corpus planning in language policy*. Mahwah, NJ: Lawrence Erlbaum Associates.

Fishman, J. (2006b). Good conferences in a wicked world: On some worrisome problems in the study of language maintenance and language shift. In N. Hornberger & M. Pütz (Eds.), *Language loyalty, language planning and language revitalization: Recent writings and reflections from Joshua A. Fishman* (pp. 133–39). Clevedon, England: Multilingual Matters.

Fodor, I., & Hagège, C. (Eds.). (1983/4). *Language reform: History and future*, 3 vols. Hamburg, Germany: Buske Verlag.

Fodor, I., & Hagège, C. (Eds.). (1990). *Language reform: History and future* (Vol. 5). Hamburg, Germany: Buske Verlag.

Fonseca-Greber, B., & Reagan, T. (2008). Developing K–16 student standards for language learning: A critical examination of the case of Esperanto. *Critical Inquiry in Language Studies, 5*, 44–63.

Foran, S. (1996). *The Irish Sign Language* (rev. ed.). Dublin, Ireland: National Association for Deaf People.

Forster, P. (1982). *The Esperanto movement*. The Hague, The Netherlands: Mouton.

Forster, P. (1987). Some social sources of resistance to Esperanto. In *Serta Gratvlatoria in Honorem Juan Régulo, II (Esperantismo)* (pp. 203–211). La Laguna, Spain: University de La Laguna.

Foucault, M. (1969). *L'archéologie du savoire* [The archeology of knowledge]. Paris: Gallimard.

Frishberg, N. (1988). Signers of tales: The case for literary status of an unwritten language. *Sign Language Studies, 59*, 149–170.

Fromkin, V., Rodman, R., & Hyams, N. (2003). *An introduction to language* (7th ed.). Boston, MA: Thomson Heinle.

Frost, R. (1969). *Stopping by woods on a snowy evening.* New York, NY: Dutton Children's Books.

Gabrielová, D. (1988). *Slovník znakové reci* [Sign language dictionary]. Prague, Czech Republic: Horizont.

Gannon, J. (Ed.). (1981). *Deaf heritage: A narrative history of deaf America.* Silver Spring, MD: National Association of the Deaf.

Garibova, J., & Asgarova, M. (2009). Language policy and legislation post-Soviet Azerbaijan. *Language Problems and Language Planning, 33*, 191–217.

Gibson, H. (2006). American Sign Language curriculum for first-language ASL students. In H. Goodstein (Ed.), *The Deaf Way reader II: Perspectives from the Second International Conference on Deafness* (pp. 100–106). Washington, DC: Gallaudet University Press.

Glenny, M. (1996). *The fall of Yugoslavia: The Third Balkan War* (3rd ed.). New York, NY: Penguin.

Gomes de Matos, F. (1995). The linguistic rights of language learners. *Language Planning Newsletter, 11*, 1–2.

Gómez, L., & Javier, J. (1997). *Diccionario del idioma de señas de Nicaragua* [Dictionary of Nicaraguan Sign Language]. Managua, Nicaragua: Asociación Nacional de Sordos de Nicaragua.

Goodman, T. (1978). Esperanto: Threat or ally? *Foreign Language Annals, 11*, 201–3.

Goodstein, H. (Ed.). (2006). *The Deaf-Way reader II: Perspectives from the Second International Conference on Deafness.* Washington, DC: Gallaudet University Press.

Greenwald, B. (2004). The real "toll" of A. G. Bell: Lessons about eugenics. In J. Van Cleve (Ed.), *Genetics, disability, and deafness* (pp. 35–41). Washington, DC: Gallaudet University Press.

Greenwald, B. (2007). Taking stock: Alexander Graham Bell and eugenics, 1883–1922. In J. Van Cleve (Ed.), *Deaf history unveiled: Interpretations form the new scholarship* (pp. 136–52). Washington, DC: Gallaudet University Press.

Gregor, D. (1976). Der kulturelle Welt des Esperanto [The cultural world of Esperanto]. In R. Haupenthal (Ed.), *Plansprachen* [Planned languages] (pp. 297–304). Darmstad, Germany: Wissenschaftliche Buchgesellschaft.

Gregory, S. (1992). The language and culture of deaf people: Implications for education. *Language and Education, 6*, 183–97.

Gregory, S., & Hartley, G. (Eds.). (1991). *Constructing deafness.* London, England: Pinter Publishers.

Grenoble, L., & Whaley, L. (Eds.). (1998a). *Endangered languages: Current issues and future prospects.* Cambridge, England: Cambridge University Press.

Grenoble, L., & Whaley, L. (1998b). Toward a typology of language endangerment. In L. Grenoble & L. Whaley (Eds.), *Endangered languages: Current issues and future prospects* (pp. 22–54). Cambridge, England: Cambridge University Press.

Grin, F. (2005). Linguistic human rights as a source of policy guidelines: A critical assessment. *Journal of Sociolinguistics, 9*, 448–60.

Grinevald. C. (1998). Language endangerment in South America: A programmatic approach. In L. Grenoble & L. Whaley (Eds.), *Endangered languages: Current issues and future prospects* (pp. 124–59). Cambridge, England: Cambridge University Press.

Grosjean, F. (1992). The bilingual and bicultural person in the hearing and deaf world. *Sign Language Studies, 77*, 307–320.

Guillorel, H., & Koubi, G. (Eds.). (1999). *Langues et droits* [Languages and rights]. Brussels, Belgium: Bruylant.

Gustason, G., & Woodward, J. (Eds.). (1973). *Recent developments in manual English*. Washington, DC: Department of Education, Gallaudet College.

Gustason, G., & Zawolkow, E. (1993). *Signing Exact English*. Los Alamitos, CA: Modern Signs Press.

Gutiérrez, P. (1994). A preliminary study of deaf educational policy. *Bilingual Research Journal, 18*, 85–113.

Hagège, C. (2000). *Halte à la mort des langues* [Stop the death of languages]. Paris, France: Editions Odile Jacob.

Hagège, C. (2009). *On the death and life of languages*. New Haven, CT: Yale University Press.

Hale, K. (1998). On endangered languages and the importance of linguistic diversity. In L. Grenoble & L. Whaley (Eds.), *Endangered languages: Current issues and future prospects* (pp. 192–216). Cambridge, England: Cambridge University Press.

Hall, J. K., & Eggington, W. (Eds.). (2000). *The sociopolitics of English language teaching*. Clevedon, England: Multilingual Matters.

Haller, M. (1963). *Eugenics: Hereditarian attitudes in American thought*. New Brunswick, NJ: Rutgers University Press.

Hamel, E. (1995a). Indigenous education in Latin America: Policies and legal frameworks. In T. Skutnabb-Kangas & R. Phillipson (Eds.), *Linguistic human rights* (pp. 271–87). Berlin, Germany: Mouton de Gruyter.

Hamel, E. (1995b). Linguistic rights for Amerindian peoples in Latin America. In T. Skutnabb-Kangas & R. Phillipson (Eds.), *Linguistic human rights* (pp. 289–303). Berlin, Germany: Mouton de Gruyter.

Hamm, C. (1989). *Philosophical issues in education: An introduction*. New York, NY: The Falmer Press.

Hansen, B. (1987). Sign language and bilingualism: A focus on an experimental approach to teaching deaf children in Denmark. In J. Kyle (Ed.), *Sign and school* (pp. 81–88). Clevedon, England: Multilingual Matters.
Hansen, B. (1990). Trends in the progress towards bilingual education for deaf children in Denmark. In S. Prillwitz & T. Vollhaber (Eds.), *Sign language research and application: Proceedings of the International Congress on Sign Language Research and Application* (pp. 51–62). Hamburg, Germany: Signum.
Harbert, W., with McConnell-Ginet, S., Miller, A. & Whitman, J. (Eds.). (2009). *Language and poverty*. Clevedon, England: Multilingual Matters.
Harries, L. (1983). The nationalisation of Swahili in Kenya. In C. Kennedy (Ed.), *Language planning and language education* (pp. 118–28). London, England: George Allen & Unwin.
Harris, J. (1995). *The cultural meaning of deafness: Language, identity and power relations*. Aldershot, England: Ashgate.
Harrison, K. D. (2007). *When languages die: The extinction of the world's languages and the erosion of human knowledge*. Oxford, England: Oxford University Press.
Harshav, B. (1993). *Language in time of revolution*. Berkeley: University of California Press.
Hassanpour, A. (1999). Language rights in the emerging world linguistic order: The state, the market, and communication technologies. In M. Kontra, R. Phillipson, T. Skutnabb-Kangas, & T. Várady (Eds.), *Language: A right and a resource* (pp. 223–41). Budapest, Hungary: Central European University Press.
Haualand, H., & Allen, C. (2009). *Deaf people and human rights*. Helsinki, Finland: World Federation of the Deaf.
Haugen, E. (1966). *Language conflict and language planning: The case of modern Norwegian*. Cambridge, MA: Harvard University Press.
Hawkesworth, C. (1998). *Colloquial Croatian and Serbian: The complete course for beginners*. London, England: Routledge.
Hawkins, M. (1997). *Social Darwinism in European and American thought: Nature as model and nature as threat*. Cambridge, England: Cambridge University Press.
Hayes, J., & Dilka, K. (1995). A "new" old language for credit and instruction in the schools. *Special Services in the Schools* [now published as *Journal of Applied School Psychology*], 9, 119–24.
Heap, M., & Morgans, H. (2006). Language policy and SASL: Interpreters in the public service. In B. Watermeyer, L. Swartz, T. Lorenzo, M. Schneider, & M. Priestley (Eds.), *Disability and social change: A South African agenda* (pp. 134–47). Cape Town, South Africa: Human Sciences Research Council.
Hedberg, T. (1994). Name signs in Swedish Sign Language: Their formation and use. In C. Erting, R. Johnson, D. Smith, & B. Snider (Eds.), *The DEAF WAY:*

Perspectives from the international conference on deaf culture (pp. 416–24). Washington, DC: Gallaudet University Press.

Hernández-Chávez, E. (1995). Language policy in the United States: A history of cultural genocide. In T. Skutnabb-Kangas & R. Phillipson, in conjunction with M. Rannut (Eds.), *Linguistic human rights: Overcoming linguistic discrimination* (pp. 141–58). Berlin, Germany: Mouton de Gruyter.

Herriman, M., & Burnaby, B. (Eds.). (1996). *Language policies in English-dominant countries*. Clevedon, England: Multilingual Matters.

Heugh, K. (2002). Recovering multilingualism: Recent language-policy developments. In R. Mesthrie (Ed.), *Language in South Africa* (pp. 449–75). Cambridge, England: Cambridge University Press.

Heugh, K., Siegrühn, A., & Plüddemann, P. (Eds.). (1995). *Multilingual education for South Africa*. Johannesburg, South Africa: Heinemann.

Heyd, U. (1954). *Language reform in modern Turkey*. Jerusalem, Israel: Israel Oriental Society.

Hill, J. (Forthcoming). *Language attitudes in the American Deaf Community*. Unpublished doctoral dissertation, Gallaudet University, Washington, DC.

Hindley, R. (1990). *The death of the Irish language*. London: Routledge.

Hinnebusch, T. (1979). Swahili. In T. Shopen (Ed.), *Languages and their status* (pp. 209–93). Philadelphia: University of Pennsylvania Press.

Hintermair, M., & Albertini, J. (2005). Ethics, deafness, and new medical technologies. *Journal of Deaf Studies and Deaf Education, 10*, 185–92.

Hoffman, J. (2004). *In the beginning: A short history of the Hebrew language*. New York: New York University Press.

Hoffmeister, R. (1990). ASL and its implications for education. In H. Bornstein (Ed.), *Manual communication: Implications for education* (pp. 81–107). Washington, DC: Gallaudet University Press.

Hoffmeister, R. (2008). Language and the deaf world: Difference not disability. In M. Brisk (Ed.), *Language, culture, and community in teacher education* (pp. 71–98). New York, NY: Lawrence Erlbaum Associates.

Holborow, M. (1999). *The politics of English: A Marxist view of language*. London: Sage.

Howe, M. (1992). Untruths in advertising: Cochlear implants. In M. Garretson (Ed.), *Viewpoints on deafness: A Deaf American monograph*: *Vol. 42* (pp. 67–68). Silver Spring, MD: National Association of the Deaf.

Humphries, T. (2004). The modern deaf self: Indigenous practices and educational imperatives. In B. Brueggemann (Ed.), *Literacy and deaf people: Cultural and contextual perspectives* (pp. 29–46). Washington, DC: Gallaudet University Press.

Humphries, T., & Padden, C. (2004). *Learning American Sign Language* (2nd ed.). Boston: Pearson.

Hutchins, S., Poizner, H., McIntire, M., & Newkirk, D. (1990). Implications for sign research of a computerized written form of ASL. In W. Edmondson & F. Karlsson (Eds.), *SLR '87: Papers from the Fourth International Symposium on Sign Language Research* (pp. 255–268). Hamburg, Germany: Signum.

Hymes, D. (1996). *Ethnography, linguistics, narrative inequality: Toward an understanding of voice*. London, England: Taylor and Francis.

Irwin, J. (1996). *Empowering ourselves and transforming schools: Educators making a difference*. Albany, NY: State University of New York Press.

Iz, F. (1991). Atatürk and Turkish language reform. *Turkish Review Quarterly Digest, 5*, 69–82.

Janesick, V., & Moores, D. (1992). Ethnic and cultural considerations. In T. Kluwin, D. Moores, & M. Gaustad (Eds.), *Toward effective public school programs for deaf students: Context, process, and outcomes* (pp. 49–65). New York, NY: Teachers College Press.

Jankowski, K. (1997). *Deaf empowerment: Emergence, struggle, and rhetoric*. Washington, DC: Gallaudet University Press.

Jansen, W. (2007). *Woordvolgorde in het Esperanto: Normen, taalgebruik en universalia* [Word order in Esperanto: Norms, language use and universalism]. Utrecht, The Netherlands: Netherlands Graduate School of Linguistics.

Jansen, W. (2008). *Inleiding in de Interlinguïstiek* [Introduction to interlinguistics]. Amsterdam, The Netherlands: Universiteit van Amsterdam.

Janton, P. (1993). *Esperanto: Language, literature, and community*. Edited and rev. by H. Tonnkin, trans. by H. Tonkin, J. Edwards, & K. Weiner-Johnson. Albany, NY: State University of New York. (Original French work published 1973; Esperanto version published 1988)

Jernudd, B. (1977). Linguistic sources for terminological innovation: Policy and opinion. In J. Rubin, B. Jernudd, J. Das Gupta, J. Fishman, & C. Ferguson (Eds.), *Language planning processes* (pp. 215–36). The Hague, The Netherlands: Mouton.

Jernudd, B., & Shapiro, M. (Eds.). (1989). *The politics of language purism*. Berlin, Germany: Mouton de Gruyter.

Johnson, R., Liddell, S., & Erting, C. (1989). *Unlocking the curriculum: Principles for achieving access in deaf education* (Gallaudet Research Institute Working Paper 893). Washington, DC: Gallaudet University.

Johnston, T. (1989). *AUSLAN Dictionary: A dictionary of the sign language of the Australian deaf community*. Petersham, New South Wales: Deafness Resources Australia.

Johnston, T., & Schembri, A. (2007). *Australian Sign Language: An introduction to sign language linguistics*. Cambridge, England: Cambridge University Press.

Jokinen, M. (2000). The linguistic human rights of sign language users. In R. Phillipson (Ed.), *Rights to language: Equity, power, and education* (pp. 203–13). Mahwah, NJ: Lawrence Erlbaum Associates.

Jones, M. (2002). Deafness as culture: A psychological perspective. *Disability Studies Quarterly, 22*, 51–60.

Jordan, I. K. (2002). Bill Stokoe: An ASL trailblazer. In D. Armstrong, M. Karchmer, & J. Van Cleve (Eds.), *The study of signed languages: Essays in honor of William C. Stokoe* (pp. 1–6). Washington, DC: Gallaudet University Press.

Joseph, J., & Taylor, T. (Eds.). (1990). *Ideologies of language*. London, England: Routledge.

Juaristi, P., Reagan, T., & Tonkin, H. (2008). Language diversity in the European Union. In X. Arzoz (Ed.), *Respecting linguistic diversity in the European Union* (pp. 47–72). Amsterdam, The Netherlands: John Benjamins.

Kachru, B. (Ed.). (1982). *The other tongue: English across cultures*. Oxford, England: Pergamon Press.

Kamwangamalu, N. (2004). The language policy/language economics interface and mother-tongue education in post-apartheid South Africa. *Language Problems and Language Planning, 28*, 131–46.

Kamwangamalu, N., & Reagan, T. (Guest Eds.). (2004). *Language Problems and Language Planning: Special Issue on South Africa 28*(2).

Kannapell, B. (1985). *Language choice reflects identity choice: A sociolinguistic study of deaf college students*. Unpublished doctoral dissertation, Georgetown University, Washington, DC.

Kaplan, R., & Baldauf, R. (1997). *Language planning: From practice to theory*. Clevedon, England: Multilingual Matters.

Karmani, S. (1995). Islam, politics, and English language teaching. *Muslim Education Quarterly, 13*, 12–32.

Kazmi, Y. (1997). The hidden political agenda of teaching English as an international language. *Muslim Education Quarterly, 15*, 45–59.

Kendon, A. (1990). Signs in the cloister and elsewhere. *Semiotica, 79*, 307–29.

Kenneally, C. (2007). *The first word: The search for the origins of language*. London, England: Penguin Books.

Kennedy, C. (Ed.). (1983). *Language planning and language education*. London, England: George Allen & Unwin.

Kennedy, G. (Ed.). (1997). *A dictionary of New Zealand Sign Language*. Auckland, New Zealand: Auckland University Press.

Kennedy, G. (Ed.). (2002). *A concise dictionary of New Zealand Sign Language*. Auckland, New Zealand: Bridget Williams Books.

Kerr, D. (1976). *Educational policy: Analysis, structure, and justification*. New York, NY: David McKay.

Kersting, S. (1997). Balancing between deaf and hearing worlds: Reflections of mainstreamed college students on relationships and social interactions. *Journal of Deaf Studies and Deaf Education, 2*, 252–63.

Kettrick, C. (1984a). *American Sign Language: A beginning course*. Silver Spring, MD: National Association of the Deaf.

Kettrick, C. (1984b). *American Sign Language: A beginning course, Teacher's manual*. Silver Spring, MD: National Association of the Deaf.

Khalid, A. (1977). *The liberation of Swahili from European appropriation*. Nairobi, Kenya: East Africa Literature Bureau.

King, K. (1999). Inspecting the unexpected: Language status and corpus shifts as aspects of Quichua language revitalization. *Language Problems and Language Planning, 23*, 109–132.

King, K., Schilling-Estes, N., Fogle, L., Lou, J., & Soukup, B. (Eds.). (2008). *Sustaining linguistic diversity: Endangered and minority languages and language varieties*. Washington, DC: Georgetown University Press.

King, M., & van den Berg, O. (1992). *One nation, many languages: What policy for schools?* Pietermaritzburg, South Africa: Centaur Publications.

Koenen, L., Bloem, T., Janssen, R., & van de Ven, A. (1993). *Gebarentaal: De taal van doven in Nederland* [Sign language: The language of the deaf in the Netherlands]. The Hague, The Netherlands: Vi-Taal.

Komesaroff, L. (2008). *Disabling pedagogy: Power, politics and deaf education*. Washington, DC: Gallaudet University Press.

Kontra, M., Phillipson, R., Skutnabb-Kangas T., & Várady, T. (Eds.). (1999). *Language: A right and a resource*. Budapest, Hungary: Central European University Press.

Kornilov, V. (1989). Эсперантское причастие как проблема общей и сравнительной партципологии [The Esperanto partical as a problem of general and comparative participology]. *Interlinguistica Tartuensis, 6*, 123–33.

Kramer, C. (1999a). *Macedonian: A course for beginning and intermediate students*. Madison, WI: University of Wisconsin Press.

Kramer, C. (1999b). Official language, minority language, no language at all: The history of Macedonian in primary education in the Balkans. *Language Problems and Language Planning, 23*, 233–50.

Krashen, S. (1996). *Under attack: The case against bilingual education*. Culver City, CA: Language Education Associates.

Krausneker, V. (2000). Sign languages and the minority language policy of the European Union. In M. Metzger (Ed.), *Bilingualism and identity in deaf communities* (pp. 142–58). Washington, DC: Gallaudet University Press.

Krauss, M. (1992). The world's languages in crisis. *Language, 68*, 4–10.

Krauss, M. (2006). Classification and terminology for degrees of language endangerment. In M. Brenzinger (Ed.), *Language diversity endangered* (pp. 1–18). Berlin, Germany: Mouton de Gruyter.

Krentz, C. (Ed.). (2000). *A mighty change: An anthology of deaf American writing, 1816–1864*. Washington, DC: Gallaudet University Press.
Kriel, M. (1998). Taal en identiteitskrisis, en die alternatiewe Afrikaans musiekbeweging [Language and identity crisis in the alternative Afrikaans music movement]. *South African Journal of Linguistics, 16*, 16–26.
Kroll, S., & Zahirovič, D. (1998). *Bosnian-English / English-Bosnian dictionary*. New York, NY: Hippocrene.
Kühl, S. (1994). *The Nazi connection: Eugenics, American racism, and German National Socialism*. Oxford, England: Oxford University Press.
Kunitz, S. (1994). *Disease and social diversity: The European impact on the health of non-Europeans*. Oxford, England: Oxford University Press.
Kyle, J. (Ed.). (1987). *Sign and school: Using signs in deaf children's development*. Clevedon, England: Multilingual Matters.
Kyle, J. (1990). The deaf community: Custom, culture and tradition. In S. Prillwitz & T. Vollhaber (Eds.), *Sign language research and application* (pp. 175–85). Hamburg, Germany: Signum.
Ladd, P. (2003). *Understanding deaf culture: In search of deafhood*. Clevedon, England: Multilingual Matters.
Ladd, P. (2005). Deafhood: A concept stressing possibilities, not deficits. *Scandinavian Journal of Public Health, 33* (Suppl. 66), 12–17.
Lafayette, R. (Ed.). (1996). *National standards: A catalyst for reform*. Lincolnwood, IL: National Textbook Co.
Lambert, R. (1990). *Language policy: An international perspective*. Washington, DC: Johns Hopkins University, National Foreign Language Center.
Lambert, R. (Ed.). (1994). *Foreign language policy: An agenda for change*. Thousand Oaks, CA: Sage.
Lambert, R., & Shohamy, E. (Eds.). (2000). *Language policy and pedagogy: Essays in honor of A. Ronald Walton*. Amsterdam, The Netherlands: John Benjamins.
Lampe, J. (2000). *Yugoslavia as history: Twice there was a country* (2nd ed.). Cambridge, MA: Cambridge University Press.
Lane, H. (1984). *When the mind hears: A history of the deaf*. New York, NY: Random House.
Lane, H. (1992). *The mask of benevolence: Disabling the deaf community*. New York, NY: Alfred A. Knopf.
Lane, H. (1993a). Cochlear implants: Their cultural and historical meaning. In J. Van Cleve (Ed.), *Deaf history unveiled: Interpretations from the new scholarship* (pp. 272–91). Washington, DC: Gallaudet University Press.
Lane, H. (1993b). The medicalization of cultural deafness in historical perspective. In R. Fischer & H. Lane (Eds.), *Looking back: A reader on the history of deaf communities and their sign languages* (pp. 479–93). Hamburg, Germany: Signum.

Lane, H. (2005). Ethnicity, ethics, and the DEAF-WORLD. *Journal of Deaf Studies and Deaf Education, 10*, 291–310.
Lane, H., Hoffmeister, R., & Bahan, B. (1996). *A journey into the DEAF-WORLD*. San Diego, CA: DawnSign Press.
Large, A. (1985). *The artificial language movement*. Oxford, England: Basil Blackwell.
Leigh, I. (2008). Who am I? Deaf identity issues. In K. Lindgren, D. DeLuca, & D. Napoli (Eds.), *Signs and voices: Deaf culture, identity, language, and arts* (pp. 21–29). Washington, DC: Gallaudet University Press.
Lentz, E., Mikos, K., & Smith, C. (1992). *Signing naturally: Level 2*. San Diego, CA: DawnSign Press.
Levesque, J. (2001). Let's return ASL to deaf ownership. In L. Bragg (Ed.), *DEAF-WORLD: A historical reader and primary sourcebook* (pp. 116–17). New York, NY: New York University Press.
Lewis, G. (1984). Atatürk's language reform as an aspect of modernization in the Republic of Turkey. In J. Landau (Ed.), *Atatürk and the modernization of Turkey* (pp. 195–213). Leiden, The Netherlands: Westview Press.
Liddell, S. (1980). *American Sign Language syntax*. The Hague, The Netherlands: Mouton.
Liddell, S. (1995). Real, surrogate, and token space: Grammatical consequences in ASL. In K. Emmorey & J. Reilly (Eds.), *Language, gesture, and space* (pp. 19–41). Hillsdale, NJ: Lawrence Erlbaum Associates.
Liddell, S. (2003). *Grammar, gesture, and meaning in American Sign Language*. Cambridge, England: Cambridge University Press.
LilloMartin, D. (1991). *Universal grammar and American Sign Language: Setting the null argument parameters*. Dordrecht, The Netherlands: Kluwer Academic Publishers.
Lindgren, K., DeLuca, D., & Napoli, D. (Eds.). (2008). *Signs and voices: Deaf culture, identity, language, and arts*. Washington, DC: Gallaudet University Press.
Linton, S. (1998). *Claiming disability: Knowledge and identity*. New York, NY: New York University Press.
LoBianco, J. (1987). *National policy on languages*. Canberra, Australia: Australian Government Publishing Service.
Logiadis, M. (1985). *Lexiko Noematikes glossas* [Dictionary of Greek sign language]. Athens, Greece: Potamitis.
Louw, J. (1983/4). The development of Xhosa and Zulu as languages. In I. Fodor & C. Hagège (Eds.), *Language reform*: *Vol. 2* (pp. 371–92). Hamburg, Germany: Buske Verlag.
Louw-Potgieter, J., & Louw, J. (1991). Language planning: Preferences of a group of South African students. *South African Journal of Linguistics, 9*, 96–99.
Low, W. (1992). Colors of ASL . . . A world expressed: ASL poetry in the curriculum. In *Deaf studies for educators: Conference Proceedings* (pp. 53–59). Washington, DC: College for Continuing Education, Gallaudet University.

Lubbe, J., & Truter, E. (2007). Gevalle van positiewe taalbeplanning soos gerapporteer in die gedrukte media [Cases of positive language planning as reported in the printed media]. *Southern African Linguistics and Applied Language Studies, 25*, 557–74.

Lucas, C. (Ed.). (1989). *The sociolinguistics of the deaf community*. San Diego, CA: Academic Press.

Lucas, C. (Ed.). (1990). *Sign language research: Theoretical issues*. Washington, DC: Gallaudet University Press.

Lucas, C. (Ed.). (1995). *Sociolinguistics in deaf communities*. Washington, DC: Gallaudet University Press.

Lucas, C. (Ed.). (1996). *Multicultural aspects of sociolinguistics in deaf communities*. Washington, DC: Gallaudet University Press.

Lucas, C., Bayley, R., & Valli, C. (2001). *Sociolinguistic variation in American Sign Language*. Washington, DC: Gallaudet University Press.

Lucas, C., Bayley, R., & Valli, C. (2003). *What's your sign for pizza? An introduction to variation in American Sign Language*. Washington, DC: Gallaudet University Press.

Lucas, C., & Valli, C. (1989). Language contact in the American deaf community. In C. Lucas (Ed.), *The sociolinguistics of the deaf community* (pp. 11–40). San Diego, CA: Academic Press.

Lucas, C., & Valli, C. (1991). ASL or contact signing: Issues of judgement. *Language in Society, 20*, 201–16.

Lucas, C., & Valli, C. (1992). *Language contact in the American deaf community*. San Diego, CA: Academic Press.

Luetke-Stahlman, B. (1988). The benefit of oral English-only as compared with signed input to hearing-impaired students. *Volta Review, 90*, 349–61.

Maartens, J. (1994). Teaching Afrikaans as emancipatory discourse. In R. Botha, M. Kemp, C. le Roux, & W. Winckler (Eds.), *Taalwetenskap vir die taalprofessies / Linguistics for the language professions, 2* (pp. 298–308). Stellenbosch, South Africa: Department of General Linguistics, University of Stellenbosch.

MacMillan, M. (1982). Henri Bourassa on the defence of language rights. *Dalhousie Review, 62*, 413–30.

Maguire, G. (1991). *Our own language: An Irish initiative*. Clevedon, England: Multilingual Matters.

Marchesi, A. (1987). Sign language in the education of the deaf in Spain. In J. Kyle (Ed.), *Sign and school* (pp. 143–52). Clevedon, England: Multilingual Matters.

Markowicz, H. (1980). Myths about American Sign Language. In H. Lane & F. Grosjean (Eds.), *Recent perspectives on American Sign Language* (pp. 1–6). Hillsdale, NJ: Lawrence Erlbaum Associates.

Mar-Molinero, C. (1997). *The Spanish-speaking world: A practical introduction to sociolinguistic issues*. London, England: Routledge.
Maruatona, T. (2005). Gender and minority issues in planning literacy education in Botswana. *International Journal of Lifelong Education, 24*, 149–64.
Mas, C. (1994). Bilingual education for the deaf in France. In I. Ahlgren & K. Hyltenstan (Eds.), *Bilingualism in deaf education* (pp.71–81). Hamburg, Germany: Signum.
Massone, M. I. (1993). *Lengua de señas Argentina*, tomo I [Argentine Sign Language, vol. I]. Buenos Aires, Argentina: Editorial Sopena Argentina.
Mather, S. (1992). How pathological and cultural views of deafness affect service-delivery programs. In *Deaf studies: What's up?* (pp. 21–29). Washington, DC: Gallaudet University, College for Continuing Education.
Maurais, J. (1992). Redéfinition du statut des langues en Union Soviétique [Redefinition of language law in the Soviet Union]. *Language Problems and Language Planning, 16*, 1–20.
Mawasha, A. (1996). Teaching African languages to speakers of other South African languages: Operationalising the new democratic language policy in South Africa. *Journal for Language Teaching, 30*, 35–41.
May, S. (2005). Language rights: Moving the debate forward. *Journal of Sociolinguistics, 9*, 319–47.
Maye, C., Ringli, G., & Boyes-Braeam, P. (1987). The use of signs in Switzerland: Projects in Zurich and Geneva schools. In J. Kyle (Ed.), *Sign and school* (pp. 162–70). Clevedon, England: Multilingual Matters.
Mazrui, A., & Mazrui, A. (1998). *The power of Babel: Language and governance in the African experience*. Oxford, England: James Currey.
McArthur, T. (1998). *The English languages*. Cambridge, England: Cambridge University Press.
McCarty, T. (2002). Between possibility and constraint: Indigenous language education, planning, and policy in the United States. In J. Tollefson (Ed.), *Language policies in education: Critical issues* (pp. 285–307). Mahwah, NJ: Lawrence Erlbaum Associates.
McCaskill, C., Lucas, C., Bayley, R., & Hill, J. (In press). The hidden treasure of Black ASL: Its history and structure. Washington, DC: Gallaudet University Press.
McKay, S. (1993). *Agendas for second language literacy*. Cambridge, England: Cambridge University Press.
McKee, R., & McKee, D. (2000). Name signs and identity in New Zealand Sign Language. In M. Metzger (Ed.), *Bilingualism and identity in deaf communities* (pp. 3–40). Washington, DC: Gallaudet University Press.
McKee, R., McKee, D., Smiler, K., & Pointon, K. (2007). Maori signs: The construction of indigenous deaf identity in New Zealand Sign Language. In D. Quinto-Pozos (Ed.), *Sign languages in contact* (pp. 31–81). Washington, DC: Gallaudet University Press.

McRae, K. (1978). Bilingual language districts in Finland and Canada: Adventures in the transplanting of an institution. *Canadian Public Policy, 4*, 331–51.

McWhorter, J. (2001). *The power of Babel: A natural history of languages.* New York, NY: Times Books.

McWhorter, J. (2009). Most of the world's languages went extinct. In S. Blum (Ed.), *Making sense of language* (pp. 192–206). New York, NY: Oxford University Press.

Meadow, K. (1977). Name signs as identity symbols in the deaf community. *Sign Language Studies, 16*, 237–46.

Medoff, M. (1980). *Children of a lesser god.* New York, NY: Dramatists Play Service.

Meir, I., & Sandler, W. (2008). *A language in space: The story of Israeli Sign Language.* New York, NY: Lawrence Erlbaum Associates.

Metzger, M. (Ed.). (2000). *Bilingualism and identity in deaf communities.* Washington, DC: Gallaudet University Press.

Myers, S., & Fernandes, J. (2010). Deaf Studies: A critique of the predominant U.S. theoretical direction. *Journal of Deaf Studies and Deaf Education, 15*(1), 30–49.

Miller, B., Sonnenstrahl, D., Wilhite, A., & Johnston, P. (2006). Deaf View Image Art: A manifesto revisited. In H. Goodstein (Ed.), *The DEAF WAY II reader* (pp. 251–263). Washington, DC: Gallaudet University Press.

Miller, K. (2008). American Sign Language: Acceptance at the university level. *Language, Culture and Curriculum, 21*, 226–34.

Ministry of Education, Science and Culture (Iceland). (2004). *The national curriculum guide for compulsory school: General section, 2004.* Reykjavík, Iceland: Author.

Mitchell, R., Young, T., Bachleda, B., & Karchmer, M. (2006). How many people use ASL in the United States? Why estimates need updating. *Sign Language Studies, 6*, 390–401.

Mithun, M. (1998). The significance of diversity in language endangerment and preservation. In L. Grenoble & L. Whaley (Eds.), *Endangered languages: Current issues and future prospects* (pp. 163–91). Cambridge, England: Cambridge University Press.

Mkilifi, A. (1978). Triglossia and Swahili-English bilingualism in Tanzania. In J. Fishman (Ed.), *Advances in the study of societal multilingualism* (pp. 129–49). The Hague, The Netherlands: Mouton.

Monaghan, L., Schmaling, C., Nakamura, K., & Turner, G. (Eds.). (2003). *Many ways to be deaf: International variation in deaf communities.* Washington, DC: Gallaudet University Press.

Morgan, R. (Ed.). (2008). *"DEAF ME NORMAL": Deaf South Africans tell their life stories.* Pretoria, South Africa: University of South Africa Press.

Motoyoshi, M. (1990). The experience of mixed-race people: Some thoughts and theories. *Journal of Ethnic Studies, 18*(2), 77–94.
Msimang, C. (1992). The future status and function of Zulu in the new South Africa. *South African Journal of African Languages, 12*, 139–43.
Murray, J. (2004). "True love and sympathy": The deaf-deaf marriages debate in transatlantic perspective. In J. Van Cleve (Ed.), *Genetics, disability, and deafness* (pp. 42–71). Washington, DC: Gallaudet University Press.
Mutasa, D. (1996). Constraints on the promotion of African languages to the level of English, French and Portuguese. *South African Journal of Linguistics* (Suppl. 32), 23–34.
Muzsnai, I. (1999). The recognition of sign language: A threat or the way to a solution? In M. Kontra, R. Phillipson, T. Skutnabb-Kangas, & T. Várady (Eds.), *Language: A right and a resource—Approaching linguistic human rights* (pp. 279–96). Budapest, Hungary: Central European University Press.
Myklebust, M. (1957). *The psychology of deafness.* New York, NY: Grune & Stratton.
Nahir, M. (1977). The five aspects of language planning. *Language Problems and Language Planning, 1*, 107–24.
Nahir, M. (1988). Language planning and language acquisition: The "great leap" in the Hebrew revival. In C. Paulston (Ed.), *International handbook of bilingualism and bilingual education* (pp. 275–95). New York, NY: Greenwood Press.
Nahir, M. (2002). Corpus planning and codification in the Hebrew revival. *Language Problems and Language Planning, 26*, 271–98.
Nakamura, K. (2006). *Deaf in Japan: Signing and the politics of identity.* Ithaca, NY: Cornell University Press.
Nash, J. (1987). Policy and practice in the American Sign Language community. *International Journal of the Sociology of Language, 68*, 7–22.
National Association of the Deaf. (2009). *2008 NAD Conference Priorities.* Retrieved April 21, 2010, from *http://www.nad.org/about-us/priorities.*
Neisser, A. (1983). *The other side of silence: Sign language and the deaf community in America.* New York, NY: Alfred Knopf.
Nettle, D. (1999). *Linguistic diversity.* Oxford, England: Oxford University Press.
Nettle, D., & Romaine, S. (2000). *Vanishing voices: The extinction of the world's languages.* Oxford, England: Oxford University Press.
Newman, P. (2003). The endangered languages issue as a hopeless cause. In M. Janse & S. Tol (Eds.), *Language death and language maintenance: Theoretical, practical and description approaches* (pp. 1–13). Amsterdam, The Netherlands: John Benjamins.
Nichols, J. (1998). The origin and dispersal of languages: Linguistic evidence. In N. Jablonski & L. Aiello (Eds.), *The origin and diversification of language* (pp. 127–170). San Francisco, CA: California Academy of Sciences.

Niño-Murcia, M. (1997). Linguistic purism in Cuzco, Peru: A historical perspective. *Language Problems and Languaeg Planning, 21*, 134–61.

Nitschke, A. (1997). Sign language and gesture in medieval Europe: Monasteries, courts of justice, and society. In U. Segerstråle & P. Molnár (Eds.), *Nonverbal communication: Where nature meets culture* (pp. 263–74). Hillsdale, NJ: Lawrence Erlbaum Associates.

Norris, D. (1993). *Serbo-Croat: A complete course for beginners*. London, England: Hodder Headline.

Novak, P. (2008). Visual Shakespeare: *Twelfth Night* and the value of ASL translation. In K. Lindgren, D. DeLuca, & D. Napoli (Eds.), *Signs and voices: Deaf culture, identity, language, and arts* (pp. 220–31). Washington, DC: Gallaudet University Press.

Nover, S. (1993). *Our voices, our vision: Politics of deaf education*. Paper presented at the convention of CAIS/CEASD, Baltimore, Maryland.

Nover, S. (1995). Politics and language: American Sign Language and English in deaf education. In C. Lucas (Ed.), *Sociolinguistics in deaf communities* (pp. 109–63). Washington, DC: Gallaudet University Press.

Nover, S. (2000). *History of language planning in deaf education in the 19th century*. Unpublished doctoral dissertation, University of Arizona, Tucson, AZ.

Nover, S., & Ruiz, R. (1994). The politics of American Sign Language in deaf education. In B. Schick & M. Moeller (Eds.), *The use of sign language in instructional settings: Current concepts and controversies* (pp. 73–84). Omaha, NE: Boys Town National Research Hospital.

Nuessel, F. (2000). *The Esperanto language*. New York, NY: Legas.

Nwachukwu, P. (1983). *Towards an Igbo literary standard*. London, England: Kegan Paul.

Oates, E. (1992). *Linguagem das mãos* [Language of hands]. Aparecida, Brazil: Editora Santuário.

Ogbu, J. (1978). *Minority education and caste: The American system in cross-cultural perspective*. New York, NY: Academic Press.

Ogbu, J. (1987). Variability in minority school performance: A problem in search of an explanation. *Anthropology and Education Quarterly, 18*, 312–34.

Ogbu, J. (1988). Class stratification, racial stratification, and schooling. In L. Weis (Ed.), *Class, race and gender in American education* (pp. 106–25). Albany, NY: State University of New York Press.

Ogbu, J. (1992). Understanding cultural diversity and learning. *Educational Researcher, 21*, 5–14.

Ogbu, J. (Ed.). (2008). *Minority status, oppositional culture and schooling*. Mahwah, NJ: Lawrence Erlbaum Associates.

Ogilvy-Foreman, D., Penn, C., & Reagan, T. (1994). Selected syntactic features of South African Sign Language: A preliminary analysis. *South African Journal of Linguistics, 12*, 118–23.

Ohna, E. (2003). Education of deaf children and the politics of recognition. *Journal of Deaf Studies and Deaf Education, 8*, 5–10.

O'Huallacháin, C. (1991). *The Irish language in society*. Coleraine, Ireland: University of Ulster.

O'Huallacháin, C. (1994). *The Irish and Irish: A sociolinguistic analysis of the relationship between a people and their language*. Baile Átha Cliath, Ireland: Irish Franciscan Provincial Office.

Okrent, A. (2006). A visit to Esperantoland. *The American Scholar, 75*, 93–108.

Okrent, A. (2009). *In the land of invented languages*. New York, NY: Spiegel & Grau.

Oladejo, J. (1991). The national language question in Nigeria: Is there an answer? *Language Problems and Language Planning, 15*, 255–67.

O Laoire, M. (1995). An historical perspective on the revival of Irish outside the Gaeltacht, 1880–1930, with reference to the revitalization of Hebrew. *Current Issues in Language and Society, 2*, 223–35.

Omagio Hadley, A. (2001). *Language teaching in context* (3rd ed.). Boston, MA: Heinle & Heinle.

Ó Riagáin, P. (1997). *Language policy and social reproduction: Ireland, 1893–1993*. Oxford, England: Clarendon Press.

Oviedo, A. (2004). *Classifiers in Venezuelan Sign Language*. Hamburg, Germany: Signum.

Ozolins, U. (2003). The impact of European accession upon language policy in the Baltic states. *Language Policy, 2*, 217–38.

Padden, C. (1980). The deaf community and the culture of deaf people. In C. Baker & R. Battison (Eds.), *Sign language and the deaf community* (pp. 89–103). Silver Spring, MD: National Association of the Deaf.

Padden, C. (2008). The decline of Deaf Clubs in the United States: A treatise on the problem of place. In H. Bauman (Ed.), *Open your eyes: Deaf Studies talking* (pp. 169–76). Minneapolis, MN: University of Minnesota Press.

Padden, C., & Humphries, T. (1988). *Deaf in America: Voices from a culture*. Cambridge, MA: Harvard University Press.

Padden, C., & Humphries, T. (2005). *Inside deaf culture*. Cambridge, MA: Harvard University Press.

Padden, C., Humphries, T., & O'Rourke, T. (1994). *A basic course in American Sign Language* (2nd ed.). Silver Spring, MD: T. J. Publishers.

Padden, C., & Rayman, J. (2002). The future of American Sign Language. In D. Armstrong, M. Karchmer & J. Van Cleve (Eds.), *The study of signed languages: Essays in honor of William C. Stokoe* (pp. 247–61. Washington, DC: Gallaudet University Press.

Paget, Lady G., & Gorman, P. (1976). *The Paget-Gorman sign system*. London, England: Association for Experiments in Deaf Education.

Paget, R. (1951). *The new sign language*. London, England: The Welcome Foundation.

Panara, R. (1992). Lip service. In J. Jepson (Ed.), *No walls of stone: An anthology of literature by deaf and hard of hearing writers*. Washington, DC: Gallaudet University Press.

Pan-South African Language Board. (2005). *Annual report: 2004/2005*. Pretoria, South Africa: Author.

Papaspyrou, C., & Zienert, H. (1990). The syncWRITER computer programme. In S. Prillwitz & T. Vollhaber (Eds.), *Sign language research and application: Proceedings of the International Congress* (pp. 275–93). Hamburg, Germany: Signum.

Parasnis, I. (Ed.). (1998). *Cultural and language diversity and the deaf experience*. Cambridge, England: Cambridge University Press.

Partridge, M. (1972). *Serbo-Croat: Practical grammar and reader*. Belgrade, Serbia [Yugoslavia]: Izdavački Zavod Jugoslavija.

Patrick, D. (2005). Language rights in indigenous communities: The case of the Inuit of Arctic Québec. *Journal of Sociolinguistics, 9*, 369–89.

Paul, P. (N.d.). ASL to English: A bilingual minority-language immersion program for deaf students. Unpublished manuscript.

Paul, P. (2001). *Language and deafness* (3rd ed.). San Diego, CA: Singular Thomson.

Paul, P. (2003). Processes and components of reading. In M. Marschark & P. Spencer (Eds.), *Oxford handbook of deaf studies, language and education* (pp. 97–109). Oxford, England: Oxford University Press.

Paul, P., & Jackson, D. (1993). *Toward a psychology of deafness: Theoretical and empirical perspectives*. Boston, MA: Allyn & Bacon.

Paul, P., & Quigley, S. (1987). Using American Sign Language to teach English. In P. McAnally, S. Rose, & S. Quigley (Eds.), *Language learning practices with deaf children* (pp. 139–166). San Diego, CA: College-Hill.

Paulston, C. B. (2003). Language policies and language rights. In C. B. Paulston & G. R. Tucker (Eds.), *Sociolinguistics: The essential readings* (pp. 472–83). Oxford, England

Peet, H. P. (1853). Elements of the language of signs. *American Annals of the Deaf and Dumb, 5*, 83–95.

Pelletier, L. (2005). *American Sign Language as a second language in elementary education: A critical perspective on curriculum and policy*. Unpublished doctoral dissertation, University of Connecticut, Storrs, CT.

Penn, C. (1992). *Dictionary of Southern African signs, Volume 1*. Pretoria, South Africa: Human Sciences Research Council.

Penn, C. (1993). *Dictionary of Southern African signs, Volume 2*. Pretoria, South Africa: Human Sciences Research Council.

Penn, C. (1994a). *Dictionary of Southern African signs, Volume 3*. Pretoria, South Africa: Human Sciences Research Council.

Penn, C. (1994b). *Dictionary of Southern African signs, Volume 4*. Pretoria, South Africa: Human Sciences Research Council.

Penn, C. (1994c). *Dictionary of Southern African signs, Volume 5*. Pretoria, South Africa: Human Sciences Research Council.

Penn, C., & Reagan, T. (1990). How do you sign "apartheid"? The politics of South African Sign Language. *Language Problems and Language Planning, 14*, 91–103.

Penn, C., & Reagan, T. (1991). Toward a national policy for deaf education in the "new" South Africa. *South African Journal of Communication Disorders, 38*, 19–24.

Penn, C., & Reagan, T. (1994). The properties of South African Sign Language: Lexical diversity and syntactic unity. *Sign Language Studies, 85*, 319–27.

Penn, C., & Reagan, T. (1995). On the other hand: Implications of the study of South African Sign Language for the education of the deaf in South Africa. *South African Journal of Education, 15*, 92–96.

Penn, C., & Reagan, T. (2001). Linguistic, social and cultural perspectives on sign language in South Africa. In E. Ridge, S. Makoni, & S. Ridge (Eds.), *Freedom and discipline: Essays in applied linguistics from Southern Africa* (pp. 49–65). New Delhi, India: Bahri Publications.

Penny, R. (2002). *A history of the Spanish language* (2nd ed.). Cambridge, England: Cambridge University Press.

Pennycook, A. (1994). *The cultural politics of English as an international language*. London, England: Longman.

Pennycook, A. (1998). *English and the discourses of colonialism*. London, England: Routledge.

Pennycook, A. (2000). The social politics and cultural politics of language classrooms. In J. Hall & W. Eggington (Eds.), *The sociopolitics of English language teaching* (pp. 89–103). Clevedon, England: Multilingual Matters.

Pennycook, A. (2001). *Critical applied linguistics: A critical introduction*. Mahwah, NJ: Lawrence Erlbaum Associates.

Pennycook, A. (2004). Performativity and language studies. *Critical Inquiry in Language Studies, 1*, 1–19.

Pennycook, A. (2008). Translingual English. *Australian Review of Applied Linguistics, 31*, 30.1–30.9.

Perelló, J., & Frigola, J. (1987). *Lenguaje de signos manuales* [Hand sign language]. Barcelona, Spain: Cientifico Medi.

Perlmutter, D. (2008). *Nobilior est vulgaris*: Dante's hypothesis and sign language poetry. In K. Lindgren, D. DeLuca, & D. Napoli (Eds.), *Signs and voices: Deaf culture, identity, language, and arts* (pp. 189–213). Washington, DC: Gallaudet University Press.

Perry, J. (1985). Language reform in Turkey and Iran. *International Journal of Middle East Studies, 17*, 295–311.

Peters, C. (2000). *Deaf American literature: From carnival to the canon.* Washington, DC: Gallaudet University Press.

Petersen, A., & Hansen, B. (1982). *Den lille Tegn-Dansk Ordbog* [The small Sign-Danish dictionary]. Copenhagen, Denmark: DCTK.

Pharies, D. (2007). *A brief history of the Spanish language.* Chicago, IL: University of Chicago Press.

Phillips, J. (Ed.). (1999). *Foreign language standards: Linking research, theories, and practices.* Lincolnwood, IL: National Textbook Co.

Phillipson, R. (1992). *Linguistic imperialism.* Oxford, England: Oxford University Press.

Phillipson, R. (Ed.). (2000). *Rights to language: Equity, power and education.* Mahwah, NJ: Lawrence Erlbaum Associates.

Phillipson, R. (2003). *English-only Europe? Challenging language policy.* London, England: Routledge.

Phillipson, R., Rannut, M., & Skutnabb-Kangas, T. (1995). Introduction. In T. Skutnabb-Kangas & R. Phillipson, in conjunction with M. Rannut (Eds.), *Linguistic human rights: Overcoming linguistic discrimination* (pp. 1–22). Berlin, Germany: Mouton de Gruyter.

Pilleux, M., Cuevas, H., & Avalos, E. (Eds). (1991). *El lenguaje de señas* [The language of signs]. Valdivia, Chile: Universidad Austral de Chile.

Plaza-Putz, C., & Morales-López, E. (Eds.). (2008). *Sign bilingualism: Language development, interaction, and maintenance in sign language contact situations.* Amsterdam, The Netherlands: John Benjamins.

Polomé, C., & Hill, C. (Ed.). (1980). *Language in Tanzania.* Oxford, England: Oxford University Press.

Popper, K. (2002). *The logic of scientific discovery.* London, England: Routledge. (Original German work published 1935)

Posner, R. (1996). *The Romance languages.* Cambridge, England: Cambridge University Press.

Pratt, L. (1868). Introductory. *American Annals of the Deaf and Dumb, 13,* 129–47.

Pratte, R. (1988). *The civic imperative: Examining the need for civic education.* New York, NY: Teachers College Press.

Prendergast, C. (2008). *Buying into English: Language and investment in the new capitalist world.* Pittsburgh, PA: University of Pittsburgh Press.

Preston, P. (1994). *Mother father deaf: Living between sound and silence.* Cambridge, MA: Harvard University Press.

Prillwitz, S. (1987). Is the time of the "German Method" over in Germany? On sign language research and practice in the FRG. In J. Kyle (Ed.), *Sign and school* (pp. 89–99). Clevedon, England: Multilingual Matters.

Prillwitz, S., & Zienert, H. (1990). Hamburg Notation System for sign language: Development of a sign writing with computer application. In S. Prillwitz &

T. Vollhaber (Eds.), *Current trends in European sign language research* (pp. 355–379). Hamburg, Germany: Signum.

Prucha, F. (Ed.). (1990). *Documents of United States Indian policy* (2nd ed.). Lincoln, NE: University of Nebraska Press.

Quintela, D., Ramírez, I., Robertson, X., & Pérez, A. (1997). ¿Por qué una educación bicultural bilingüe para las personas sordas? [Why a bilingual bicultural education for deaf people?] *Revista de la Universidad Metropolitana de Ciencias de la Educación*, 3, 43–52.

Radutzky, E. (Ed.). (19892). *Dizionario della lingua italiana dei segni* [Dictionary of Italian Sign Language]. Rome, Italy: Edizioni Kappa.

Ramsey, C. (1989). Language planning in deaf education. In C. Lucas (Ed.), *The sociolinguistics of the deaf community* (pp. 123–46). New York, NY: Academic Press.

Ramsey, C. (2004). What does culture have to do with the education of students who are deaf or hard of hearing? In B. Brueggemann (Ed.), *Literacy and deaf people: Cultural and contextual perspectives* (pp. 47–58). Washington, DC: Gallaudet University Press.

Reagan, T. (1983). The economics of language: Implications for language planning. *Language Problems and Language Planning, 7*, 148–61.

Reagan, T. (1984). Language policy, politics and ideology: The case of South Africa. *Issues in Education, (61)2*, 155–64.

Reagan, T. (1986a). Creating artificial sign languages: Guidelines and constraints. *Sign Language Studies, 52*, 219–34.

Reagan, T. (1986b). "Language ideology" in the language planning process: Two African case studies. *South African Journal of African Languages, 6*, 94–97.

Reagan, T. (1987). The politics of linguistic apartheid: Language policies in black education in South Africa. *Journal of Negro Education, 56*, 299–312.

Reagan, T. (1988). Multiculturalism and the deaf: An educational manifesto. *Journal of Research and Development in Education, 22*, 1–6.

Reagan, T. (1989). Nineteenth century conceptions of deafness: Implications for contemporary educational practice. *Educational Theory, 39*, 39–46.

Reagan, T. (1990a). Cultural considerations in the education of the deaf. In D. Moores & K. Meadow-Orlans (Eds.), *Educational and developmental aspects of deafness* (pp. 73–84). Washington, DC: Gallaudet University Press.

Reagan, T. (1990b). The development and reform of sign languages. In I. Fodor & C. Hagège (Eds.), *Language reform: History and future: Vol. 5* (pp. 253–67). Hamburg, Germany: Buske Verlag.

Reagan, T. (1991). Responding to linguistic diversity in South Africa: The contribution of language planning. *South African Journal of Linguistics, 8*, 178–84.

Reagan, T. (1995a). A sociocultural understanding of deafness: American Sign Language and the culture of deaf people. *International Journal of Intercultural Relations, 19*, 239–51.

Reagan, T. (1995b). "Neither easy to understand nor pleasing to see": The development of manual sign codes as language planning activity. *Language Problems and Language Planning, 19*, 133–50.

Reagan, T. (1996). Bilingualism and the dual culture of the deaf. *South African Medical Journal, 86*, 797–99.

Reagan, T. (1997). When is a language not a language? Challenges to "linguistic legitimacy" in educational discourse. *Educational Foundations, 11*, 5–28.

Reagan, T. (2000). But does it *count*? Reflections on "signing" as a foreign language. *Northeast Conference on the Teaching of Foreign Languages Review* (Special Issue on American Sign Language), *48*, 16–26.

Reagan, T. (2001a). Language planning and policy. In. C. Lucas (Ed.), *The sociolinguistics of sign languages* (pp. 145–80). Cambridge, England: Cambridge University Press.

Reagan, T. (2001b). The promotion of linguistic diversity in multilingual settings: Policy and reality in post-apartheid South Africa. *Language Problems and Language Planning, 25*, 51–72.

Reagan, T. (2002a). *Language, education and ideology: Mapping the linguistic landscape of U.S. schools*. Westport, CT: Praeger.

Reagan, T. (2002b). Language planning and language policy: Past, present and future. In R. Mesthrie (Ed.), *Language in South Africa* (pp. 419–33). Cambridge, England: Cambridge University Press.

Reagan, T. (2002c). Toward an "archeology of deafness": Etic and emic constructions of identity in conflict. *Journal of Language, Identity, and Education, 1*, 41–66.

Reagan, T. (2004). *Delimiting South African Sign Language: Politics, ideology, and linguistics*. Paper presented at the 21st World Congress of the Fédération Internationale des Professeurs de Langues Vivantes, Johannesburg, South Africa.

Reagan, T. (2005a). *Critical questions, critical perspectives: Language and the second language educator*. Greenwich, CT: Information Age Publishers.

Reagan, T. (2005b). The deaf as a linguistic minority: Educational considerations. Reprinted in L. Katzman, A. Gandhi, W. Harbour, & J. LaRock (Eds.), *Special education for a new century* (New ed., pp. 39–52). Cambridge, MA: Harvard Educational Review. (Original work published 1985)

Reagan, T. (2005c). Language policy and sign languages. In T. Ricento (Ed.), *An introduction to language policy: Theories and methods* (pp. 329–45). Oxford, England: Blackwell.

Reagan, T. (2007). Multilingualism and exclusion: American Sign Language and South African Sign Language. In P. Cuvelier, T. du Plessis, M. Meeuwis, & L. Teck (Eds.), *Multilingualism and exclusion: Policy, practice and prospects* (pp. 162–73). Pretoria, South Africa: Van Schaik.

Reagan, T. (2009). *Language matters: Reflections on educational linguistics*. Charlotte, NC: Information Age Publishing.

Reagan, T., & Osborn, T. A. (1998). Power, authority, and domination in foreign language education: Toward an analysis of educational failure. *Educational Foundations, 12*, 45–62.

Reagan, T., & Osborn, T. (2002). *The foreign language educator in society: Toward a critical pedagogy*. Mahwah, NJ: Lawrence Erlbaum Associates.

Reagan, T., & Penn, C. (1997). Language policy, South African Sign Language, and the deaf: Social and educational implications. *Southern African Journal of Applied Language Studies, 5*, 1–13.

Reagan, T., Penn, C., & Ogilvy, D. (2006). From policy to practice: Sign language developments in post-apartheid South Africa. *Language Policy, 5*, 187–208.

Republic of South Africa (1995). *Pan-South African Language Board Act* (No. 59). Pretoria, South Africa: Author.

Republic of South Africa (1996a). *Constitution of the Republic of South Africa*. Pretoria, South Africa: Author.

Republic of South Africa (1996b). *South African Schools Act* (No. 84). Pretoria, South Africa: Author.

Republic of South Africa. (1997). *Language in education policy* (Department of Education, 14 July). Pretoria, South Africa: Author.

Republic of South Africa. (2002). *National language policy framework* (Department of Arts and Culture, 13 November). Pretoria, South Africa: Author.

Rhodes, N., & Pufahl, I. (2010). *Foreign language teaching in U.S. schools: Results of a national survey*. Washington, DC: Center for Applied Linguistics.

Ricento, T. (Ed.). (2006). *An introduction to educational policy*. Oxford, England: Blackwell.

Ricento, T., & Burnaby, B. (Eds.). (1998). *Language and politics in the United States and Canada: Myths and realities*. Mahwah, NJ: Lawrence Erlbaum Associates.

Ridge, S. (2004). Language planning in a rapidly changing multilingual society: The case of English in South Africa. *Language Problems and Language Planning, 28*, 199–215.

Rissanen, T. (1987). Sign and school in Finland. In J. Kyle (Ed.), *Sign and school* (pp. 195–97). Clevedon, England: Multilingual Matters.

Roberts, P. (2005). A framework for analysing definitions of literacy. *Educational Studies, 31*, 29–38.

Robinson, C. (1996). Winds of change in Africa: Fresh air for African languages? Some preliminary reflections. In H. Coleman & L. Cameron (Eds.), *Change and language* (pp. 166–182). Clevedon, England: Multilingual Matters.

Romaine, S. (1994). *Language in society: An introduction to sociolinguistics*. Oxford, England: Oxford University Press.

Romaine, S. (1995). *Bilingualism* (2nd ed.). Oxford, England: Blackwell.

Rosen, R. (2008). American Sign Language as a foreign language in U.S. high schools: State of the art. *The Modern Language Journal, 92*, 10–38.

Rosen, R. (2009). The World Federation of the Deaf. In D. Moores & M. Miller (Eds.), *Deaf people around the world: Educational and social perspectives* (pp. 374–91). Washington, DC: Gallaudet University Press.

Rosenquest, B. (2002). Literacy-based planning and pedagogy that supports toddler language development. *Early Childhood Education Journal, 29*, 241–49.

Rosenstock, R. (2004). *An investigation of International Sign: Analyzing structure and comprehension*. Unpublished doctoral dissertation, Gallaudet University, Washington, DC.

Rubin, J., & Jernudd, B. (Eds.). (1971). *Can language be planned? Sociolinguistic theory and practice for developing nations*. Honolulu, HI: University Press of Hawai'i.

Rubin, J., Jernudd, B., Das Gupta, J., Fishman, J., & Ferguson, C. (Eds.). (1977). *Language planning processes*. The Hague, The Netherlands: Mouton.

Ruiz, R. (1984). Orientations in language planning. *NABE Journal, 8*, 15–34.

Ruiz, R. (1990). Official languages and language planning. In K. Adams & D. Brink (Eds.), *Perspectives on official English* (pp. 11–24). Berlin, Germany: Mouton de Gruyter.

Ruiz, R. (2010). Reorienting language-as-resource. In J. Petrovic (Ed.), *International perspectives on bilingual education: Policy, practice and controversy* (pp. 155–72). Charlotte, NC: International Age Publishing.

Rutherford, S. (1993). *A study of American deaf folklore*. Silver Spring, MD: Linstok Press.

Ryazanova-Clarke, L., & Wade, T. (1999). *The Russian language today*. London, England: Routledge.

Sacks, O. (1989). *Seeing voices: A journey into the world of the deaf*. Berkeley: University of California Press.

Sáenz-Badillos, A. (1993). *A history of the Hebrew language*. Cambridge, England: Cambridge University Press.

Safford, P., & Safford, E. (1996). *A history of childhood and disability*. New York, NY: Teachers College Press.

Sandelin, B., & Sarafoglou, N. (2004). Language and scientific publication statistics. *Language Problems and Language Planning, 28*, 1–10.

Sandler, W., & Lillo-Martin, D. (2006). *Sign language and linguistic universals*. Cambridge, England: Cambridge University Press.

Saulnier, K., & Miller, R. (1980). *Goldilocks and the three bears in Signed English*. Washington, DC: Gallaudet College Press.

Scheffler, I. (1960). *The language of education*. Springfield, IL: Charles C. Thomas.

Schein, J. (1984). *Speaking the language of sign: The art and science of signing*. Garden City, NY: Doubleday.

Schein, J. (1989). *At home among strangers: Exploring the deaf community in the United States*. Washington, DC: Gallaudet University Press.
Schein, J., & Stewart, D. (1995). *Language in motion: Exploring the nature of sign*. Washington, DC: Gallaudet University Press.
Schermer, T. (2004). Lexical variation in Sign Language of the Netherlands. In M. Van Herreweghe & M. Vermeerbergen (Eds.), *To the lexicon and beyond: Sociolinguistics in European deaf communities* (pp. 91–110). Washington, DC: Gallaudet University Press.
Schermer, T., Fortgens, C., Harder, R., & de Nobel, E. (Eds.). (1991). *De Nederlandse Gebarentaal* [The Dutch Sign Language]. Amsterdam: Nederlands Stichting voor het Dove en Slechthorende Kind.
Schick, B. (2003). The development of American Sign Language and manually coded English systems. In M. Marschark & P. Spencer (Eds.), *Oxford handbook of deaf studies, language, and education* (pp. 219–31). Oxford, England: Oxford University Press.
Schlyter, B. (1998). New language laws in Uzbekistan. *Language Problems and Language Planning, 22*, 143–81.
Schmidt, R. (2006). Political theory and language policy. In T. Ricento (Ed.), *An introduction to language policy* (pp. 95–110). Oxford, England: Blackwell.
Schubert, K. (Ed.). (1989). *Interlinguistics: Aspects of the science of planned language*. Berlin, Germany: Mouton de Gruyter.
Schubert, K. (Guest Ed.). (2001). *Interface* (Vol. 15: *Special issue on planned languages: From concept to reality*). Brussels, Belgium: Hogeschool voor Wetenschap en Kunst.
Schuchman, J. (2004). Deafness and eugenics in the Nazi era. In J. Van Cleve (Ed.), *Genetics, disability, and deafness* (pp. 72–78). Washington, DC: Gallaudet University Press.
Sebba, M. (2006). Ideology and alphabets in the former USSR. *Language Problems and Language Planning, 30*, 99–125.
Senghas, R., & Monaghan, L. (2002). Signs of their times: Deaf communities and the culture of language. *Annual Review of Anthropology, 31*, 69–97.
Serpell, R., & Mbewe, M. (1990). Dialectal flexibility in sign language in Africa. In C. Lucas (Ed.), *Sign language research* (pp. 275–87). Washington, DC: Gallaudet University Press.
Shapiro, J. (1993). *No pity: People with disabilities forging a new civil rights movement*. New York, NY: Times Books.
Shelly, S., & Schneck, J. (1998). *The complete idiot's guide to learning sign language*. New York, NY: Alpha Books.
Shohamy, E. (2006). *Language policy: Hidden agendas and new approaches*. London, England: Routledge.
Shor, I. (1992). *Empowering education: Critical teaching for social change*. Chicago, IL: University of Chicago Press.

Shorish, M. (1984). Planning by decree: The Soviet language policy in Central Asia. *Language Problems and Language Planning, 8*, 35–49.
Shrum, J., & Glisan, E. (2005). *Teacher's handbook: Contextualized language instruction* (3rd ed.). Boston, MA: Thomson Heinle.
Sibayan, B. (1974). Language policy, language engineering and literacy in the Philippines. In J. Fishman (Ed.), *Advances in language planning* (pp. 221–254). The Hague, The Netherlands: Mouton.
Siegel, L. (2008). *The human right to language: Communication access for deaf children.* Washington, DC: Gallaudet University Press.
Sign language: A way to talk, but is it foreign? (1992, 7 January). *New York Times.*
Sikosek, M. (2006). *Die neutrale Sprache: Eine politische Geschiche des Esperanto-Weltbundes* [The neutral language: A political history of the Esperanto world community]. Bydgoszcz, Poland: Skonpres.
Simms, L., & Thumann, H. (2007). In search of a new, linguistically and culturally sensitive paradigm in deaf education. *American Annals of the Deaf, 152*, 302–11.
Simon, P. (1980). *The tongue-tied American: Confronting the foreign language crisis.* New York, NY: Continuum.
Sinnott, E. (1999). *Deaf Studies VI Artworks: Brochure.* Held at the Deaf Studies VI Conference, ProArts Gallery, Oakland, CA.
Siple, L. (1994). Cultural patterns of deaf people. *International Journal of Intercultural Relations, 18*, 345–67.
Siple, P., & Fischer, S. (Eds.). (1991). *Theoretical issues in sign language research: Psychology.* Chicago, IL: University of Chicago Press.
Skelton, T., & Valentine, G. (2003). "It feels like being deaf is normal": An exploration into the complexities of defining D/deafness and young D/deaf people's identities. *The Canadian Geographer, 47*, 452–66.
Skutnabb-Kangas, T. (1994). Linguistic human rights: A prerequisite for bilingualism. In I. Ahlgren & K. Hyltenstam (Eds.), *Bilingualism in deaf education* (pp. 139–59). Hamburg, Germany: Signum.
Skutnabb-Kangas, T. (2000). *Linguistic genocide in education or worldwide diversity and human rights?* Mahwah, NJ: Lawrence Erlbaum Associates.
Skutnabb-Kangas, T. (2008). Bilingual education and sign language as the mother tongue of deaf children. In C. Bidoli & E. Ochse (Eds.), *English in international deaf communication* (pp. 75–94). Bern, Switzerland: Peter Lang.
Skutnabb-Kangas, T., & Bucak, S. (1995). Killing a mother tongue: How the Kurds are deprived of linguistic human rights. In T. Skutnabb-Kangas & R. Phillipson (Eds.), *Linguistic human rights* (pp. 347–70). Berlin, Germany: Mouton de Gruyter.
Skutnabb-Kangas, T., & Phillipson, R., in conjunction with M. Rannut. (Eds.). (1995). *Linguistic human rights: Overcoming linguistic discrimination.* Berlin, Germany: Mouton de Gruyter.

Smiler, K., & McKee, R. (2006). Perceptions of Maori deaf identity in New Zealand. *Journal of Deaf Studies and Deaf Education, 12*, 93–111.
Smit, U. (1994). Investigating language attitudes as a basis for formulating language policies: A case study. *Southern African Journal of Applied Language Studies, 3*, 23–35.
Smith, C., Lentz, E., & Mikos, K. (1988). *Signing naturally: Level 1*. San Diego, CA: DawnSign Press.
Smith, N. (2002). *Language, bananas and bonobos: Linguistic problems, puzzles and polemics*. Oxford, England: Blackwell.
Sonnenstrahl, D. (1996). De'VIA: What an odd word! In M. Garretson (Ed.), *Deafness: Historical Perspectives* (pp. 131–34). Silver Spring, MD: National Association of the Deaf.
Sonnenstrahl, D. (2003). *Deaf artists in America: Colonial to contemporary*. San Diego, CA: DawnSign Press.
Spencer, P., & Marschark, M. (2003). Cochlear implants: Issues and implications. In M. Marschark & P. Spencer (Eds.), *Oxford handbook of deaf studies, language and education* (pp. 434–48). Oxford, England: Oxford University Press.
Spolsky, B. (2004). *Language policy*. Cambridge, England: Cambridge University Press.
Spolsky, B., & Shohamy, E. (2000). Language practice, language ideology, and language policy. In R. Lambert & E. Shohamy (Eds.), *Language policy and pedagogy: Essays in honor of A. Ronald Walton* (pp. 1–41). Amsterdam, The Netherlands: John Benjamins.
Spring, J. (2008). *The American school: From the Puritans to No Child Left Behind* (7th ed.). Boston, MA: McGraw Hill.
Stack, K. (2004). Language accessibility in a transliterated education: English signing systems. In E. Winston (Ed.), *Educational interpreting: How it can succeed* (pp. 61–72). Washington, DC: Gallaudet University Press.
Stedt, J., & Moores, D. (1990). Manual codes on English and American Sign Language: Historical perspectives and current realities. In H. Bornstein (Ed.), *Manual communication: Implications for education* (pp. 1–20). Washington, DC: Gallaudet University Press.
Sternberg, M. (1998). *American Sign Language dictionary*. New York, NY: HarperPerennial.
Stevenson, P. (1997). *The German-speaking world: A practical introduction to sociolinguistic issues*. London, England: Routledge.
Stevenson, P. (1998). *The German language and the real world: Sociolinguistic, cultural, and pragmatic perspectives on contemporary German*. Oxford, England: Clarendon Press.

Stewart, D. (1992). Toward effective classroom use of ASL. In M. Walworth, D. Moores, & T. O'Rourke (Eds.), *A free hand: Enfranchising the education of deaf children* (pp. 89–118). Silver Spring, MD: T. J. Publishers.

Stewart, D. (1998). *American Sign Language: The easy way*. Hauppauge, NY: Barron's.

Stewart, L. (1992). Debunking the bilingual/bicultural snow job in the American deaf community. In M. Garretson (Ed.), *Viewpoints on deafness* (pp. 129–42). Silver Spring, MD: National Association of the Deaf.

Stokoe, W. (Ed.). (1980). *Sign and culture*. Silver Spring, MD: Linstok Press.

Stokoe, W. (1993). *Sign language structure*. Silver Spring, MD: Linstok Press. (Original work published 1960)

Stokoe, W., Casterline, D., & Croneberg, C. (1976). *A dictionary of American Sign Language on linguistic principles*. Silver Spring, MD: Linstok Press. (Original work published 1965)

Storbeck, C., Magongwa, L., & Parkin, I. (2009). Education of the deaf in South Africa. In D. Moores & M. Miller (Eds.), *Deaf people around the world: Educational and social perspectives* (pp. 133–44). Washington, DC: Gallaudet University Press.

Strike, N. (1996). Talking our way out of the *laager*: Foreign languages in South African education. *Language Matters: Studies in the Languages of Southern Africa, 27*, 253–64.

Strong, M. (1988). A bilingual approach to the education of young deaf children: ASL and English. In M. Strong (Ed.), *Language learning and deafness* (pp. 113–29). Cambridge, England: Cambridge University Press.

Strong, M. (1999). The politics of sign language: Language planning for deaf Americans. In T. Huebner & K. Davis (Eds.), *Sociopolitical perspectives on language policy and planning in the USA* (pp.193–203). Amsterdam, The Netherlands: John Benjamins.

Supalla, S. (1986). *Manually coded English: The modality question in signed language development*, Unpublished master's thesis, University of Illinois, Champaign-Urbana.

Supalla, S. (1990). The arbitrary name sign system in American Sign Language. *Sign Language Studies, 67*, 99–126.

Supalla, S. (1992). *The book of name signs*. Berkeley, CA: DawnSign Press.

Supalla, T., & Webb, R. (1995). The grammar of International Sign: A new look at pidgin languages. In K. Emmorey & J. Reilly (Eds.), *Langauge, gesture, and space* (pp. 333–351). Mahwah, NJ: Lawrence Erlbaum Associates.

Sutton-Spence, R., & Woll, B. (1998). *The linguistics of British Sign Language: An introduction*. Cambridge, England: Cambridge University Press.

Šušnjar, A. (2000). *Croatian-English / English-Croatian dictionary*. New York: Hippocrene.

Suwanarat, M., Reilly, C., Wrigley, O., Ratanasint, A., & Anderson, L. (1986). *The Thai Sign Language dictionary*. Bangkok, Thailand: National Association of the Deaf in Thailand.

Suwanarat, M., Wrigley, O., & Anderson, L. (1990). *The Thai Sign Language dictionary* (rev. and expanded ed.). Bangkok, Thailand: National Association of the Deaf in Thailand.

Sveriges Dövas Riksföbund. (1971). *Teckenordbok* [Sign dictionary]. Borlänge, Sweden: Author.

Tai, J. (1988). Bilingualism and bilingual education in the People's Republic of China. In C. Paulston (Ed.), *International handbook of bilingualism and bilingual education* (pp. 185–201). New York, NY: Greenwood Press.

Taub, S. (2001). Complex superposition of metaphors in an ASL poem. In V. Dively, M. Metzger, S. Taub, & A. Baer (Eds.), *Signed languages: Discoveries from international research* (pp. 197–230). Washington, DC: Gallaudet University Press.

Tennant, R., & Brown, M. (1998). *The American Sign Language handshape dictionary*. Washington, DC: Clerc Books, Gallaudet University Press.

Timmermans, N. (2003). *Report: A comparative analysis of the status of sign languages in Europe*. Strasbourg, France: Council of Europe.

Timmermans, N. (2005). *The status of sign languages in Europe*. Strasbourg, France: Council of Europe.

Tollefson, J. (1991). *Planning language, planning inequality: Language policy in the community*. London, England: Longman.

Tollefson, J. (Ed.). (1995). *Power and inequality in language education*. Cambridge, England: Cambridge University Press.

Tollefson, J. (Ed.). (2002). *Language policies in education: Critical issues*. Mahwah, NJ: Lawrence Erlbaum Associates.

Tollefson, J., & Tsui, A. (Eds.). (2004). *Medium of instruction policies: Which agenda? Whose agenda*? Mahwah, NJ: Lawrence Erlbaum Associates.

Tomkins, L. (2004). Cultural and linguistic voice in the deaf bilingual experience. In B. Brueggemann (Ed.), *Literacy and deaf people: Cultural and contextual perspectives* (pp. 139–56). Washington, DC: Gallaudet University Press.

Tonkin, H. (Ed.). (1997). *Esperanto, interlinguistics, and planned languages*. Lanham, MD: University Press of America.

Tse, L. (2001). *"Why don't they learn English?" Separating fact from fallacy in the U.S. language debate*. New York, NY: Teachers College Press.

Tsunoda, T. (2006). *Language endangerment and language revitalization: An introduction*. Berlin, Germany: Mouton de Gruyter.

Turner, G. (2006). Why protect heritage sign languages? *International Journal of Applied Linguistics, 16*, 409–13.

Turner, G. (2009). Sign language planning: Pragmatism, pessimism, and principles. *Current Issues in Language Planning, 10*, 243–54.

Tutu, D. (1983). *Hope and suffering*. Grand Rapids, MI: William Eerdmans.
Umiker-Sebeok, J., & Sebeok, T. (Eds.). (1987). *Monastic sign language*. Berlin, Germany: Mouton de Gruyter.
Uzicanin, N. (1996). *Bosnian-English / English-Bosnian compact dictionary*. New York, NY: Hippocrene.
Valli, C. (1990). The nature of a line in ASL poetry. In W. Edmondson & F. Karlsson (Eds.), *SLR '87: Papers from the Fourth International Symposium on Sign Language Research* (pp. 171–82). Hamburg, Germany: Signum.
Valli, C. (Ed.). (2005). *The Gallaudet dictionary of American Sign Language*. Washington, DC: Gallaudet University Press.
Valli, C., Lucas, C., & Mulrooney, J. (2005). *Linguistics of American Sign Language: An introduction* (4th ed.). Washington, DC: Gallaudet University Press.
Van Cleve, J. (Ed.). (1993). *Deaf history unveiled: Interpretations from the new scholarship*. Washington, DC: Gallaudet University Press.
Van Cleve, J. (Ed.). (2004). *Genetics, disability, and deafness*. Washington, DC: Gallaudet University Press.
Van Cleve, J. (Ed.). (2007). *The deaf history reader*. Washington, DC: Gallaudet University Press.
Van Cleve, J., & Crouch, B. (1989). *A place of their own: Creating the deaf community in America*. Washington, DC: Gallaudet University Press.
Van Herreweghe, M., & Vermeerbergen, M. (2009). Flemish Sign Language standardisation. *Current Issues in Language Planning, 10*, 308–26.
van Rensburg, C. (1993). Die demokratisering van Afrikaans [The democratization of Afrikaans]. In *Linguistica: Festschrifit E. B. van Wyk* (pp. 141–53). Pretoria, South Africa: J. L. van Schaik.
van Rensburg, C. (Ed.). (1997). *Afrikaans in Afrika* [Afrikaans in Africa]. Pretoria, South Africa: J. L. van Schaik.
van Uden, A. (1986). *Sign languages of deaf people and psycholinguistics*. Lisse, The Netherlands: Swets & Zeitlinger.
Verhoef, M. (1998a). Funksionele meertaligheid in Suid-Afrika: 'n onbereikbare ideaal? [Functional multilingualism in South Africa: An unachievable ideal?]. *Liberator, 19*, 35–50.
Verhoef, M. (1998b). 'n teoretiese aanloop tot taalgesindheidsbeplanning in Suid-Afrika [A theoretical trade for language health planning in South Africa]. *South African Journal of Linguistics, 16*, 27–33.
Vernon, M., & Andrews, J. (1990). *The psychology of deafness: Understanding deaf and hard-of-hearing people*. New York, NY: Longman.
Vitas, D. (1998). *Croatian*. Hauppauge, NY: Barron's Educational Series.
Vivolin-Karén, R., & Alanne, K. (2003). *Draft curriculum and structure of Finnish Sign Language*. Helsinki: Finnish Association of the Deaf.
Walker, L. (1986). *A loss for words*. New York, NY: Harper & Row.

Walworth, M., Moores, D., & O'Rourke, T. (Eds.). (1992). *A free hand: Enfranchising the education of deaf children*. Silver Spring, MD: T. J. Publishers.

Wardhaugh, R. (1999). *Proper English: Myths and misunderstandings about language*. Oxford, England: Blackwell.

Webb, V. (Ed.). (1992). *Afrikaans ná apartheid* [Afrikaans after apartheid]. Pretoria, South Africa: J. L. van Schaik.

Webb, V. (2002). *Language in South Africa: The role of language in national transformation, reconstruction, and development*. Amsterdam, The Netherlands: John Benjamins.

Webb, V. (2004). African languages as media of instruction in South Africa: Stating the case. *Language Problems and Language Planning, 28*, 147–73.

Weinreich, M. (1945). צײַט אונדזער פֿון פראָבלעמען די און ייִוואָ דער [The YIVO and the problems of our time]. *YIVO-Bleter, 25*, 3–18.

Weinstein, B. (1980). Language planning in francophone Africa. *Language Problems and Language Planning, 4*, 55–77.

Weinstein, B. (Ed.). (1990). *Language policy and political development*. Norwood, NJ: Ablex Publishing Corporation.

Wesemaël, R. (1985). L'interprétation simultanée en langage gestuel [Simultaneous interpretation in sign language]. *Language Problems and Language Planning, 9*, 105–14.

Wilbur, R. (1979). *American Sign Language and sign systems*. Baltimore, MD: University Park Press.

Wilbur, R. (1990). Metaphors in American Sign Language and English. In W. Edmondson & K. Karlsson (Eds.), *SLR '87: Papers from the Fourth International Symposium on Sign Language Research* (pp. 163–70). Hamburg, Germany: Signum.

Wilbur, R. (2008). Success with deaf children: How to prevent educational failure. In K. Lingren, D. DeLuca, & D. Napoli (Eds.), *Signs and voices: Deaf culture, identity, language, and arts* (pp. 117–38). Washington, DC: Gallaudet University Press.

Wilcox, P. (2000). *Metaphors in American Sign Language*. Washington, DC: Gallaudet University Press.

Wilcox, S. (Ed.). (1988). *Academic acceptance of American Sign Language*. Burtonsville, MD: Linstok Press.

Wilcox, S. (Ed.). (1989). *American deaf culture: An anthology*. Silver Spring, MD: Linstok Press.

Wilcox, S. (2003). The multimedia dictionary of American Sign Language: Learning lessons about language, technology, and business. *Sign Language Studies, 3*, 379–92.

Wilcox, S., & Wilcox, P. (1997). *Learning to see: American Sign Language as a second language* (2nd ed.). Washington, DC: Gallaudet University Press.

Wiley, T. (2002). Accessing language rights in education: A brief history of the U.S. context. In J. Tollefson (Ed.), *Language policies in education: Critical issues* (pp. 39–64). Mahwah, NJ: Lawrence Erlbaum Associates.

Willard, T. (1993). I've had enough of the I-LOVE-YOU sign, thanks. *Silent News, 25*, 2.

Winefield, R. (1981). *Bell, Gallaudet, and the sign language debate: An historical analysis of the communication controversy in education of the deaf.* Unpublished doctoral dissertatBion, Harvard University, Cambridge, MA.

Winefield, R. (1987). *Never the twain shall meet: Bell, Gallaudet, and the communications debate.* Washington, DC: Gallaudet University Press.

Winston, E. (Ed.). (1999). *Storytelling and conversation: Discourse in deaf communities.* Washington, DC: Gallaudet University Press.

Wittgenstein, L. (1980). *Culture and value.* Chicago, IL: University of Chicago Press. (Original work published 1946)

Wolff, H. E. (2000). Language and society. In B. Heine & D. Nurse (Eds.), *African languages: An introduction* (pp. 298–347). Cambridge, England: Cambridge University Press.

Wong, L. (1999). Authenticity and the revitalization of Hawaiian. *Anthropology & Education Quarterly, 30*, 94–115.

Woodbury, A. (1998). Documenting rhetorical, aesthetic, and expressive loss in language shift. In L. Grenoble & L. Whalely (Eds.), *Endangered languages: Current issues and future prospects* (pp. 234–58). Cambridge, England: Cambridge University Press.

Woodcock, K. (2001). Cochlear implants vs. deaf culture? In L. Bragg (Ed.), *DEAF-WORLD: A historical reader and primary sourcebook* (pp. 325–32). New York: New York University Press. (Original work published 1993)

Woodward, J. (1973). Manual English: A problem in language standardization and planning. In G. Gustason & J. Woodward (Eds.), *Recent developments in manual English* (pp. 1–12). Washington, DC: Department of Education, Gallaudet College.

Woodward, J. (1982). *How you gonna get to heaven if you can't talk with Jesus: On depathologizing deafness.* Silver Spring, MD: T. J. Publishers.

World Federation of the Deaf. (2007). *WFD statement on the unification of sign languages.* Helsinki, Finland: World Federation of the Deaf.

World Federation of the Deaf. (2009). *Open letter with regard to the unification project of sign languages in the arab region.* Helsinki, Finland: World Federation of the Deaf.

Wright, L. (2002). Why English dominates the central economy: An economic perspective on "elite closure" and South African language policy. *Language Problems and Language Planning, 26*, 159–77.

Wright, L. (2004). Language and value: Towards accepting a richer linguistic ecology for South Africa. *Language Problems and Language Planning, 28*, 175–97.

Wright, S. (1996). *Language and the state: Revitalization and revival in Israel and Eire*. Clevedon, England: Multilingual Matters.

Wright, S. (2004). *Language policy and language planning: From nationalism to globalization*. New York, NY: Palgrave Macmillan.

Wright, S. (2007). The right to speak one's own language: Reflections on theory and practice. *Langauge Policy,* 6, 203–24.

Yau, S. (1982). Creation d'anthroponymes gestuels par une sourde amérindienne isolée [The creation of name signs by the isolated deaf American Indian]. *Amérindia: Revue d'Éthnolinguistique Amérindienne,* 7, 7–22.

Yau, S. (1990). Lexical branching in sign language. In S. Fischer & P. Siple (Eds.), *Theoretical issues in sign language research: Linguistics* (pp. 261–78). Chicago, IL: University of Chicago Press.

Yau, S., & He, J. (1990). How do deaf children get their name signs during their first month in school? In W. Edmondson & F. Karlsson (Eds.), *SLR '87: Papers from the Fourth International Symposium on Sign Language Research* (pp. 242–54). Hamburg, Germany: Signum.

Yoel, J. (2007). Evidence for first-language attrition of Russian Sign Language among immigrants to Israel. In D. Quinto-Pozos (Ed.), *Sign languages in contact* (pp. 153–91). Washington, DC: Gallaudet University Press.

Zaitseva, G. (1987). Problems of sign language in Soviet deaf education. In J. Kyle (Ed.), *Sign and school* (pp. 100–108). Clevedon, England: Multilingual Matters.

Zeshan, U. (2000). *Sign language in Indo-Pakistan: A description of a signed language*. Amsterdam, The Netherlands: John Benjamins.

Index

Figures and notes are indicated by f and n following page numbers.

ABC story, 14–15
acquisition planning, 49, 51*f*, 53, 58, 170–71
ActionAid International, 70
Agnon, Shmuel Yosef, 61
Alabama legislation on ASL, 114
Allen, Shannon, 150
alphabets, manual, 131, 132–34*f*
Altbach, P., 48
American Manual Alphabet, 131, 132*f*
American School for the Deaf (ASD), 97
American Sign Language (ASL), 97–128
  artistic and literary tradition and, 13–18
  compared to manual sign codes, 147
  Congress of Milan and, 104–6
  in continuum with contact sign and manual sign codes, 7–8, 8*f*, 30*n*6, 42
  criticisms of, 111–12
  dictionaries, 117–18
  as foreign language program in schools, 119–21
  future concerns, 123–28
  glosses for word "manage," 141, 141*f*
  initialized signs, 102–3, 165, 166*f*
  as language of DEAF WORLD, 11–13
  language planning in nineteenth century and, 99–104
  law enforcement provision of interpreters for, 116
  legitimation of, in twentieth century, 5–6, 28, 111–13
  lexical diversity of, 7
  name signs in, 12
  origins of, 97–98
  poetry in, 16–17
  signing vs., 42
  state treatment of, 113–16
  as threat to other sign languages, 161
American Sign Language Handshape Dictionary (Tennant & Brown), 118
American Sign Language Teachers Association (ASLTA), 123
Anglophone Africa, 81
Anthony, David, 136
Arab Federation of Organizations Working with the Deaf (AFOOD), 168
Arabic language, 61, 81, 168
Arab Sign Language, 168
Aramaic language, 60
artificial languages, 132–35
artistic and literary tradition, 13–18
ASL. *See* American Sign Language
assimilation, 110–11. *See also* linguistic assimilation
Atatürk, 72
A-to-Z story, 14–15
attitude planning, 49, 50, 51*f*, 53–54, 58, 72, 103, 171–72
attitudinal deafness, 19
audiological vs. cultural deafness, 10, 19
audism, 28
Australian Sign Language, 160, 164–65, 167

Bahan, B., 9–10
Bailey, C., 117
Baker, Charlotte, 9
Baldauf, R., 49, 52–53, 55, 71
Baltic states, post-Soviet breakup, 51–52
Baxter, Robert, 76
Becker, Carl, 37
behavioral norms in DEAF WORLD, 20–21
Bell, Alexander Graham, 106–8, 110
Bell, Alexander Melville, 106
Bell, Eliza, 107
Bell, Mabel Hubbard, 107, 110
Ben-Yehuda, Eliezer, 60
Bienvenu, MJ, 118
bilingualism
  ASL dictionary and, 118–19
  bilingual countries, 80
  Connecticut Asylum approach, 100
  in educational settings, 149, 150, 170–71
  elitism and, 93
biotechnological innovations, 123–26
Bishop, M., 29
Blackledge, Adrian, 182
Blommaert, Jan, 47
Bokmål language, 72
Bornstein, Harry, 142
borrowing from another language, 57, 74, 165–66
Bosnian language, 41
Bouvet, Danielle, 170
Brandeis, Louis, 111
brand names adopted in language lexicon, 74
Brazilian Sign Language, 160
Brien, David, 130–31
British Sign Language, 136, 164, 165, 167
British Sign Language for Dummies, 168
Brown, N., 118
Burke, Teresa, 125
Canadian Dictionary of ASL, 117
Can Language Be Planned? (Rubin & Jernudd), 32
Carroll, J., 113
CASE. *See* Conceptually Accurate Signed English
Casterline, D., 117
children of deaf adults (Codas), 10, 19, 29*n*3
Chinese characters, simplification of, 72
Chomsky, N., 96*n*1
civil rights issues, 4
Clarke Institution for Deaf-Mutes, 100–101
Clerc, Laurent, 97–98, 99, 105, 135
closed-caption televisions, 21
Cobarrubias, Juan, 77, 79
cochlear implants, 23–29, 124–25
cognition, study of, 69
Cogswell, Alice, 22
Cogswell, Mason, 99
Cohen, L., 29
colonial settlement
  internationalization and, 81
  language loss as result of, 66
  linguistic assimilation during, 79
Colorado legislation on ASL, 115
"Combined System," 101–2, 103, 110, 128*n*3
compounding of signs, 164
Conceptually Accurate Signed English (CASE), 143, 146
Conference of Principals of the American Institutions for the Education of the Deaf and Dumb (May 1868), 101–2
Conference of Superintendents and Principals of American Schools for the Deaf, 104
Congress of Milan (1880), 104–6. *See also* oralism
  in Deaf Art, 18

Conley, Willy, 15
Connecticut Asylum for the Education and Instruction of Deaf and Dumb Persons, 97, 99–100
constitutional recognition of national languages, 160, 177
contact sign languages, 6, 8, 12, 143
Cooper, James, 50
Cooper, Robert, 32, 35
Cornett, R. Orin, 143–44
corpus planning
  described, 52–53
  detailed analysis of sign language as, 103
  dictionaries, development of, 117, 118
  initialized signs as, 102–3
  international perspective, 162–70
  as language planning activity, 49, 51*f*
  language purification as, 56
  language reform as, 72
  language revitalization as, 58
  language standardization as, 73
Corson, David, 85, 94
Costello, E., 117
Croatian language, 39, 41
Croneberg, C., 117
Crouch, B., 105
Cubberley, Elwood P., 110–11
cued speech, 8*f*, 143–44, 145*f*
culture of DEAF WORLD, 9–23
  artistic and literary tradition, 13–18
  ASL as language of, 11–13
  deaf clubs, 22–23, 126–27
  deaf humor, 20
  identity of deaf people, 9–11
  manual sign codes and, 147–48
Cummins, Jim, 26

Deaf Art, 13–14, 18
Deaf Artists of America, 14
Deaf children of deaf parents, 4, 5
Deaf children of hearing parents. *See* hearing parents of deaf children
Deaf clubs, 22–23, 126–27
Deaf culture. *See* DEAF WORLD
Deaf education. *See also* residential schools
  Bell's opinion of, 107–8
  deaf teachers, hiring of, 105
  decision making about, 182–83
  founding of schools for deaf students, 99–101
  in late nineteenth century, 103–4
  manual sign codes in, 148–51, 153
  oralism in. *See* oralism
  repressive nature of, 18
  sign language use in, 100
Deaf Heritage: A Narrative History of Deaf America (Gannon), 22
Deaf humor, 20
deafness
  attitudinal deafness, 19
  conceptions of, 3–4
  different kinds of hearing loss, 4–5
  not a disability, 1, 9
Deaf social and cultural organizations, 22–23, 126–27
Deaf Studies as university discipline, 27
Deaf (capital D) vs. deaf (lower-case d), 29*n*1
DEAF WORLD
  artistic and literary tradition of, 13–18
  ASL as language of, 11–13
  attitudinal deafness, 19
  behavioral norms in, 20–21
  Bell's opposition to, 107–8
  culture of, 9–23
  deaf humor, 20
  historical awareness and, 22
  as special case, 1–30
  in tension with hearing world, 23–29
  voluntary network of deaf social and cultural organizations, 22–23

decolonization in Asia and Africa, effect on language, 44–45
De Haerne, M., 103
de Lacharriere, Ladreit, 106
de l'Epee, Abbé Charles-Michel, 99, 135
Department of Justice Regulations, 115–16
derivational signs, 167
Developing a Prototype for a Monolingual ASL Dictionary (Bienvenu), 118
developing countries and official language policies, 80
De'VIA (Deaf View/Image Art) Manifesto, 14
dictionaries
  of ASL, 117–18
  of British Sign Language, 130–31, 162
  of international sign languages, 162–63
  of Signed English, 143
Dictionary of British Sign Language/English (Brien), 130–31, 162
directionality of language planning process, 84
disability, deafness not considered as, 1, 9
diversity, 7–8, 88, 93. *See also* linguistic pluralism
Dixon, R., 65–66, 67
Dolby, K., 117
Dupor, Susan, 18

Early Hearing Detection and Intervention Program, 143
Eastman, G., 49
Ecuador and national sign languages, 160
education. *See also* Deaf education
  ASL–English bilingual/bicultural education programs, 118, 149
  foreign language education in U.S., 54–55, 120–23, 122*f*
  Hawai'ian immersion programs, 71
  language policy and, 48–49, 54, 94–96
  language revival and, 72
  language rights and, 92, 116–17
  limited English proficiency students, 92–93
  linguistic assimilation and, 79
  mainstreaming, 126, 149
  Maori educational programs, 70–71
  secondary schools offering ASL, 115
Edwards, John, 91
elderly deaf, 5, 10, 29*n*1
elitism, 93
e-mail, 21
empowerment of deaf people, 183–84
endangered languages, 61–72, 64*f*, 127
"The Endangered Languages Issue as a Hopeless Cause" (Newman), 68–69
English language
  collection of ideolects making up, 43
  de facto national language of U.S., 56, 92
  in Ireland, 59–60, 68
  as "Language of Wider Communication," 45–46
  Latin alphabet, use of, 34
  linguistic imperialism of, 90
  in Nigeria, 45
  Saxonist movement to purify, 57
Esperanto, 91, 96*n*4, 123, 133–34
etic vs. emic constructions of deafness, 11, 19
eugenics, 109–10
European Charter of Regional or Minority Languages (1992), 173
European Parliament "Resolution on Sign Languages" (1988), 159–60, 161, 186–88
European Union (EU) and national sign languages, 157–60, 158–59*f*

evaluation
of language planning, 84
of language policies, 86–87
explicit language policies, 56
extinct languages, 63, 64*f*
eye contact, 20

facial expressions, 21
Ferguson, G., 47
Fernandes, Jane K., 27–28
fingerspelling, 117, 130–32, 144, 164
Finland's recognition of sign language, 157
Finnish Sign Language, 164, 165, 167, 178–79*n*2
Fishman, Joshua, 71–72, 180
Flemish Sign Language, 159
Fodor, I., 73
forced language loss, 66–67
foreign language education in U.S., 54–55, 120–23, 122*f*
foreign language programs of ASL, 119–21
former Soviet states and language policy, 50–52
Foucault, Michel, 26
Fourth International Congress on the Education and Welfare of the Deaf (Paris 1900), 105
Francophone Africa, 45, 79, 81
Franglais, 57
French, Daniel Chester, 22
French language. *See also* Francophone Africa
Anglicisms in, 57
as "Language of Wider Communication," 45–46
linguistic imperialism of, 90
French Sign Language, 97–98, 135
Fromkin, V., 74
Frost, Robert, 29

Gaeltacht (Ireland), 59
Gallaudet, Edward Miner, 101, 102, 106, 110, 128*n*3
Gallaudet, Sophia Fowler, 107
Gallaudet, Thomas Hopkins, 22, 99, 101, 105
Gallaudet University, 167
Gannon, Jack, 22
genetic testing, 125–26
Gestuno, 156, 175–76
gestural lexicons, 9
gesturing, 21
Gomes de Matos, F., 87
Gorman, Pierre, 135
grassroots involvement, 184
Gustason, G., 136, 137, 139, 146

Hagège, C., 73
Hamburg Notation System, 169–70
"hard of hearing," choice of term, 27
Harrison, K. David, 62, 69
Haugen, Einar, 43
Hawai'ian language, 71
HEAFIE sign, 19, 19*f*
hearing children of deaf parents. *See* children of deaf adults (Codas)
hearing hegemony, 181
"hearing impaired," choice of term, 27
hearing loss, degree of, 29–30*n*5
hearing parents of deaf children, 4, 5, 29*n*3
cochlear implants, information and decisions about, 23–29
hearization, 26–27
Hebrew language revitalization, 59, 60–61, 81, 96*n*3
Heugh, K., 176–77
Hicks, S., 29
Hindi language, 45–46
historical awareness of DEAF WORLD, 22
Hoffmeister, R., 9–10
Holcolmb, Roy, 118
"home" signing systems, 4

human rights, 87, 89, 92, 172–73
humor, 20
Humphries, T., 25, 118, 144
Hyams, N., 74
Hymes, Dell, 93–94

Ibo language, reform of, 72
Icelandic Sign Language, 160
identity and language, 33–34
identity of deaf people, 9–10
ASL use and, 13
deaf constructions of, 11
ideological monolingualism, 93–94, 128*n*2
I-LOVE-YOU sign, 21, 21*f*
IMA. *See* International Manual Alphabet
immigration
assimilation of immigrants, 110–11
voluntary language shift and, 68
implicit language policies, 56
Indiana School for the Deaf, 126
Indian Peace Commission Report of 1868, 67
Individualized Educational Program (IEP), 116
Individuals with Disabilities Education Act (IDEA), 116
initialized signs, 102–3, 165, 166*f*
Institution Nationale des Sourds-Muets à Paris, 99
internationalization, 77, 81, 83*f*
International Journal of Bilingual Education and Bilingualism, 26
International Manual Alphabet (IMA), 131, 133*f*
international perspectives, 155–79
acquisition planning, 170–71
activities for sign languages, 156–72
attitude planning, 171–72
corpus planning, 162–70
Gestuno, 175–76
manual sign codes, 151–52
sign languages and language rights, 172–75
South Africa, 176–78
status planning, 157–62
International Sign, 175–76
Internet, lexicographical use of, 163
interpreted performances in theater, 15
interpreters, legislation for providing, 115–16
Irish language
revitalization, 59–60, 96*n*3
voluntary language shift, 68
Islay (novel), 14
Israel. *See* Hebrew language revitalization
Israeli Sign Language, 151–52, 164, 165
"I've Had Enough of the I-LOVE-YOU Sign, Thanks" (Willard), 21

Jankowski, Katherine, 104, 106
Jernudd, B., 32, 73
Jews. *See* Hebrew language revitalization
Johnston, T., 165
jokes, 20
Jokinen, Markku, 170
Jordan, I. King, 23, 112–13, 183
Journal of Deaf Studies and Deaf Education, 27
A Journey into the DEAF-WORLD (Lane, Hoffmeister, & Bahan), 9–10
Julius Caesar, 33
Kansas legislation on ASL, 115
Kaplan, R., 49, 52–53, 55, 71
Kerr, Donna, 86
Kerth, Thomas, 121
Khalid, Abdallah, 56–57
King, K., 58
King, Martin Luther, Jr., 185
KiSwahili language, 45, 57, 74, 81
Kiunguja (Zanzibar dialect of Swahili), 72–73

Kohanga Reo ("language nest")
Maori-medium preschools, 70–71
Krausnecker, V., 156
Krauss, Michael, 63–65

Ladino language, 60
Lampe, John, 39
Lane, Harlan, 9–10, 13, 25, 26, 97, 108
"language-as-a-problem" orientation, 76–77, 78*f*, 181
"language-as-a-resource" orientation, 76, 77, 78*f*, 181
Language Conflict and Language Planning: The Case of Modern Norwegian (Haugen), 43
language endangerment. *See* endangered languages
Language in Education Policy (South Africa), 178
language loss, 61–70
forced language loss, 66–67
population loss as cause of, 66
significance of, 68–69
voluntary language shift, 67–68
ways to confront, 70
language modernization, 55, 73–76
language planning and language policies, 31–96
acquisition planning, 50, 51*f*, 53, 58, 170–71
activities associated with, 35, 156–72
types of activities, 49–55, 51*f*, 156
attitude planning and, 50, 51*f*, 53–54, 58, 72, 103, 171–72
collection of ideolects making up a language, 43
corpus planning. *See* corpus planning
deaf people not part of, 181
definition of language planning, 31, 35
definition of language policies, 35
directionality of, 84
in education, 94–96
evaluation of, 86–87
functions of, 55–76
modernization, 55, 73–76
purification, 55, 56–58
reform, 55–72
revival. *See* language revival and revitalization
standardization. *See* language standardization
historical development of, 43–48
language loss. *See* language loss
language rights and, 87–94
nature and purposes of, 1–2, 31, 48–49
orientations and ideologies of, 76–82, 78*f*, 83*f*
planning distinguished from policy, 85
problematic nature of "language," 35–43
process, 79*f*, 82–86
evaluation phase, 84
factfinding phase, 82
goals and strategies phase, 82
implementation phase, 82–83, 84
social implications of, 184–85
stakeholders' role, 85
status planning and, 50–52, 51*f*, 58, 73, 157–62
Language Problems and Language Planning (journal), 44, 96*n*4
language purification, 55, 56–58
language reform, 55, 72
Language Reform: History and Future (Fodor & Hagège), 73
language revival and revitalization, 55, 58–66, 70–72. *See also* language loss
language rights
ASL study and, 115
deaf students in public schools, 116–17
international sign languages, 172–75
"language-as-a-right" orientation, 76–77, 78*f*, 181
in language planning and policy, 87–94

"Languages of Wider Communication" (LWCs), 45–46, 46*f*, 91
language spread, 50
language standardization, 55, 72–73
"standard language," 34
The Last Supper (Sinnott), 18
Latin alphabet, English's use of, 34
Latin language
evolution of Romance languages from, 37–38
use by Romans, 33
law enforcement and provision of interpreters, 116
legislation
on ASL, 113–16
on deaf people's rights internationally, 172–73
lexical creation of new signs, 164
lexicography for sign languages. *See* dictionaries
The Liberation of Swahili from European Appropriation (Khalid), 56–57
Libras (Brazilian Sign Language), 160
Liddell, S., 5–6
limited English proficiency students in U.S. schools, 92–93
Lincoln Memorial statue, 22
linguicism, 91
linguistic assimilation, 77, 79, 83*f*, 180–81
linguistic imperialism, 90–91, 161–62
linguistic legitimacy, 91
linguistic pluralism, 77, 80, 83*f*, 88
Linguistics of Visual English (LOVE), 142, 146
"Lip Service" (Panara), 28–29
literacy, 32
The Logic of Scientific Discovery (Poppin), 36
LOVE. *See* Linguistics of Visual English
Luetke-Stahlman, Barbara, 138
LWCs. *See* "Languages of Wider Communication"
Macedonian language, 41
Maine legislation on ASL, 114–15
mainstreaming, 126, 149
Malay language, 46
Mancing, Howard, 120
Mandarin language, 46
manual coded English (MCE), 130
"Manual Method," 101
manual sign codes, 129–54
artificial languages, 132–35
compared to ASL, 147
in continuum with ASL and contact sign, 7–8, 8*f*, 30*n*6, 42
cultural limitations of, 147–48
development of, 8, 135–46
Conceptually Accurate Signed English (CASE), 143, 146
cued speech, 143–44, 145*f*
manual alphabets, 131, 132–34*f*
Paget Gorman Sign System, 135–36, 151
Seeing Essential English (SEE-1), 136–37, 138*f*, 146
Signed English, 142–43, 146
Signing Exact English (SEE-2), 137–40, 139*f*, 146
educational limitations of, 148–51, 153
fingerspelling. *See* fingerspelling
international uses of, 151–52
linguistic limitations of, 146–47
rejection by deaf community, 12
Maori language, 70–71, 160
marriage within group of deaf community, 19, 108
The Mask of Benevolence (Lane), 10
MCE (manual coded English), 130
McGregor, Robert P., 97
McRae, Kenneth, 88
McWhorter, John, 62
medical innovations, 123–24
medical view of deafness, 3

Medium of Instruction Policies: Which Agenda? Whose Agenda? (Tollefson & Tsui), 48–49
Meir, I., 151
metaphors in ASL, 17
Milan Italy, 1880 (Thornley), 18
Miller, Betty, 13–14
minority languages, 180
modernization. *See* language modernization
monastery use of signing, 9
moribund languages, 63, 64*f*
morphological processes, 167
Morphological Sign System, 137
multilingual official policy, 80
Multimedia Dictionary of American Sign Language, 118
Myers, Shirley Shultz, 27–28
Myklebust, M., 111–12

name signs, 12
National Association of the Deaf (NAD), 22, 114, 124
National Consortium of Interpreter Education Centers, 123
National Cued Speech Association, 143–44
National Curriculum Guide for Compulsory School (Iceland), 160
National Institutes of Health planning group, 23
nationalism and language planning, 52, 59
national languages. *See* official languages
National Park Service, 22
National Technical Institute for the Deaf (NTID), 167
National Theatre of the Deaf, 15
Native American languages, replacing with English, 66–67, 71
natural sign languages, 5–7, 42. *See also* American Sign Language (ASL)
  borrowings by, 164
Navajo language, 67
Nebraska School for the Deaf, 126
Newman, Paul, 68–69
New Zealand and Maori language, 70–71, 160
New Zealand Sign Language, 164, 165
Nigeria, languages used in, 45, 72, 81
No Child Left Behind, 123
Norwegian language, 43, 72
Novak, Peter, 16
Nover, Stephen
  on bilingual approach, 100
  chronological approach of, 99
  on Combined System, 101
  on Congress of Milan, 104
  on deaf teachers, 105
  on hearization, 26
  on signacy, 119
Nynorsk language, 72

O'Brien, Conor Cruise, 91
Office for Civil Rights, U.S. Department of Education, 116
official languages, 44–45, 56, 72, 80, 92, 157
oralism, 101, 102, 103, 105, 110
  manualism vs., 129–30
orthography and language, 34, 39
Ozolins, U., 51–52

Padden, C., 25, 144
Paget, Grace, 135
Paget, Richard, 135
Paget Gorman Sign System, 135–36, 151
Panara, Robert, 28–29
Pan-South African Language Board (PANSALB), 177
pathological view of deafness, 3
Peet, Isaac, 102–3
Pelletier, Linda, 123
People's Republic of China, 72
Perú and Quechua language, 58, 81

Philippines, 57, 79
Phillipson, Robert, 90
phonology, 154*n*3
Pidgin English, 45
pidgin sign, 8
Pidgin Signed English (PSE), 143
Plains Indians, 9
poetry in ASL, 16–17
political ideology determining written language, 34
Popper, Karl, 36
population loss in relation to language loss, 66
Posner, Rebecca, 38–39
postivism, 36
poverty and language loss, 69–70
Preston, P., 29
The Psychology of Deafness (Myklebust), 112
Puerto Rico, 79
purists. *See* language purification

Quechua language in Perú, 58, 81

Ramsey, Claire, 146–47, 148
Rehabilitation Act of 1973 (Section 504), 116
residential schools, 5, 108, 126
revival. *See* language revival and revitalization
Rhode Island legislation on ASL, 115
Roberts, P., 32
Rochester Method, 8*f*, 117, 131–32
Rodman, R., 74
Romaine, Suzanne, 60, 70
Romance languages, 37–39, 40–41*f*
Roman Empire, 33, 62
Rubin, J., 32
Rubino, Francesco, 175
Ruiz, Richard, 76–77
Russian language
  linguistic imperialism of, 90
  modernization, 75
safe languages, 63–65, 64*f*
Sandler, W., 151
SASL. *See* South African Sign Language
Schein, Jerome, 13
Schembri, A., 165
Schick, Brenda, 144
Second International Congress of Instructors of Deaf-Mutes. *See* Congress of Milan (1880)
Section 504, Rehabilitation Act of 1973, 116
Seeing Essential English (SEE-1), 136–37, 138*f*, 146
Serbo-Croatian language, 39, 41
Shakespeare, 15–16
Shohamy, Elana, 85
Sibayan, B., 57
Sicard, Abbé Roch-Ambroise, 99, 135
Siegel, Lawrence, 116–17
signacy, 119
signed communication, 6, 9
Signed English, 8*f*, 142–43, 146
Signed Hebrew, 151–52
Signing Exact English (SEE-2), 137–40, 139*f*, 146
sign languages. *See also* American Sign Language (ASL); manual sign codes
  kinds of signing, 6–9
  language planning activities for, 156–72
  nature and characteristics of, 5–9
  number of, 7
  signing vs., 7–8, 42
  as threatened languages, 127
Sign Language Structure (Stokoe), 5, 112–13
SignWriting, 169, 170
Simon, Paul, 54–55
Simultaneous Communication (SimCom), 118, 154*n*2
Sinnott, Ethan, 18
Skutnabb-Kangas, Tove, 7, 77, 91, 161–62, 173–74, 183

Smith, Neil, 36
social class and language purity, 58
Social Darwinism, 109
sociocultural perspective on deafness, 3–4, 9, 23
South Africa
attitude planning, 54
isiZulu vs. isiXhosa, 39
language planning and policy, 47, 156
language planning for sign language, 42, 176–78
multilingual official policy, 80, 81
South African Sign Language (SASL), 7, 42, 156, 160, 177–78
Spanglish, 57
Spanish language, 37–38
Anglicisms in, 57
hierarchy in, 93
as "Language of Wider Communication," 46
linguistic imperialism of, 90
Spectrum: Focus on Deaf Artists, 13
Spectrum Visual Arts Institute, 13
spoken languages, number of, 7
stable languages, 65
"standard language," 34, 55
Standards for Foreign Language Learning (ACTFL), 121–23, 122*f*
state legislation on ASL, 113–23
status planning, 49, 50–52, 51*f*, 58, 73, 157–62
sterilization of deaf children, 109
Sternberg, M., 117
Stewart, Larry, 98
Stokoe, William, 5, 112–13, 117, 128*n*1, 169
Stokoe System, 169
storytelling, 14
Strong, Michael, 183
Summer Institute of Linguistics, 63
Supalla, S., 146
Sutton, Valerie, 170
Swahili language, 72–73. *See also* KiSwahili language

Tagalog language, 57, 81
Tanzania and KiSwahili language, 45, 72–73, 81
TC. *See* Total Communication
TDD/TTYs, 21
technology, use of, 21
The Tempest (Shakespeare), 15
Tennant, R., 118
tension with hearing world, 23–29
Terry, S. T., 100
textbooks, 167–68
text messaging, 21
Thailand and national sign languages, 160
theatrical productions, 15–16
Third European Congress on Sign Language Research (1989), 161, 189–91
Thornley, Mary, 18
threatened languages, 64*f*, 91. *See also* endangered languages
Tollefson, James, 46, 48–49, 95–96, 181
The Tongue-Tied American: Confronting the Foreign Language Crisis (Simon), 54–55
Total Communication, 102, 118, 130, 154*n*2
touching, 21
trilingual countries, 80
Tsui, Amy, 48–49
Turkish language, 34, 72
Turkish Sign Language, 160–61
Turner, Graham, xvii, 127, 174
Tutu, Desmond, 184, 185
Twain, Mark, 69–70
Twelfth Night (Shakespeare), 16
"two-out-of-three" rule, 140

Uganda and national sign languages, 160

Unification of Signs Commission, 175
United Nations Convention on the Rights of Persons with Disabilities, 169
United Nations Declaration on the Rights of Persons Belonging to National or Ethnic, Religious and Linguistic Minorities (1992), 89, 93
United Nations Educational, Scientific and Cultural Organization (UNESCO) Institute for Statistics, 75
United States
  de facto national language in, 56
  foreign language education, 54–55
  hierarchy of languages in, 93
  ideological monolingualism of, 93–94, 128*n*2
  limited English proficiency students in, 92–93
  manual sign codes developed in, 136
Universal Declaration of Human Rights, 89
Utah School for the Deaf, 126

Valli, Clayton, 16–17, 117
Van Cleve, J., 105
Veditz, George, 109
Venezuela and national sign languages, 160
vernacularization, 77, 81, 83*f*
videophones and video teleconferencing, 21
Vienna Circle, 35–36
voluntary language shift, 67–68
voluntary network of deaf social and cultural organizations, 22–23

Walker, L., 29
Wampler, Dennis, 142
Weinreich, Max, 41–42, 43, 96*n*2
Westervelt, Zenas, 131
WFD. *See* World Federation of the Deaf
"Why Protect Heritage Sign Languages?" (Turner), 174
Wikipedia, 76
Wilbur, Ronnie, 139
Wilcox, P., 119–20
Wilcox, S., 119–20
Willard, Tom, 21
"Windy, Bright Morning" (Valli), 16
Winefield, Richard, 109
Wittgenstein, Ludwig, 134
Wolff, H. Ekkehard, 38
Woodward, J., 136, 147
word order, 144
World Deaf Congress (1951), 175
World Federation of the Deaf (WFD), 131, 160, 169
  Commission on Sign Language recommendations (1991), 161, 192–95
  human rights survey (2009), 172
  International Sign, use of, 176
Wright, Sue, 87

Yiddish language, 60, 61

Zawolkow, Esther, 137, 139, 146
Zinser, Elizabeth, 183
Zionism and revival of Hebrew language, 60–61